Bob Bly has to be one of the greatest marketers . . . a true master. I offer as evidence: "Edu-Marketing," the key idea behind *The White Paper Marketing Handbook*. Edu-Marketing is one of the most important strategies for marketing to a business or technical audience today. I'm proud to say that I have been a "student" of Bob's for almost 20 years . . . yet I have only met him once in person. How did I learn so much? Through the solid guidance of educational materials he has sent me as a practitioner in the science of Edu-Marketing. It works—and I'm living proof! I'm happy to say I've already picked up a bunch of new ideas from *The White Paper Marketing Handbook*.

Al Bredenberg
Broad Mountain Associates, LLC Strategic Consulting

Bob's done it again! This is the most comprehensive and only one-of-its-kind reference book on writing powerful white papers. Don't write another white paper until you've read Bob's book.

Joan Damico
Copywriter & Integrated Marcom Consultant
J. Damico Marketing Communications

Bob Bly, consummate expert in business communications, adds this worthy volume on "white papers" to his long list of books packed with excellent advice. Follow Bob's crisp writing and comprehensive step-by-step recommendations to beef up your sales with the powerful "edu-marketing" approach.

Bob Donath
B2B Marketing Consultant and Writer

Much of our success is attributable to giving our clients and prospects free relevant information. We sponsor free multi-day client conferences, publish white papers, special reports, books and booklets. As such, we are disciples of what Bob Bly calls "Edu-Marketing." This practice lends significant credibility to our consultative selling and, as such, we can't do enough of it. Now comes

Mr. Bly's new "how-to" masterpiece, *The White Paper Marketing Handbook*, and it is a cornucopia of compelling Edu-Marketing strategies and tactical advice that will help us continue growing as trusted advisors to our clients.

> **Ralph Drybrough**
> **Chief Executive Officer**
> **MeritDirect**

Robert Bly's advice is reliable and can help give a marketing professional an edge in today's competitive environment.

> **Michele Favaro**
> **Director of Public Relations**
> **Passlogix**

Bob Bly's mastery of the nuances of B2B marketing is second to none. He has deep, personal experience with every strategy and technique he shares in this meaty, incredibly detailed, totally up-to-date volume. What's more, his book is highly readable—no surprise since Bob is one of today's most successful and gifted marketing copywriters. This *White Paper Marketing Handbook* will be at arm's reach on my bookshelf—I know I'll reference it often!

> **Susan K. Jones**
> **Professor of Marketing, Ferris State University**
> **Partner, The Callahan Group, LLC**
> **Author, *Creative Strategy in Direct and Interactive Marketing***

At first glance this looks like a niche book. But it's a lot more. It's an entire course in marketing, which in a way makes sense, since the central subject is "edu-marketing." And who better to write about than "Professor" Bly?

Rick Kean
Executive Director
Business Marketing Association

With this book, companies will be able to reach new customers for a whole lot less money than any other method I know of. Not only is this a terrific guide to marketing to executives, engineers and B2B professionals, the tips on content creation, article writing, publicity, white paper alternatives and case studies are all worth the cost of admission. In fact a freelance writer could build an entire consulting business just by following the advice in this book—and they wouldn't be selling mere writing services to their clients, they'd be selling hot prospects. For the sales driven company, what could be more valuable than that?

Perry Marshall
Perry S. Marshall & Associates

I have a big problem with *The White Paper Marketing Handbook*. I didn't write it. Bob not only proves that information has replaced boasting and bombast as the most powerful marketing tactic. He shows, with examples, checklists, recommendations and expert opinions—and 10 contemporary case studies—how savvy "edu-marketers" can attract new business by giving away free information.

Alan Sharpe
President
Sharpe Copy Inc.

Bob Bly has done it again. A highly valuable contribution to the world of business-to-business marketing. With some ground-breaking new concepts, like "edu-marketing," and "bait piece." I'm just sorry he didn't write this for us 5 years ago.

Ruth P. Stevens
President, eMarketing Strategy
Author, *Trade Show and Event Marketing*

The White Paper Marketing Handbook

*How to Generate More Leads and Sales
with White Papers, Special Reports,
Booklets, and CDs*

Robert W. Bly

AMERICAN
MARKETING
ASSOCIATION

RĀC⊛M
COMMUNICATIONS

THOMSON

Australia · Brazil · Canada · Mexico · Singapore · Spain · United Kingdom · United States

THOMSON

White Paper Marketing Handbook:
How to Generate More Leads and Sales with White Papers, Special Reports, Booklets, and CDs
Robert W. Bly

COPYRIGHT © 2006 by Texere, an imprint of Thomson/South-Western, a part of The Thomson Corporation. Thomson and the Star logo are trademarks used herein under license.

Consulting Editor in Marketing: Richard Hagle

Composed by: Sans Serif Inc.

Printed in the United States of America by R.R. Donnelley

1 2 3 4 5 08 07 06
This book is printed on acid-free paper.

ISBN: 0-324-30082-4

Library of Congress Cataloging in Publication Number is available. See page 230 for details.

For more information about our products, contact us at:

Thomson Learning Academic Resource Center
1-800-423-0563

Thomson Higher Education
5191 Natorp Boulevard
Mason, Ohio 45040
USA

To Rick Kean—
The Consummate Marcom Professional

"Do not covet your ideas. Give away everything you know and more will come back to you." Paul Arden, It's Not How Good You Are, It's How Good You Want to Be (Phaidon)

"The true measure of your education is not what you know, but how you share what you know with others." Kent Nerburn, *Simple Truths* (MJF Books)

"For it is in the totality of experience reckoned with, filed, and forgotten, that each man is truly different from all others in the world. And when a man talks from his heart, in his moment of truth, he speaks poetry." Ray Bradbury, *Zen in the Art of Writing* (Capra Press)

"If I have an apple and you have an apple and we exchange apples, then you and I will still each have one apple. But if you have an idea and I have an idea and we exchange these ideas, then each of us will have two ideas." George Bernard Shaw (from his play, *The Apple Cart*, 1929)

Contents

Acknowledgments

I'd like to thank Rich Hagle and Margaret Maloney, my editors, for making this book much better than it was when the manuscript first crossed their desks, and for Rich's patience in waiting for its arrival.

Special thanks to all the marketers who allowed me to reprint their white papers, ads, e-zines, and other materials in this book.

DILBERT: © Scott Adams/Dist. by United Features Syndicate, Inc.

Introduction

We live in an information society. So it makes sense that *information* has replaced hype and puffery as the most powerful marketing tool. The *White Paper Marketing Handbook* is the first how-to marketing book to show you, the marketer, how to maximize your marketing results—especially leads, orders, and sales—using "free information" offers.

What free information do we offer? In the 1990s, the dominant form of marketing collateral was the glossy, four-color sales brochure, and occasionally, a reprint of a trade journal article or technical paper.

In the 21st century, brochures have been replaced by a new, yet less understood, marketing medium: the "white paper."

A *white paper* is a promotional piece in the guise of an informational article or report. How does it work?

Just as many infomercials convey the look and feel of an informative, unbiased TV program rather than a paid commercial, a white paper attempts to convince the reader that he is being educated—about the issue or problem your product addresses (e.g., computer security, improving customer service, managing your sales force, saving for retirement), rather than being sold on a specific product.

The white paper serves the same sales purpose as a brochure . . . to sell or help sell a product or service . . . but reads and looks like an article or other important piece of authoritative, objective information.

Unlike a sales brochure, a white paper must contain useful "how-to" information that helps the reader solve a problem, or make or justify a key business decision (e.g., whether to install a new firewall or build a facility instead of leasing).

But make no mistake, both the brochure and the white paper have the same ultimate objective: to sell or help sell your company's product or service.

For instance, a company selling beds through direct response TV commercials uses TV spots to generate leads. They offer a free "information kit" that includes both a video demonstrating the bed's superior construction and a guide on how to get a good night's sleep.

Where white papers and brochures differ is their approach to making the sale: brochures contain a straightforward presentation of product features and benefits, while white papers take more of a "soft sell" approach which we will examine more fully in Chapter 1.

Marketing by offering customers and prospects free, useful information—not only white papers but booklets, special reports, checklists, guides, manuals, newsletters, monographs, books, CD-ROMs, audios, and videos—has been a proven, effective sales tool for decades.

For example, financial planners give free talks to library or church groups on how to save for retirement . . . and by giving advice, they get clients in return. Software marketers offer information technology (IT) professionals free white papers and seminars to educate them on specific issues their products address.

Direct marketers refer to the free booklet or white paper as a "bait piece," since the free information is the bait used to hook the reader into responding to your advertisement. We might call this educational approach to marketing *edu-marketing*—seeking to market a product or service by educating the prospect about a problem and its solutions.

"A free white paper or guide is a powerful offer that can stimulate high click-through rates, capture essential company and contact information, and result in successful lead generation," says online marketing guru Deb Weil. "According to February 2001 stats compiled by eMarketer, white papers are the second most consulted source of information by corporate end users; the first is employee phone directories."[1]

Jonathan Kantor, president of The Appum Group, says the term *white paper* originated during World War II to describe high-level classified information. Jonathan Jackson of eMarkter says that *white paper* is a term used to describe official British parliamentary reports on an issue delivered before action is taken. According to copywriter Michael Stelzner, the term *white paper* is an offshoot of the term *white book*, which is an official publication of a national government. He cites as an example the *Winston Churchill White Paper of 1922*, which addressed political conflict in Palestine.

Says Stelzner, in his white paper, *How to Write a White Paper*: "A white paper typically argues a specific position or solution to a problem. Although white papers take their roots in governmental policy, they have become a common tool used to introduce technology innovations and products."[2]

Since the rise of desktop publishing and the Internet, the use of bait pieces in general and white papers in particular has exploded. White papers are relatively easy to produce and post as a downloadable Adobe® Portable Document Format (PDF) file on the Web.

The growth of electronic marketing has also created other new bait-piece formats, including CD-ROMs, e-zines (online newsletters), Web conferences or "Webinars" (seminars held over the Web), and content-rich Web sites (all discussed in Chapters 7 and 9).

Marketers hoping to sell more of their products and services flood the Internet with new white papers each month, at significant expense and effort. Yet there has been no book to guide them in how to effectively use this new medium and form of marketing—until now.

The White Paper Marketing Handbook: How to Generate More Leads and Sales By Offering Your Customers Free White Papers, Special Reports, Booklets, and CDs is the first and only book to tell marketers in any industry—from software and medical equipment, to life insurance and home improvement—how to create effective white papers (and other bait pieces) . . . and how to build a successful marketing campaign around them.

The Internet has now created a consumer who is increasingly more sophisticated and educated about the products and services he is evaluating. Both online and offline, marketers who acknowledge the buyer's higher degree of sophistication—and provide the education the buyer seeks—are winning market share and customer loyalty.

The White Paper Marketing Handbook will show you, step by step, how to plan, implement, and measure this type of information-based, edu-marketing campaign. The result: dramatically higher response, more inquiries of better quality, more qualified prospects, higher closing ratios, and increased sales and profits.

I do have one favor to ask. If you have created a successful white paper or other information-based marketing program, why not send it to me so I can share it with readers of the next edition of this book? You will receive full credit, of course.

You can contact me at:

Bob Bly
22 E. Quackenbush Avenue
Dumont, NJ 07628
Phone: 201-385-1220
Fax: 201-385-1138
Web: *www.bly.com*
E-mail: *rwbly@bly.com*

1

The "Edu-Marketing" Revolution

Syms, the retailer, advertises that "an educated consumer is our best customer." But is it the role of advertising to educate that customer?

Many advertisers seem to think so, and have had great success with ad campaigns that inform and educate their target audience. And thanks in large part to the Internet, this kind of education marketing—*edu-marketing*—is growing in both popularity and effectiveness.

The practice of using advertising to educate customers goes back at least to the early 20th century, and probably well before that. For instance, the Hercules Manufacturing Company successfully sold stump pullers to farmers and other landowners by pointing out to them that removing tree stumps increases the value of their property. The headline of their ad read, "Increase Value of Land from $30 to $125 Per Acre by Pulling Stumps" (this was decades ago when land in rural and wooded areas was much cheaper than today).

Today the Internet has trained consumers to demand and respond to informational, content-rich marketing materials (like white papers) rather than traditional "hard-sell" advertising.

Remember, the Internet was originally founded as a computer network for university and government scientists to share information, not as a commerce channel. And that culture of pure and free information exchange, rather than selling, has carried over to today.

Traditional marketing approaches, especially the hard sell, don't work well on the Internet or with consumers in the Internet Age. To get readership and response, marketers have to create marketing messages that look, feel, and sound like objective, unbiased, useful information. And Internet marketers have quickly moved to accommodate this preference. They have to, if they want to generate results.

Customers increasingly want to be educated, if not universally than at least in a large number of industries and markets. These information-seeking prospects do not want to make decisions without having important facts, and they want to be treated respectfully, as the intelligent, thinking beings they are. Edu-marketing is perhaps the most effective type of marketing for today's marketplace of increasingly savvy buyers.

Does this mean today's buyer is logical, not emotional? On the contrary, thousands of buying decisions are made every day driven primarily by emotion. However, customers want facts—information, statistics, and proof—so they can justify their decision to themselves and others. Edu-marketing convinces them that their gut instincts are right and they are not making an error in buying from you. It also allows them to justify their emotional purchase decision to others, such as a spouse, by backing it up with facts.

It's common marketing and selling knowledge: Selling is educating. It's getting that person to understand why a product is beneficial. It's not convincing someone to buy.

This book's premise is that, in the Information Age, today's potential customers often respond best to marketing they perceive to be informational rather than promotional. For example, on the Internet, users overwhelmingly flock to sites that give them useful information rather than make a "sales pitch." White papers and other edu-marketing promotions educate the consumer about his or her problem and the solution to that problem. In some cases it makes the consumer aware that he or she actually has a problem.

In the 1920s, the Lambert Pharmacal Company built Listerine from zero sales into a national brand by educating the public on an obscure condition that previously most people had never heard of, "halitosis," which is the medical name for bad breath. Gerald Lambert tells the story in the 1957 book, *The Amazing Advertising Business*:

> I closed the door [and] announced that we would not leave the room until we had an advertising idea for Listerine. Marion spoke up apologetically. "How about bad breath?" he said.
>
> I asked Mr. Deacon if Listerine was good for bad breath. "It says in this clipping from the *British Lancet* that in cases of halitosis . . . "
>
> "What's halitosis?" I interrupted.
>
> "Oh!" he said, "that is the medical term for bad breath."

"There," I said, "is something to hang our hat on." We all agreed that we had found a way to refer to bad breath without quite so much offense . . . ."[1]

Listerine wasn't sold with white papers, but the idea was the same: commercials educated the consumer on a medical condition (halitosis) and its cure (Listerine).

Edu-marketing positions the marketer's product as an essential component of the solution provided. The consumer's awareness of the problem has been heightened, making him highly receptive to buying your solution.

He buys your product, and not your competitor's, because (a) he feels loyalty to you for being the one to educate him and (b) your marketing program has convinced him that your product is in fact the ideal solution.

Edu-Marketing Versus Traditional Marketing

Traditional marketing is product, service, or company-oriented. Edu-marketing is solutions oriented.

An example is a recent radio commercial for Advent, a company that helps amateur inventors bring their inventions to the marketplace.

If the commercial had merely said, "We charge a consulting fee to advise inventors on how to patent and promote their inventions," it probably wouldn't have gotten much of a response.

But this commercial made the offer of a specific educational bait piece. The announcer urged listeners to call a toll-free number, 1-800-681-IDEA, to request a "FREE Inventor's Kit."

Why does this approach work so much better than merely talking about the service?

1. It makes a free offer. And people love getting stuff for free.
2. It makes a specific offer that sounds valuable . . . an "Inventor's Kit" . . . even though you really aren't told what is in the kit. (It turns out to be a four-page color brochure combining a few tips for inventors about bringing their inventions to market with some information on Advent's services.)
3. It gives you the impression that you are going to get useful information and guidance on marketing your invention, rather than a hard sell for a consulting service.

The Hair Club for Men, a company selling hair replacement systems, takes a similar approach in its radio commercial: they urge the listener to call

1-800-500-4814 for a free special report on what to do about your thinning hair. They call it a "consumer awareness guide to hair replacement" to create a perception of value and objectivity.

Traditional marketing focuses on selling the consumer. Edu-marketing focuses on educating the consumer about his problem and the solution to his problem, with your product being part of the solution.

Connect Direct, a California company specializing in direct marketing for technology clients, advises: "Use offers that educate rather than sell. An effective information offer says 'here's how to solve a problem' versus 'here's why you should buy our product.'"[2]

Although the majority of white papers are produced by high-tech, business-to-business marketers, edu-marketing has wide applicability to both business and consumer marketing campaigns.

To promote its new 2005 SLK 350, Mercedes-Benz offered a free "SLK 350 Rush Kit" during its Fall 2004 advertising campaign. The kit was actually a nicely packaged CD-ROM, which was graphically designed to look like one of the car's tires and hub caps (easy to do because both the CD and the tire and hub cap are round).

Edu-marketing is most often used in direct response campaigns, but it also has its applications in retail. In a recent visit to my local CVS pharmacy, I picked up a free 32-page color magazine. Articles cover such topics as surviving allergy season, getting rid of acne, restricting dietary carbohydrates, and keeping a scrap book. But it also includes advertisements for products sold in CVS such as over-the-counter and prescription medications, nutritional supplements, and supplies for creating scrap books.

Consumers have an avid interest in health topics, and health care marketers increasingly see marketing opportunity in providing content to them. A full-page ad in *Reader's Digest* for ZOCOR, a cholesterol medication, offers a free copy of a "Heart Protection Study" to consumers who call a toll-free number or visit Merck's Web site. On another page in the same issue of the magazine, Pfizer's ad for Zoloft, an anti-depressant, offers a free information kit with a CD-ROM.

"When I was doing a direct mail promotion for *Campaigns & Elections* magazine some years ago, I noticed that there was a lot of editorial content about raising money for campaigns," says copywriter John Clausen. "We selected a bunch of the more promising articles and put them together in a booklet called, *Filling the War Chest: How to Raise Money for Political Campaigns.* "It was a huge hit; the client told me it was phenomenal."[3]

Nicole Riegel, Marketing Director of Better Buys for Business, says that while the primary goal of her company's Web site is to get visitors to buy on their first visit, others want to learn more about the products before doing so.

To meet this need, Riegel developed a series of free reports that provide useful and objective information prospects can use to make better buying decisions. All the prospect has to do to get a free report is provide an e-mail address, which allows Riegel to track whether those who request the freebie purchase later. According to Riegel, the conversion rate for customers who download the reports is 12 percent.[4]

Go to my Web site, *www.bly.com*, and you can see that I use the same free report strategy as Nicole. There are more than half a dozen how-to reports on various aspects of marketing, everything from direct mail and online marketing, to selling information products and software.

The reports are free. But to download them, you must give me your e-mail address, which helps me build a list of people interested in the types of problems and tasks that I handle as a freelance copywriter. Building a large "house file" (list of prospect e-mail addresses) is the key to successful online marketing, and we discuss this notion further in Chapter 9.

Why White Papers Work

Nick Copley, an executive with Bitpipe, a Web site that serves as an online clearinghouse for IT-oriented white papers, says that one reason for the popularity of white papers is the difficulty technology companies have getting coverage in the trade press: "The big publishers—the Ziffs, the IDGs, the CMPs—are scaling back the amount of editorial space they have to offer, and everyone is getting squeezed out."[5]

As a result, says Copley, many technology companies have chosen to bypass the trade press and reach their customers directly, usually with company-written "white papers," stand-alone articles about products and technology, case studies, market analysis, and strategy advice.

Bitpipe syndicates thousands of these white papers, and Copley says white paper readers are generally willing to accept a less-than-objective vendor perspective in such papers in exchange for getting useful information. "People are looking to get up to speed on technology anyway they can, and a little bias seems to be okay."[6]

There's no doubt about it: white paper marketing gets results. "I have been giving away a free white paper for the last three years while marketing online and I can assure you that it is an amazing strategy that delivers results," writes Donny Lowy of *www.closeoutexplosion.com*. "When used correctly it can increase your sales conversion ratio from 1 percent to as high as 3 percent. And in online marketing, even a 1 percent sales conversion would be satisfactory."[7]

White paper marketing works in two ways: It educates the buyer and it increases lead generation.

The first role is buyer education. This has two benefits: (a) it builds customer loyalty (they will buy from you instead of your competitors because you are their trusted advisor) and (b) it "sets the specs" for products in your category.

Setting the specs means your educational materials give guidelines for product selection, and these guidelines are written so that your product fits them best. Once the buyer gets the guidelines from your edu-marketing materials, he will use them to evaluate all products in your category—and of course yours will come out best, since you wrote the requirements to begin with.

For instance, one of the first things marketing expert Joe Polish did when he opened his carpet cleaning service was to write a booklet, *Consumers Guide to Carpet Cleaning*. The booklet warned consumers about the most common carpet-cleaning scams. "It provided a service to customers, taught them about my business, and increased my average sale by 100 percent," says Joe.[8] The text is now posted at *www.ethicalservices.com* (click on "Consumer Guide").

The other benefit of white paper marketing is that offering free, useful content increases response to lead-generating direct marketing including e-mail marketing, direct mail, print ads, and broadcast commercials. You can maximize response rates by offering your white papers as "bait pieces" (incentives for responding) to these promotions.

"I think the best way to attract potential customers is to give away free information," writes marketing consultant Jeffrey Dobkin. "It's valuable to the respondents, they can't get it anywhere else, and it's cheap to produce."[9] Why is offering free white papers and related informational pieces so effective? There are several reasons:

- It begins the relationship on a positive note, with you giving a valuable free gift to those you want to do business with.
- It acknowledges that the prospect is a thinking, decision-making human being who wants to make up his own mind; it does not talk down to people, as much advertising does.
- Marketers who educate their customers build better relationships with their marketplace and project a positive, leadership-oriented image. They are seen as more honest and credible than marketers whose only

objective seems to be to sell their product rather than solve the customer's problem.

- Consumers prefer to buy from vendors who seemingly put the customer first. When you educate the consumer, you demonstrate to her that you put her first.

- Marketers who educate their customer "sets the specs" for the purchase, and therefore have the best chance of closing the sale. If your marketing campaign teaches prospects the seven things to look for in a widget, and your widget has all seven, you will be the buyer's first choice.

- Manufacturers, service providers, and other vendors who provide educational materials on the selection, application, and proper usage of their products and services are perceived as recognized experts in their fields.

- People love to get free stuff, and so free offers increase response to marketing communications. When IBM sent out a direct mail piece offering three free golf balls to a target audience of CAD/CAM manufacturing engineers, the response rate exceeded 8 percent. On another IBM mailing offering Web services and products, a direct mail package offering a free information audiocassette generated six times greater response than the identical package without the free cassette offer. [10]

Are these leads worth anything? Do these bait piece requesters actually buy products? Or do they just want free stuff?

The Starch Reports analyzed 5 million inquiries received by 165 firms over a period of 12 years. They found that advertisements that generated the most inquiries usually brought in the most sales:

- Many prospects hesitate to call an 800-number in response to a mailing or advertisement, either because they are afraid of sales pressure or they're not exactly sure what to say or ask for. When you offer a free booklet in your ad, the prospect knows exactly what to say: "I'm calling to get your free booklet." When you make clear to the reader what the next step is, he is more likely to take it.

- When you advertise only a product or service, you only get responses from those prospects who are ready to buy today. When you add a free information offer, you also get responses from those prospects who are good candidates for what you are selling, but have a future rather than an immediate need. [11]

This last point warrants some amplification. Let's stop to examine its ramifications for your marketing program.

Reaching Prospects with Both Immediate and Future Needs

In my quarter century as a marketer, I have observed the following rule of thumb:

When you market to a group of target prospects, all of whom are qualified and can benefit from what you are selling, only 10 percent will have an immediate need for your product or service today; the other 90 percent will have a future need.

Therefore, if your marketing only targets those who are ready to buy today, you are missing 90 percent of the potential market for your product. As Connect Direct observes, "Focusing on only the most qualified prospects leaves many potential (albeit, more long-term) deals on the table. A potential customer might have precisely the problem that a particular product or service solves and are anxious to solve that problem, yet may not feel as through they're ready to buy and so fail to respond to the campaign."[12]

A marketing manager at H-P comments,

> Customers are like submarines. They spend most of their time 'underwater,' i.e., not in a buying mode. They surface every few months or years to buy. The goal of an edu-marketing campaign is to keep them thinking about your company and your products while they are in the underwater phase.[13]

Think about a printing firm, for example. Most businesses have only periodic needs to have materials printed. Let's say you are one of those businesses.

If you get a mailing from a printer and you do not need printing that week, you are likely to throw it away without responding. You are only likely to call and ask for a quote if the timing is right: the mailing arrives on your desk the very same day you have a need for some printing.

However, if the printer added the offer of a free booklet to the mailing, *10 Mistakes to Avoid When Preparing Your Next Job for the Printer*, you might say, "I don't have an immediate need, but this booklet sounds interesting and useful." So you call up to request it.

By doing so, you go from being a complete stranger to the printer to a becoming at least a "suspect," someone who may become a prospect for their printing services. After all, why would you request a booklet on how to prepare your next job for the printer unless you were going to have a "next job" at some point?

When you request it, the person answering the phone asks you questions. He probes deeper, and finds out that you're gearing up to do a new color catalog in a couple of months.

Based on that need, he tells you about his catalog printing capabilities, gets the details of your catalog from you, and sends you a quotation. If you approve it, he has just made a sale he would not have otherwise made . . . because he offered you "bait" and you took it!

If you rent a mailing list, you can only use those names one time; if you want to mail to them again, you have to rent the names again. The exception is those who respond to your mailing. If a person replies, you can add their name to your own list, and from then on you "own" that name, and can mail to it as often as you like without paying an additional fee to the mailing list owner.

When you only generate response from those who have a need for your product or service today, the number of replies received is small, and so you build your "house list" slowly.

But when you offer a bait piece, you get responses not only from those who need to buy today but also from a larger audience—those who may have a need in the future. When they reply, you can add their names to your own list, reducing your future list rental costs because you now own those names.

The best way to reduce marketing costs and increase return on investment (ROI) from your marketing is to concentrate on building up your house list. And you can do that much more rapidly by constantly offering different bait pieces in your promotions.

Positioning Yourself as the Expert

It is a mistake to imagine that writers are experts on the things they write about," says Parker Palmer, a senior adviser to the Fetzer Institute, in his book *The Active Life*:

> I write about things I am still wrestling with, things that are important to me but that I have not yet figured out. Once I master something, I put it behind me. I lose the passionate curiosity that writing a book requires. I write to explore vexing questions and real dilemmas, to take myself into territories I have never seen before in hopes of understanding myself and the world a bit better.[14]

Nevertheless, publishing and disseminating advice and information on a particular topic creates the impression that you are an expert in that topic. Says publisher Edward Uhlan in his book *The Rogue of Publishers Row*, "Simply because what a man says appears in print, people assume he has something to say."

We are inundated with information today, but starved for knowledge, wisdom, and solutions. Consumers increasingly turn to those they perceive as experts for this knowledge, wisdom, and solutions.[15]

"There is nothing wrong with deferring to genuine expertise," says writer Jamie Whyte. "You need to defer to some people because you simply can't do all the research on everything yourself."[16]

Ironically, creating edu-marketing campaigns helps make you a genuine expert in your topic. Consider the five ways of learning something:

1. Doing the thing.
2. Observing the thing.
3. Teaching others to do the thing.
4. Doing primary research (e.g., interviewing experts).
5. Doing secondary research (e.g., reading about the thing).

To create information-rich white papers with genuinely valuable and accurate content involves at least three of these five learning methods (numbers three, four, and five). Therefore, the more you write about a topic, the more you learn about it. Eventually, without even being aware of it, your knowledge level increases to where you know more about the subject than 90 percent of the people interested and involved in it.

Consultant Hubert Bermont suggests that free reports and other bait piece offers can effectively sell prospects regardless of whether they find the content helpful.

Bermont suggests making a follow-up call a week or so after you send out your free report and asking whether the information was useful to the prospect.

If the prospect says "yes," then you can suggest an appointment so they can learn how you can help them apply the ideas or methods in the report to solving their specific problem.

If the prospect says "no," you can explain that the report was necessarily written in general terms, because you do not know their specific problem. But by meeting with them, you can learn their specific problem and recommend an effective and appropriate solution. So either way, sending a bait piece can move the sale forward.[17]

The Edu-Marketing Mindset

Edu-marketers are solutions-focused and information-oriented. You must identify a core market, then thoroughly understand a pressing problem of theirs that your product is really good at solving.

You also need to act as an "information advocate" for these customers, taking on the job of educating them about the problem and its solutions. Yet you are in business to sell products, not give away free information. The key is to selectively disseminate information that appears unbiased, but in fact forwards the goal of getting the customer to choose your product over the competition.

It's impossible to sell a product or service without demand—no matter how low the price or how big the discount. Edu-marketing creates demand by showing prospects why they need your products and services, how to make intelligent buying decisions, and how to best use it after they buy.

Edu-marketing creates a "halo" surrounding everything you sell. When you promote an individual product or service, only that particular product or service benefits. But, empowering customers and prospects benefits every product and service you sell.

Information pre-sells and differentiates. It builds customer confidence and positions you as credible, knowledgeable, and trusted. Information sets you apart. You become a unique, trusted adviser.

A successful white paper answers questions that must be answered before prospects will buy:

- Who benefits from the product or service?
- What benefits does the product or service offer?
- When is the product or service needed?
- Why is the product or service better than other products and services designed for the same application?
- Where is the product or service used?
- How do you choose and use it?

Conventional advertising is hard to create because it's judged by its creativity—how effectively it attracts attention, how clearly it delivers its message, and how memorable it is. By comparison, edu-marketing is easier to create because the goal is to inform, rather than interrupt, manipulate, or show off.

All you have to do is answer the six questions listed above. If you understand your market and can sell in face-to-face situations, you can create your own effective content.

Thanks to the Internet and desktop publishing, you can do most of the production yourself using your PC, saving on expensive outside production costs.

In the past, you had to advertise, mail, or deliver marketing messages in person. Advertising involved expensive newspaper space or radio station time charges. Mailing involved printing, addressing, and postage costs. Presentations involved travel, lodging, and conference room rentals.

Today, you can distribute educational messages for free as Web site downloads or as e-mail attachments. Options include:

- *White papers.* These analyze challenges and trends, and show how to benefit from your products and services.
- *E-books.* These offer in-depth, procedural descriptions that demonstrate your competence and communicate how-to-buy and how-to-use tips.
- *E-mail newsletters.* You can keep in constant touch with customers without addressing, printing, and postage costs.
- *E-courses.* You can automatically deliver information in chunks over a period of several days—or even weeks.[18]

You can also present teleseminars, which permit prospects to get to know you in an informal, interactive environment. Free line rentals are available; others cost about $25 an hour.

Edu-marketing works best when you keep in touch and deliver information at frequent intervals. Once created, you can recycle your newsletters as articles, columns, and presentations to drive Web site traffic.

The effect of disseminating free content as a marketing tool is cumulative. The more information you share, the more your market will look forward to your messages and refer coworkers and friends to you. Customers and prospects give you their total attention when you offer information that helps them achieve their goals. Education messages last far longer than promotional or price advertising, which your market quickly forgets.

My colleague Joe Vitale is a master of edu-marketing, not only creating and disseminating valuable free content to build his reputation, but converting those who request his free information into paying customers for his products and services.

Joe calls this his "karma" model (©copyright 2004 Joe Vitale and Bob Serling):

I have this model that I'm going to call almost a "karma model." It's one where I give now in order to receive later. And there's a big focus on giving information. A lot of it is just tips, articles, white papers, and excerpts from white papers.

If people go to my Web site at *www.mrfire.com* they'll see dozens and dozens of articles and interviews and audios and book excerpts, along with my catalog, of course, but the whole idea is I am giving and giving and giving and giving.

Why am I doing that? One thing I learned, maybe 15 years ago when I first went online, is that the Internet began with this gift culture mentality. People went on there to receive things. They wanted information, and they wanted it for free.

So they were trained right away that they didn't have to buy anything on the Internet, that they would go looking around and they could find any answers that they wanted, solutions that they wanted, information, white papers, whatever it happens to be, and they were used to not paying for it.

So my model was really modeled after that whole concept, and I continued it. Of course, why do I continue it? Because it works for me.

What I do is build relationships with people, I build trust with people. I establish my own credibility with these people, and through these freebies, where they like my articles and they like my excerpts.

Underneath it all, almost unconsciously, they start to conclude, "Wow, Joe really knows a lot about Internet marketing," or, "Wow, Joe really knows a lot about hypnotic writing," or, "Wow, when it comes to doing anything online, when I want to hire somebody, I better go see this guy, because he knows what he's talking about."

Well, how do they come to those conclusions? By all the free information that they saw on my Web site, as well as all the free information which I distributed across the Internet, which is something we'll touch on a little bit later.

But my whole model, if I had to sum it up, is: I give now in order to receive later. And there are key benefits that I've mentioned—the trust, the credibility, building rapport, building a relationship, getting my name out there. I'm almost building a brand, because people become familiar with Joe Vitale.

I'm giving information that solves a problem. It's not fluff. It's not hype. It's not something that somebody might read and say, "Oh, that was boring," or, "That wasn't very interesting," or "That wasn't very helpful."

It's important that whatever is being given is really meaty, so that people feel, "This is something I can use. This is something that solves a problem that I have right now." So a sense of respect is going on.

You can give all kinds of things out there that are garbage, and it's not going to build rapport or credibility or trust or a relationship, and people won't care if they do business with you later when you ask for money. So whatever you give needs to be relevant to your target audience. That's an important fundamental first step.

The other is with everything that I give, there's always a subtle call to buy at the end of it. This again began with the Internet being an information-exchange type of media. So I focus on giving something like 95 percent information and maybe about 5 percent or even less of a sales plug.

The best example I can give is the various articles that I've been distributing online for 15 years, most of which are at *www.mrfire.com*. Read any of those articles, and when you get to the very end of it, you're going to see what you and I know as a "resource box." That can also be called an "advertisement," but we won't say that on the Internet, because that's a bad word.

In the resource box, it says something to the effect of, "If you want to know more about Joe Vitale's products or services, or want to hire him as a copywriter, or get his latest package of goods, go to this Web site." So there's always a subtle call to action. It's almost subliminal, but it's acceptable in the way that I just described it.

So while I am teaching people that I'm going to give them something for free, I'm also teaching them that I'm the expert when you want something more, and here's how to find it, or reach me, or find this product, through the resource box that's always at the end of what I just gave out.

So those are some of the things that I'm doing. So I'm training people to receive, but I'm also training them to buy.[19]

Common Objections to White Papers

Some marketing departments shy away from developing white papers, despite the many benefits they offer. Common objections to white papers include the following:

- *"White papers are not marketing collateral, so why should the marketing department be involved? Let the engineers write them; they understand the technology."*

In the past, white papers were written by technical staff to explain the intricate details of new technologies to those charged with implementing them. But times have changed.

According to some analysts, corporate decision-makers rely on white papers more than almost any other source of information available to them. The solid technical information contained in such collateral helps decision-makers understand the business case of the offering. This goal fits squarely in the bailiwick of marketing, not engineering.

There is an old argument in technical writing about whether it is better to have engineers do the writing, and then let technical writers clean up the grammar and language; or have professional technical writers interview the engineers, write the draft, and have engineers check it for accuracy. We will explore the various options for developing content, especially on technical subjects, in Chapter 4.

- *"We already have sufficient marketing collateral. Look at our data sheets and product brochures!"*

White papers combine with brochures, data sheets, and case studies to provide a comprehensive portfolio of collateral. Product brochures generate interest in the offering. Data sheet specifications demonstrate that the offering can be integrated into a potential customer's environment. Case studies demonstrate that the offering has worked successfully for other users. But only the depth of detail available in a white paper can convince technical decision-makers that the offering actually works.

- *"White papers take forever to write. We need to go to market immediately."*

It's true that an effective white paper can take longer to develop than some forms of collateral. But with a committed team of developers and content providers, it can be written, edited, illustrated, laid out, and distributed in as little time as three weeks.[20]

Why White Papers Fail . . . and Succeed

People often view white papers as bafflingly complex documents that only engineers, scientists, or other professionals in specialized fields can understand. Sadly, this reputation isn't entirely unearned. Some companies that recognize the potential benefits of white papers publish documents that create more marketing harm than good. Some white papers fail because they:

- *Lack objectivity.* Biased information alienates readers and instills doubt about the paper's validity. Instead of making unsubstantiated claims about a specific offering's suitability and benefits, a high-quality white paper educates the audience about solutions to their problems. Writers should cite outside sources such as analyst research or industry reports whenever possible to strengthen the credibility of the business case and to demonstrate the technical prowess of the offering.
- *Provide inadequate or inappropriate technical detail.* A white paper that glosses over the details of how an offering helps solve a business problem is little more than a lengthy brochure. By contrast, a

document that focuses solely on technical detail without placing the offering in a larger business context fails to make a persuasive case. Effective white papers explain innovative technologies in a compelling way that helps potential customers understand both how and why the offering will improve their business climate.

- *Offer sub par writing.* An effective white paper clearly communicates a wealth of technical detail without condescending to the audience or making unreasonable assumptions about their prior knowledge. The communication skills needed to write white papers differ significantly from those required for marketing and advertising copy or for technical documents such as user manuals and training materials.

- *Uses inappropriate information density for the intended audience.* "Information density" refers to the technical depth and level of detail in a document. Often white papers on technical subjects written for an executive audience have too high an information density (too much technical detail), while white papers written for engineers and scientists have too low an information density (they are too superficial).

- *Takes too much time and work to produce.* The problem with white papers is that somebody has to write them. However, by following the directions in this book, you will be able to produce effective white papers without an unreasonable expenditure of time and labor.

- *White papers and other free information offers are so common and overused today, they don't work any more.* This statement sounds logical, but fortunately, it isn't true. If your white paper is specific to the interests of your target audience, and promises a useful benefit as a reward for reading, prospects will respond to it. Having said that, if you are in a market where white papers are proliferating, there are alternative formats that can generate response when white papers seem to be overused; these are discussed in Chapter 7.[21]

One solution is simply to call your white paper something other than a "white paper." Ivan Levison, a copywriter specializing in the software industry, prefers the term "guide" to "white paper."[22] Other alternatives include "bulletin," "special report," "monograph," and "executive briefing."

Case Study: International Paper

In 1979, International Paper (IP) launched—in *BusinessWeek*, among other publications—what has come to be recognized as one of the most successful corporate advertising programs of all time. Titled "The Power of the Printed Word," the campaign's ostensible objective was "to help young people read faster, write more clearly, and communicate better." Exhibit 1.1 shows one of the ads in the series.

"The Power of the Printed Word" won virtually every major advertising award, attracted requests for more than 39 million reprints, and earned for the company public praise from literacy groups and librarians, teachers' organizations, editors and publishers, the President of the United States and the First Lady. Decades later, some or all of the ads are still in use in all levels of schools, in churches and prisons, in the military and in industrial training.

All of this approbation, however, has to do with its success as advertising, which is not the business of the International Paper Company. The company's senior management did not summon its corporate communications staff one morning and say, "Please develop an award-winning corporate advertising program." Nor, for that matter, did management give what one corporate advertising veteran calls "the dog-catcher's lament"—to wit: "Nobody out there understands us, so why don't you develop a program that will make us famous?"

That "The Power of the Printed Word" became an award-winning corporate advertising program and that awareness of and favorable feeling toward the company increased were by-products of the program's real mission, which was deeply rooted in the profitability of one of IP's core businesses.

In fact, the company did not start out with a commitment to do advertising at all. The genesis of the program was an explication by a policy-level executive of a threat the company was facing, and an invitation to corporate communications and other departments to suggest solutions.

The threat had to do with the perception—not inaccurate—by the company's most important single group of customers—publishers of books, magazines and newspapers, and commercial printers—that International Paper was making major investments in other segments of its business and neglecting their needs.

In fact, the company had invested five billion dollars over the previous seven years to become both the leading producer of paper-based packaging and a player in wood products. IP had even acquired an oil company.

Meanwhile, postal rate increases were having a negative impact on the profits of its customers in the publishing business, and one remedy for this would have been production of a lighter-weight magazine paper. Publishers resented the fact that the dollars IP could have invested in a new paper mill for their benefit were being allocated elsewhere.

Some leaders in the publishing industry had begun to publicly question IP's commitment to the printing and publishing industries, and to privately threaten to drop the company from its position as the number one or two supplier to third or fourth. This would have had a disastrous effect on International Paper's own profitability at a time when the company was already having difficulty making money.

The company's problem, reduced to its simplest terms, was "How can we maintain our market share in this business for the next five years so we can make the billion-dollar investment a new paper mill will ultimately require?"

A routine advertising "solution" might have been a campaign in trade magazines proclaiming that "International Paper is committed to printing and publishing." Corporate advertising of this kind is common . . . and valueless. Even if true, such advertising—one expert calls it "we-we" advertising—is empty and patently self-serving. It insults the intelligence of the customer and embarrasses employees who must still deal with whatever problems caused the ads to be run in the first place.

What was required in this case was to reaffirm International Paper's historic commitment to printing and publishing, but to do so in a credible way. Concerned customers had to be given reasons to believe that the company ultimately would make the investment they wanted.

Instead of looking only at what corporate officials in the paper business wanted to say, advertising management and the ad agency looked at what issues, besides those related to the cost and availability of paper, the leaders of the customer group were concerned about.

Extensive research turned up a common denominator among printing and publishing business executives everywhere: they were worried about the ability and propensity of young people to read and write as well as earlier generations had, leading to a shared fear that the next generation would be less dependent on the printed word for information, entertainment, and communication.

Again, the usual Pavlovian advertising response to this discovery would have been another wave of ads in trade magazines saying "Look at this declining S.A.T. verbal curve: we who care about printing and publishing have a problem."

This is another common category of corporate advertising, dubbed by one observer "the politics of noble concern," which points with alarm at a problem, but doesn't do anything to solve it. But International Paper's leaders thought customers would respond better to actions than to words, if a way could be found to genuinely help.

Eventually, two of several creative ideas were merged and the concept of credible celebrities, sponsored by IP, actually teaching language skills, was born.

But this still was only the advertising—an essential element—but still only one element of the total program it was going to take to produce a basic change in not only what customers thought, but how they were planning to behave.

Wrapped around the advertising was an integrated marketing communications program, comprising major publicity, public relations, and merchandising efforts to every important customer, influence, and potential ally externally; plus a similarly coherent effort internally, before the advertising ran, to explain the program to employees throughout the company.

Salespeople calling on the customer group the campaign was designed to reach were given a two-and-a-half hour briefing, with training sessions on how to use the campaign to achieve the company's objectives. Salespeople calling on other kinds of customers were also exposed to the program in advance and taught how to use it in different ways.

Plant and mill community relations people were given kits to use with local school systems. Employees everywhere were encouraged to use the program to help their own children and grandchildren. So were shareowners.

Clearly, this campaign incorporated a specific business objective important to the company; performing a service to the reader, executed in a fresh, noncliché way; and integrating a total program involving the entire organization.

Research before the program ran showed that printing and publishing industry leaders rated most paper companies alike—poorly. None were perceived as "putting anything back into the industry."

Six months after the launch of "The Power of the Printed Word" advertising program, a significant perceptual gap had opened between International Paper and its competitors, a gap that still existed a decade later.

For several years, until the company was finally able to invest significantly in the publishing segment of its business, as well as solve quality problems that had further complicated relationships with some customers, the only difference was "The Power of the Printed Word."

Not only did International Paper keep threatened business, but some customers actually said that if all other factors—price, delivery, terms, etc.—were equal, they would use "The Power of the Printed Word" as a tiebreaker for selecting a vendor.

The program's return on investment could be measured in more than the usual soft terms, such as increases in awareness and favorable attitudes in the marketplace, community approval, even employee morale gains. It could be measured in hard dollars saved. In effect, the company had used a $1.5 million dollar yearly corporate advertising program to defer a billion dollar investment for five years, without losing market share at a time when the cost of money was astronomical, even for "most favored borrowers."

Bait Pieces

To promote his freelance business, Swiss copywriter Aurel Gergey decided to offer a bait piece to attract potential clients:

> I thought it would be a good idea to compress some of the voluminous German style guide books into a handy white paper, says Aurel. This I did one year ago, and it worked from the beginning on very well. It's now one of my self-marketing work horses.
>
> Since beginning to offer my brief white paper online, I have had more than 10,000 downloads. These have brought me dozens of interesting contacts and several new clients.
>
> And, the white paper spreads itself, via word of mouth on the Internet. The only thing I have to do is watch it spreading like a virus and to smile. Quite a nice way to promote my business.
>
> I run Google Ads, which bring me another 50 to 100 downloads a month, with a click-through rate of around 2 percent. Also, several newsletters and magazines asked me if they could reprint my white paper in their pages, and of course I agreed. I ordered an International Society for Strategic Marketing (ISSM) number for my white paper too, which gives more credibility.[23]

Aurel is writing more white papers and has launched a new Web site and a free e-zine to promote them. For details, visit *www.gergey.com/konzentrate.php*.

I have used a similar strategy, with minimal cost and effort, to successfully promote my freelance copywriting services here in the U.S.

On my Web site, *www.bly.com*, there is an *Articles* page where I have posted several dozen articles I have written over the years on a variety of marketing topics. All are available as downloadable Word files.

I assigned a freelance desktop designer to create a series of special reports. Each consists of six to ten of these articles grouped by topic and designed as a downloadable PDF. For instance, one title, "Secrets of Successful Software and Technology Marketing," is aimed at marketing managers of high-tech companies.

Each report is approximately 50 pages. Although these individual articles also can be downloaded from the *Articles* page on my Web site, many of my prospects and clients tell me they prefer the PDF format.

The point is that people will seek out, whether for free or fee, the same content in a variety of different formats. So it makes sense to offer your information packaged in different ways (see Chapter 7).

Content as a Marketing Tool

Business-to-business (b-to-b) marketing professionals, including those in the technology industry, routinely rate content-driven activities, such as their Web site, webcasts, and white papers, as their most effective means of generating qualified sales leads. Yet these activities currently represent less than 25 percent of their total marketing spent—about the same portion allocated to the least effective lead-generation tools.

This paradox—less spending being allocated to the most effective tools—is largely explained by the lack of a content strategy at most b-to-b marketing organizations. A content strategy puts the emphasis on the content instead of focusing exclusively on the marketing delivery vehicles that disseminate it. In most organizations, there is no explicit budget devoted to creating content because most marketing professionals are pursuing, either explicitly or implicitly, a delivery vehicle marketing strategy. A content strategy places the emphasis in the right place by concentrating on prospects or customers and their content and information needs.

Content marketing calls for the segmentation of customers and prospects into distinct audiences defined by their stage in the buying cycle and their role in the buying decision. Bitpipe, a Web site that distributes white papers on the Web (*www.bitpipe.com*), refers to this as a *content matrix*. In Chapter 2 you'll learn how to create and use a content matrix to plan your edu-marketing campaign.

For instance, here's how technology marketers apply a content matrix and a content marketing methodology: They create content that meets the information needs of specific prospect groups, such as CIOs or IT professionals, at different points in the sales cycle in appropriate marketing vehicles chosen to deliver the correct target audience.

Technology marketers are now discovering that content strategy and content marketing are powerful methods for acquiring and nurturing contacts, which in turn become valuable qualified sales leads in the IT enterprise-buying cycle.[24]

After all, b-to-b buyers are always searching for valuable, in-depth content to support their buying decisions. While standard "low content" advertising messages are increasingly failing to gain attention, focused and highly relevant content available on demand online is hitting home.

So next time someone says, "Let's write a white paper for this direct mail campaign" or "We need more leads, let's do a teleconference," stop and set a content strategy. Use a content matrix and content marketing to deliver the right leads from the right people at the right time in the buying cycle. Chapters 2 through 10 explain how to do a content-based, edu-marketing campaign in detail.

2

What Makes for an Effective Bait Piece?

It's a paradox.

"Edu-marketing"—educational marketing—is the most successful type of marketing being done today. And the basis of edu-marketing is to provide content, written material, and information to potential customers.

Yet, isn't the most common complaint we hear from people is that there is too much to read . . . and not enough time to read it? That we are living in an Information Age in which we are mercilessly and continually bombarded by more reading material, commercial messages, and data than we could ever hope to absorb?

And I'm sure you have heard people dismiss your suggestion of offering a free report or booklet as a premium with this objection: "Engineers (or farmers, or computer programmers, or whoever your target audience is) don't read."

Oh, yeah? Says who?

For example, I am a chemical engineer and have been writing marketing materials aimed at engineers for 25 years. Just the other day, a client (himself an engineer) proclaimed to me, as if it were a fundamental truth, "Engineers don't read."

Yet consider these realities:

- After telling me "engineers don't have time to read," he then told me, "I spend most of my day writing." His customers, the people he is writing to, are engineers. If nobody reads, who is reading all that writing and why is he doing it?
- To earn a college degree in engineering, or anything else, required an

enormous amount of reading. This is even true for getting a high school diploma. So unless your market consists solely of high school dropouts, your prospects are accustomed to reading.

- Many large companies take writing skills into account when hiring and when making promotions. Each year, corporations spend significant amounts of money to remedy their employees' writing deficiencies.
- To keep current in almost any specialized field, whether you are a manager, accountant, engineer, or programmer, you have to read industry trade journals.
- To keep up with the business world, you have to read business magazines and newspapers.
- Much of the information we need on products, technologies, and vendors is posted on Web sites. All of it is written, and needs to be read.
- One can make an argument that the growing popularity of e-mail as the primary communication tool used by businesspeople, especially those in the corporate world, is raising reading and writing skills to a higher level.

When I started out in corporate marketing departments in the late 1970s, no self-respecting executive would be caught dead using a keyboard; that's what your secretary was for. As a staff writer in the marketing communications department at Westinghouse, I literally had to beg to be given an old typewriter; all of the other people in my department wrote by hand on legal yellow pads and gave their copy to our secretary, Mrs. H., to type.

Today, almost every manager in corporate America has a computer and uses e-mail, and they all type their own e-mail messages. As e-mail's usage increases, the volume of phone calls and face-to-face meetings declines; it's just much easier to send an e-mail. Therefore, thanks to e-mail, we are becoming more of a "reading and writing" society than we were a generation ago.

Of course, the assertion that "nobody reads today" is utter nonsense. The fact is that all of us read, all of the time.

When somebody says "nobody reads today," what he really means is that people are busier than ever before, work longer hours, and have more responsibilities. Therefore, the time they can devote to any task—whether it's reading, lawn care, or home maintenance—is more limited than it might have been years or decades ago.

As edu-marketers providing content to prospects and customers as a marketing gambit, how do we adjust our writing style to accommodate today's busy, time-pressed reader?

Here are four quick suggestions:

1. *Be concise.* Say what you have to say in the fewest possible words. When you are wordy, you waste the busy reader's time.
2. *Write for scanners and skimmers.* Increasingly people skim and scan rather than read the entire document. Use heads, subheads, bullets, numbers, tables, charts, and graphs so that the reader who skims quickly can get the gist of the message.
3. *Make the content relevant.* Eliminate nuggets of information and facts that, while interesting, do not prove or clarify your key points. If the reader wants extraneous information, he can get more than his fill on the Web. Don't waste space in your white paper with such facts; present only the most germane information.
4. *Use a value-added approach.* We are drowning in information but starved for knowledge. Most readers don't need more data and facts. What they need—and what your white paper should give them—is ideas, tips, guidance, wisdom, advice, and solutions.

Are Words Necessary?

Related to the "people don't read" argument is the "one picture is worth a thousand words" argument: that people don't have time to read, and prefer instead to look at a picture.

My client told me, "Engineers don't like to read, but they like to look at pictures." He implied that as long his marketing documents featured lots of color pictures of his product (gears and rollers), those promotions would be successful.

The problem with this approach is the assumption that a picture without accompanying words communicates the point you want to make to the reader, which in fact, it almost never does.

The "people don't read" crowd is wary of words for two reasons: first, because they believe people don't have time to read. And second, because of the rising illiteracy rate, they fear that people don't know how to read.

What they should be worried about, however, is "visual illiteracy," the fact that people don't know how to accurately read and interpret graphs, charts, schematics, drawings, blueprints, and other forms of visual communication.

Rudolph Flesch eloquently explained this concept of visual illiteracy in his classic 1949 book, *The Art of Readable Writing*:

"Easy writing's vile hard reading," wrote Sheridan. The reverse is equally true: easy reading is difficult to write. In fact, it seems to be so difficult that most people would rather try anything else but write when they face a job of simple explanation. They escape from words into pictures, symbols, graphs, charts, diagrams—anything at all as long as it's "visual." They point to the movies, the comics, the picture magazines. Obviously, they say, the trend nowadays is away from reading. People would rather just look.

That may be so; but unfortunately the idea that you can explain things without explaining them in words is pure superstition. If that surprises you, look at the evidence. There's the psychologist, for instance, who tried to find out whether children understood the charts and diagrams in the Britannica Junior Encyclopedia. It turned out that they did not. Most of the devices used blithely by the encyclopedia writers were way over the heads of the children. They have been taught how to read, but nobody had ever bothered to tell them anything about how to look at flow charts, statistical graphs, process diagrams, and the like.

Naturally, that doesn't mean that you should never illustrate visually what you have to say. Not at all: anything pictorial or graphic does help as long as there is enough text to back it up. I don't mean captions; I mean that the running text has to tell the reader what the illustration means, how he should look at it, and why. Tell the reader what to see. Remember that graphs and charts reading is not one of the three R's.[1]

In my client's case, for instance, he was promoting a unique technology—plastic gears with metal cores—that had major technical advantages over all-plastic and all-metal gears. These included greater dimensional stability, longer life, greater durability, lighter weight, reduced noise and vibration, less maintenance, and no need for lubrication. Other plastic gears absorbed water, which caused swelling; his did not. Metal gears require oil or grease and therefore must be enclosed in a gear box; his needed no oil and no gear box was required.

As he told me these facts and I took notes for some copy I was writing for him, I looked at a board in his office where a dozen pictures of different gears were pinned to the wall. The photos were of professional quality, clearly showing the gears. And what struck me is how these photos *did not communicate a single key advantage or feature of the plastic and metal gears* that he was telling me about.

By looking at the photos in his product brochure, you could get a clearer idea of how the metal and plastic were arranged in the gear. But this merely helped the reader see what the text had already made clear.

When people are given tools that are quick and easy, they tend to overuse them, and that has certainly been the case these last few years with desktop publishing software, digital imaging, Microsoft® PowerPoint®, Adobe® Photo-

Shop®, and html. Businesspeople who produce printed and online documents have gone "visual-crazy," over designing their presentations, Web sites, and communications to the nth degree.

Judicious use of visuals and graphics is more effective than overuse. Include photos, charts, and graphs not because your software makes it easy to do so, but because these visuals illustrate, clarify, demonstrate, or prove a point in the text. Despite what the picture people say, visuals are most effective when they support text, rather than attempt to replace it.

The same advice applies to document formatting and templates: Documents written by the average corporate middle manager today are top-heavy with formatting and graphics, which they believe are impressive, but are actually unnecessary and add nothing to the communication.

Take a look today at a few books, magazines, and newspapers. Notice the simplicity of the page layout and design. This simplicity is not by accident; professional graphic designers know that a clean, uncluttered page makes copy easier to read than a graphically busy and crowded page. Take a tip from their book and keep your page layouts clean, simple, and uncluttered.

Do not overestimate the reader's ability to interpret charts and graphs. Follow Flesch's advice and provide explanatory text. Annotate the graphs with call-outs and arrows. If you are showing a graph of commodity prices to demonstrate their cyclical nature, have one call-out that says "Low here—buy" and another pointing to the top of the curve that says "High here—sell."

Creating the Basis Document

If you are just getting started with white paper marketing, I recommend that you spend some time now creating a "basis document."

The *basis document* is a first, straightforward informational piece, typically 1,500 to 2,500 words long, from which you can spin off a variety of press releases, articles, booklets, tip sheets, and other bait pieces. It is meant to give an audience unfamiliar with your product a basic understanding of the problem your product solves, how the product works, and perhaps a few tips on selection and implementation.

There are two formats you can use for your basis document: list and FAQ (frequently asked questions).

List Format

To create a basis document in the *list format*, start with a headline that reads, "10 Tips for _____." In the blank, fill in your basic topic. For instance, if you are a Web site designer, your headline would read, "10 Tips for Designing an Effective Web Site."

Under the headline, write the numbers one through ten in a vertical column as follows:

Exhibit 2.1: List Format

Now fill in ten simple facts you know about your topic. Don't worry about their order, weight, or importance. One of the items can be a major concept; the next can be a common-sense tip; and the one after that could be a technical point.

After you list the ten facts, go back to your list and fill in a little more detail and explanation about each—no more than two or three paragraphs. Now take a look at it. You have just created your first bait piece, a tip sheet. You can print copies on your laser printer, and begin offering a free copy of "10 Tips for More Effective Web Design" (or whatever your topic) to prospects and customers.

Tip: run off copies on colored stock instead of white paper. I recommend canary yellow. Then in your ads, offer one or a series of "yellow sheets" (or whatever color you choose); the use of colored paper makes the tip sheet stand out from the other pieces of paper on the prospect's desk.

Want to capture business cards from potential customers when giving a speech or presentation at an association meeting? Reference your tips and then say, as you hold up your yellow tip sheet, "If you want a hard copy of these tips, write 'Yellow Sheet' or 'YS' on your business card and give it to me." Fifty to 90 percent of the people in attendance will give you their cards to get this sheet, which you can send them in the mail along with your catalog or sales brochure.

Question and Answer Format

Another format that works well for this basic document is a question and answer (or FAQ) format.

First, write the headline, "10 Questions About ____—and One Good Answer to Each. In the blank, fill in your topic; for instance, "10 Questions About Designing Effective Web Sites—and One Good Answer to Each."

Next, type a vertical column of ten pairs of Qs and As under the headline as shown in Exhibit 2.2.

Now, next to each Q, write a question that prospects commonly ask you about your topic (e.g., "Should I use animation on my home page?," "How do I optimize my site for search engines?," "Will having a blog improve my rankings in the search engines?," "Should my pages be php or html?").

Next to the A under each Q, write a short (two to three paragraphs) answer to the question. Edit, proofread, and your FAQ tip sheet is done!

In today's marketplace, a bait piece is highly recommended, if not an absolute necessity, for lead generation campaigns. Without a bait piece, most lead generation campaigns are lucky to generate a 1 percent response rate. With a bait piece offer, your lead generation campaign can realistically generate response rates of 2 percent to 3 percent or even higher. Therefore, adding a bait piece offer can double or triple response to the same letter or e-mail versus not offering a bait piece.

What does this mean for you? If you are using direct mail and getting a 1 percent response rate, you must mail 10,000 pieces to produce 100 leads. But if you can double your response rate to 2 percent by adding a bait piece, you can generate the same 100 leads by mailing only 5,000 pieces. If your cost in the mail is a dollar per mailing, offering the bait piece saves you $5,000 in printing, postage, and list rental costs.

Most marketers doing lead generation know they should offer some type of bait piece, but what stops them is the lack of an appropriate bait piece to give away. When you go through the above exercise and create the text for a basis document, that problem is solved.

Exhibit 2.2: Question and Answer Format

Q:
A:

Q:
A:

Q:
A:

Q:
A:

Q:
A:

Q:
A:

Q:
A:

Q:
A:

Q:
A:

Q:
A:

Once you have the basis document, you can package it in a variety of formats and media, e.g., a special report, booklet, tip sheet, audiocassette, giving you the bait piece you need for your lead generation campaign to generate significantly greater response.

Choosing the Topic for Your Bait Piece

The key to choosing a topic for a successful white paper is to narrow the focus. *Horizontal topics*—those that appeal to a wide audience—don't work as well for white papers and for informational writing in general as *vertical topics*—those that appeal to a narrow, specific audience.

The strongest white papers target a narrow niche. Speaker Wally Bock defines a niche as the intersection of a topic (e.g., customer service) with an industry (e.g., banking).[2] Therefore, if your audience is banking executives, "Improving Customer Service in Your Bank" is likely to generate a higher readership than a paper titled "Improving Customer Service."

The broader the topic you select, the more difficult the writing task ahead of you. For instance, if your topic is safety, well . . . hundreds of books, articles, and Web sites have already been written about safety. What will you cover that they do not? What added value can you provide the reader to justify his time spent with your white paper?

Another problem with a broad topic is how to do justice to it in the limited space available to you. You cannot begin to cover the whole of safety in a five or ten-page white paper. The idea of tackling this daunting task may result in a bad case of writer's block for you.

When the topic you have selected seems too big, use the "What about?" technique. How this works: if the topic is safety, ask yourself, "What about safety?" Say you work for a company that manufactures industrial gases. The answer could be, "I want to write a white paper about safety when using industrial gases."

Better, but could you narrow it further? Ask yourself, "What about industrial gas safety?" What aspect do you really want to cover? It should ideally be one (a) in which you have some special expertise or knowledge and (b) related to your product.

In our example, the answer might have been, "I want to write a white paper about safe handling of compressed gases stored in cylinders." Now you have a manageable topic about which you can say something meaningful in the limited space a white paper affords you.

There are several benefits to performing the "What about?" exercise and narrowing your topic. As a rule, the narrower your topic the better, and here is why:

1. The narrower your topic, the more specific your topic. Specifics attract readers more powerfully than generalities.

2. When the topic is well defined, you can give some meaningful, practical advice and information about it. When you have to cover everything, you often end up saying nothing because you have space for only the most superficial commentary on each point.

3. All documents have limited space. With a narrow topic, you can cover that topic more than adequately in the space allotted.

4. If you pick a broad topic such as "safety" for your white paper, then you have essentially used it up and doing more papers on safety would be duplicating the first. When you cover a specific niche within safety in your paper, you can then produce a series of safety-related white papers, each covering a different aspect.

Here are some additional tips for selecting a topic for your white paper (the title is also important, and Chapter 5 shows how to write an attention-grabbing title):

- Pick a topic that moves the prospect forward in the buying process. For instance, if you sell valves, your topic might be "how to size and select valves."

- Look for fresh territory not already exhausted by other white papers, articles, and Web sites. If "how to size and select valve" white papers are all over the Internet, consider a fresh angle, perhaps using the "What about" technique to narrow the topic, e.g., "How to size and select valves for viscous fluid and slurry applications."

- Favor subjects that lend themselves to quick tips, how-to advice, and easy explanations. Usually it's best to avoid topics that require in-depth analytical thinking, since your white paper reader is not likely to stick with you while you work through the argument. White papers should be quick reads and scannable. Exceptions? Of course.

- An effective strategy for topic selection is to ask salespeople what are the common objections and questions from prospects, and then produce white papers overcoming the objections or answering the questions; salespeople can provide the white papers to prospects to support their answers and arguments when they give them in a meeting or presentation. Even if the prospect never reads the white paper, the presentation of an official-looking document supporting the salesperson's point can go a long way toward convincing the prospect to accept the salesperson's claims.

What Makes for an Effective Bait Piece?

So, what makes for an effective bait piece? While there is no authoritative, definitive answer, decades of experience writing bait pieces have led me to the following guidelines:

1. *Practical.* Readers do not turn to white papers for theory or for intellectual stimulation or entertainment (though offering the latter two can be a plus).

   The number one thing your readers want is practical information—suggestions, ideas, tips, and techniques to help them do something better, faster, cheaper, or more efficiently. In essence, they crave practicality, which R. Nicolle defines in his book, *Practicality: How To Acquire It* as:

   > . . . the sense of seeing things as they are and of doing things as they ought to be done. Specifically, it is defined as the science of being skilled in the application of means to attain particular ends, especially in dealing with the common affairs of life.
   >
   > Practicality is acquired through the exercise of good nature, patience, insight, and perspicacity, and by experience. Practicality consists of judgment, attention, perception, patience, perseverance, will, decision, finesse, and foresight.[3]

2. *Clear.* Readers are impatient with fancy language, jargon, and big words used to impress them. They want their information in plain English. Many writers mistakenly think that if they use complex language, they will impress the reader. The only thing complex language does is to cause people to stop reading and toss your document in the trash. Don't try to be clever or intellectual or impressive. Say what you have to say in the simplest language possible: small words, short sentences, short paragraphs.

   Write in a natural, conversational style. Do not fall back on technical jargon. Avoid a stiff or pompous style. Write your white paper like one person talking to another about a really interesting subject—as if you are sharing something useful and exciting with a friend. Let some of your enthusiasm and personality shine through in the writing.

3. *Concise.* Your readers' time is limited. They may be willing to invest hours or days of study in a textbook, novel, or home study course that they paid for and are reading for education or entertainment,

but they do not have as strong an interest in or motivation to complete your bait piece, which they realize, at its core, has a marketing objective.

Make your white paper easy to scan, easy to read, and easy to reference. Use short paragraphs, bullets, numbers, and plenty of subheads. Put important material that you want to highlight in a box, sidebar, or in the margin.

If your bait piece is very brief, like a short booklet, this may be used as a selling point in the sales copy offering the piece to prospects. For instance, I often say something like "Reading time: 7 minutes" in my ad offering the booklet, and even on the cover, to let prospects know that reading the material won't take much of their time.

For a white paper, length varies, but typically is anywhere from four to 15 pages, with four to nine pages ideal. A tip sheet is usually one or two sides of a single sheet of 8 ½ by 11-inch paper. Audio programs, whether on audiocassette or CD, can range from ten minutes to 60 minutes in recorded length.

My experience is that prospects do not give bait pieces repeat or in-depth readings. When they get your bait piece, they either (a) throw it away, (b) skim or read it quickly, or (c) file it for future reference.

It's not critical, in all cases, that the prospect read your material. In some edu-marketing campaigns (see Chapter 3), the main purpose the bait piece serves is to increase inquiry generation; the primary reason to offer the booklet is to get more people to respond and identify themselves as prospects for your product or service.

Filing it can also be a profitable response for you. Reason: people keep reference files of information on specific topics to guide them on future purchases. When the time comes that the prospect is in the market for a new pump, and he reaches into his "Pumps" file and pulls out your booklet, there's a good chance doing so can prompt him to call you for a sales visit or price quote. I have had prospects call and hire me based on material I had sent them one or two years ago, which they had kept on file.

4. *Accurate.* Should the prospect discover inaccuracies, errors, or obsolete information in your white paper, it will reflect poorly upon you and may diminish his interest in dealing with you as a vendor. Take painstaking care to make sure your white paper is free of errors. Have

a subject matter expert read it over and correct any mistakes. Check material taken from reference sources to make sure you did not make an error in copying facts from the source document to yours.

5. *Authoritative.* Since the purpose of writing and publishing a white paper is to establish you as the authority in a particular topic, do not be afraid to write in an authoritative tone and manner.

   "Your reader respects—and expects—conviction," says copywriter John Forde. "Readers don't want more information. They can get that anywhere. Instead, they want someone to make a judgment about information so they can know what's essential and what is not."[4]

   Unlike a front-page news article in the New York Times, your white paper is not expected to be neutral reportage. You, as the author, are expected to be an expert in your topic, and you should come across as such. Don't apologize for having opinions, ideas, a strong point of view, original thoughts, or a unique methodology or approach. Those are the reasons ultimately why a prospect will choose you instead of your competitor.

   Avoid weakening your text with too many qualifiers such as "in my opinion," "it may be possible to," "maybe," and "might." Assume the manner of a confident teacher imparting knowledge to an eager student.

6. *Correct in spelling, punctuation, and grammar.* Make sure your copy is free of typos, spelling mistakes, and improper grammar. Use a spell checker, but realize that your PC won't catch all errors. On one spell-checked document, the computer let the phrase "certified pubic accountant" slip into the final draft.

   Once you have written and rewritten and reread a document half a dozen or more times, you lose the ability to accurately proof it; your mind becomes bored and cannot focus. The best solution is to let someone else proof it for you. I have a professional freelance proofreader on call for just this purpose; I pay him $20 an hour. Easier and less expensive is to have an assistant or someone else on your staff who is a good proofreader check all manuscripts.

   If there is no one else to help you and you are the sole proofreader of your own writing, there are two things you can do to ensure clean copy. First, read the copy aloud; when you reach a poorly constructed phrase or sentence, you tongue will trip over it, and you'll know to go back and fix it.

   As for finding typos, read the copy backwards. When you

proofread backwards, your mind can no longer focus on the meaning, and is forced to concentrate instead on each word one at a time, which increases the likelihood of catching typos.

7. *Binder-level reference value.* This means that the information in your document is so valuable, the readers will want to save it in a reference binder or file. *Example:* a color brochure promoting a casino was kept for years by some of the recipients because it had the rules of black jack printed on the back cover.

   Other material that can add to the reference value of your white paper include a bibliography, a list of the URLs of Web sites related to the topic, and a glossary, tables of useful data, or lists of resources such as vendors or suppliers of relevant products or services.

8. *Opinionated.* Much corporate writing tends to be bland and neutral, and this tone is death to a white paper. The reader views the author/publisher of the white paper as an expert and authority. Therefore, he expects to find your opinions of a topic or issue expressed in your white paper.

   For instance, if you are a sales trainer, and you think the colorful sales brochures produced by marketing departments are a waste of money and should never be used, say so. But be sure to explain your reasoning and provide alternative solutions (i.e., if the reader should not be giving prospects sales brochures, what should he do instead?).

9. *Non-promotional.* Although the reader expects you to be opinionated, he does not want your white paper to be a blatant or even a thinly disguised sales pitch for your product.

   The reader is not a fool. He knows your purpose in publishing the white paper is ultimately self-serving: to promote your product. But since you have chosen the white paper format, he expects your document to deliver what white papers promise: useful information and advice on a specific business or technical topic.

   If your intention is purely to sell a product, write a brochure or catalog instead. A white paper achieves its ultimate goal of helping to sell a product by informing and educating readers.

10. *Proof.* Whether you are stating an opinion, presenting a conclusion, making a recommendation, or giving advice, you have to prove to the reader that what you say is correct. Even though you are positioning yourself as an authority, that credibility only goes so far. To actually

change the reader's beliefs, attitudes, thoughts, or ideas or get them to take action or follow your suggestions, you have to prove that you are right.

There are a variety of standard methods for proving claims both in advertising copy and journalism, the two media of which white papers and other bait pieces are a hybrid.

These "proof mechanisms" include:

- Testimonials.
- Case studies.
- Benchmark test performance.
- Method of operation.
- Reviews and third-party endorsements.
- Number of users or installed systems.
- Number of years the system or method has been in operation.
- Awards (e.g., selected "Best New Product of the Year" by XYZ Magazine).
- Features, design innovations, materials of construction.

The more directly related your bait piece to the problem your product solves, the better.

For instance, Trillium Health Products used a toll-free number in infomercials selling juicing machines. The company's spokesperson, a juicing expert, appeared as a guest on a 20-minute segment of a radio show to talk about juicing. Listeners were invited to phone for a free information booklet on juicing. The booklet contained juicing tips and recipes, but also was a promotional piece for the machine.

The radio show aired in a major market, Boston, and approximately 50,000 listeners called to request the free booklet. Of those, 10 percent bought a juicing machine. So Trillium sold 5,000 juicers at $350 each for gross sales of $1.75 million—all from people who called a radio show to get a free booklet.

At the Hair Club for Men, founder Sy Sperling used a booklet called "The Consumer's Guide to Hair Replacement" as his bait piece. It worked because the topic, a comparison of the hair replacement options available to consumers, was both educational and related to the Hair Club's product, a hair replacement system (hair weave):

> "Once, we decided to give away a book on hair loss, instead of our own consumer's guide" says Sy. "This was a book published by a

regular book publisher. The phone rang off the hook, and we thought the campaign was going to be a huge success. But we didn't convert many of those leads to sales; the campaign was a disaster and cost us a fortune. People were eager to get a free book just for the sake of getting a free book, but were not necessarily interested in hair replacement. The book, unlike our consumer's guide, did not sell Hair Club or our product enough to generate sufficient interest."[5]

Creating Your Content Matrix

Just as most marketers seldom sell to a single audience, they also seldom have just a single marketing document. Often, and this is especially true when generating leads for complex sales, there are multiple decision-makers involved. For instance, when selling high-end enterprise software to corporations, the buying influences can include the IT manager or CIO, CEO, CFO, one or more management representatives of the end-user community, and a network administrator or other technical professional responsible for installing, operating, and maintaining the system.

Therefore, a useful exercise in planning an edu-marketing campaign is to create a *content matrix* outlining which bait pieces you need to create. The matrix is a grid, with the horizontal axis being job title of prospect, and the vertical axis being the step or stage in the sales cycle at which you are contacting the prospect.

As shown in Exhibit 2.3, each of these audiences may have different questions and concerns that need to be addressed by white papers and other marketing materials. The CFO, for instance, wants to know that the expensive software will generate a rapid return on investment (ROI). The CEO is more concerned with the "big picture," especially the reliability and trustworthiness of the software vendor. The end users want to be assured that the software can perform the required tasks, while IT is concerned about integration of the new software with their existing infrastructure. How would we design bait pieces to accommodate these needs and interests? Filling in the content matrix provides the guidance.

Take another look at Exhibit 2.3. When the end user is deciding whether to make an inquiry, he wants to know whether the price/performance of your product is favorable to others he is considering. Offering him a free cost/benefit analysis, which can help him determine price/performance and solve one of his problems—making the right decision—and so it is an offer with high perceived value to him.

Exhibit 2.3: Content Matrix

	Job Function			
Sales Cycle	**CEO**	**CFO**	**End User**	**Technical**
Lead			+	
Fulfillment		*		
RFP				✓
Close				

* = Cost / Benefit ROI Analysis

+ = Problem / Solution

✓ = Selection Tips

The content matrix identifies the content documents you need to create based on audience (job title or function) and where the document is to be used in the sales cycle.
Source: Robert Bly

The technical product evaluator, on the other hand, is asked by the end user to help the company select the right solution from a technical point of view. This technical evaluator might respond well to the offer of a free booklet of product selection tips, so that he can demonstrate to management that he has the expertise to buy this solution correctly.

When your marketing campaign is small or limited in scope, you may create a single bait piece to serve all of the job functions; i.e., the CEO gets the same report or booklet as the engineer. While it is better to offer content tailored to the reader's level of interest and knowledge, you can create a basis document that can adequately serve everyone involved in the buying committee.

But what you can't do is use the same bait piece at every stage of the sales cycle, and for obvious reasons: if you offered Booklet "A" to prospects to generate a lead, obviously you cannot offer that same booklet (which they already have) again to close the sale.

Can you use a single bait piece to generate enough interest to bypass one or more stages in the sales cycle? Again, no, and for this reason: prospects move according to their own schedule and process, not according to yours.

Attempting to get the prospect to alter their timelines or buying habits to accommodate your needs seldom works.

Although the offer of a bait piece has the power to increase response at multiple stages in the sales cycle, it does not have enough value or appeal to get prospects to change their buying process or habits altogether. Attempting to get them to do so would not only be ineffective, but could actually cost you sales.

Building Your Content Matrix

Once you have created your content matrix identifying the deliverables you need, e.g., white papers and other bait pieces on specific topics aimed at specific audiences at different points in the buying cycle, the next step is to create this library of documents. We call this your *content library*.

As marketing consultant Russell Kern observes, in most business-to-business (b-to-b) sales, many parties are involved in the purchase process, but it's hardly ever clean and linear. In a typical b-to-b sale, there are strategic buyers, economic buyers, and numerous technical and decision influencers all with separate agendas—each in a different stage of the sales cycle and each looking for information that supports his or her purchase decision.[6]

With decision-makers passing through various stages of the sales cycle, it becomes clear that no single offer, deployed at any one point in time, can bring all parties' buyers into the sales funnel and drive them to engagement. Thus, successful marketers build out a library of content-rich offers that are matched not only to the stages of the sales cycle, but to the personal concerns and motivations of each buyer.

There are financially oriented libraries for the C-level executives, background and educational offers for the strategic buyers, and technical information for the decision influencers.

A basic rule of thumb is that you can't force the purchase speed of buyers, but you can offer all the information they need to move through each phase of the buy cycle as fast as they desire, using the method they desire.

Business-to-business marketers should build and deploy a content-rich knowledge center Web site. When a site contains content or links to information that addresses each stage of the buy cycle and the interest of each buyer, then it becomes a unique, exclusive, and powerful offer that supports many b-to-b marketing tactics and promotions.

For example, a large telecom technology company wanted to feed its 500-person sales force by providing leads for an evolving technology now called

Voice over Internet Protocol (VoIP). It rolled out a Web site specifically designed to capture leads.

The site design was generic, to follow corporate brand standards. This generic design allowed it to support a range of lead generation campaigns. It was rich with more than 20 pieces of content covering the breadth and depth of the buy cycle stages for a range of decision-makers. Each piece of content was mapped to the sales cycle as part of the development strategy.

The site contained the following content library:

- Four white papers worth $1,500 from nationally recognized consulting firms (interest stage).
- Links to media-sponsored Web seminars, which provided substantiation for the reasons to strongly consider this new technology evaluation (interest stage for C-level).
- A problem/solution recommender that gave customized migration (consideration stage).
- E-calculators with which a buyer could determine financial payback of development (consideration stage).
- Links to video and PDF versions of case studies (consideration stage).
- Links to checklists and guides for conducting a VoIP vendor selection (evaluation stage).

This strategy covers all the bases, at all stages of the sales cycle, while providing valuable and relevant content for each decision-maker. Under this model, a single Web site supports the lead generation efforts. Various promotions can be deployed to drive traffic to the site and harvest initial sales leads.

3

Your White Paper Marketing Plan

This chapter shows how to plan a white paper marketing campaign for your product or service. Elements of the plan include:

1. *Target markets*—the groups of buyers who share a common problem, including their demographic and psychographic profile.
2. *Problem identification*—a clear definition of the pressing problem your product can help these buyers solve.
3. *Solution identification*—why your product or methodology is a superior solution. Includes an evaluation of strengths and weaknesses of your product versus the competition.
4. *Content*—the type and format of the information you are going to provide these prospects in your marketing (e.g., online tutorials, regional seminars, online chat rooms).
5. *Media*—where to reach these buyers (i.e., lists, databases, publications, Web sites, other media).
6. *Tactics*—means by which you will reach these prospects (i.e., direct mail, advertising, e-mail marketing, print advertising, radio spots, trade shows, and other marketing communications).
7. *Schedule*—quantities of promotions and when they are to run.
8. *Budget*—what it will cost.
9. *Objectives*—your goals in terms of leads, revenues, profits, or whatever other measurements you choose.
10. *Measurement*—how you will measure results to evaluate whether the objectives have been achieved.

Step One: Determine Your Target Market

Your target market is the groups of buyers who share a common problem, including their demographic and psychographic profile. Most marketers already have a pretty good idea of their target market. For instance, if you sell dental office equipment, your prospect is the dentist and his or her office staff.

Big corporations routinely spend thousands of dollars on expensive and elaborate market research studies designed to help them get inside the minds of their customers. These can include mail and online surveys, telephone interviews, and focus groups. Entrepreneurs running small businesses become worried that if they don't do this kind of expensive market research, they won't know how to reach their prospects and will fail miserably.

But for many small companies, the cost of even one study from one of the big market research companies would wipe out their entire marketing budget for the year. Relax. The good news is that focus groups and other formal market research studies are completely unnecessary.

"But how will I understand my customers?" you may ask.

Simple: just use my colleague Michael Masterson's *BDF formula*, which stands for Beliefs, Desires, and Feelings. The BDF formula says that you can understand your prospect by asking yourself three simple questions:

1. "What do my prospects believe? What are their attitudes?"
2. "What do my prospects desire? What do they want?"
3. "What do my prospects feel? What are their emotions?"[1]

There's no market research required, because you already know these things about your prospects or else you wouldn't have chosen to start a business that caters to them. Or to quote Dr. Benjamin Spock: "Trust yourself. You know more than you think you do."[2]

For instance, a company that provides "soft skills" training to information technology (IT) professionals was promoting a new on-site seminar. They sent out a flier where the headline was the title of the program: "Interpersonal Skills for IT Professionals." It generated less than half a percent response. (The offer was more detailed information about the program.) So the marketing manager and the owner brainstormed and asked themselves the BDF questions. Here's part of what they came up with . . . .

- IT professionals BELIEVE that technology is all important . . . and that they are smarter than the non-techies they serve.

- IT professionals DESIRE recognition . . . respect . . . continuing opportunity to update their skill set in new technologies and platforms . . . job security . . . more money.
- IT professionals FEEL an adversarial relationship with end users . . . they are constantly arguing with them . . . and they resent having to explain their technology to us ignoramuses.

Based on this BDF analysis, the company rewrote the letter and tested it. This time, it generated a 3 percent response, outperforming the old mailing by six to one. And one-third of those inquiries purchased an on-site one-day training seminar for $3,000. That means for every 100 pieces mailed, at a total cost of about $100, they got three leads . . . and one order for $3,000 . . . a 30-to-1 return on their marketing investment.

Oh, and the headline based on the BDF analysis? It was this:

Important news for any IT professional who has ever felt like telling an end user, "Go to hell."

Says the company owner, "The BDF formula forced us to focus on the prospect instead of the product (our seminar), and the result was a winning promotion."[3]

Amount of money spent on market research before the mailing? Not a dime.

Step Two: Problem Identification

Next, you need a clear definition of the pressing problem your product can help these buyers solve. What are your customers most concerned about that your product can help them with? Or as my colleague Don Hauptman is fond of asking, "What's keeping these prospects up at night?"

Edu-marketing is successful when it starts with the prospect—his or her needs, problems, concerns, worries, fears, and desires—and then connects those needs and wants to the benefits the product delivers.

Note: Your advertising cannot create a need or make someone want a benefit they do not already want. As Eugene Schwartz explains in his book *Breakthrough Advertising*:

The power, the force, the overwhelming urge to own that makes advertising work, *comes from the market itself,* and not from the copy. Copy cannot create desire for a product. It can only take the hopes, dreams, fears, and desires *that already exist* in the hearts of millions of people, *and focus those already-existing desires onto a particular product.* This is the copywriter's task: not to create this mass desire—but to channel and direct it.[4]

Edu-marketing does not, for instance, create the desire among IT professionals to keep their computer systems safe from hacking and computer viruses. It was not until that desire already existed as a major concern that sales of firewalls, antivirus software, content filters, and other security solutions took off.

What edu-marketing *can* do in this instance is (a) dramatize the severity and urgency of the problem to create even greater awareness among IT professionals, and (b) educate them about the best, most reliable, and most affordable solutions for solving the problem.

For instance, SurfControl has a product that filters unwanted Internet content. One of the goals of their edu-marketing program, which includes a series of white papers, is to show network professionals the dangers that unwanted Internet content, such as that delivered by spam and instant messaging, pose to their networks.

Step Three: Solution Identification

Once you have clearly identified the problem, you want to offer a solution. In a conventional marketing campaign, this solution would clearly be the product or service you are selling. But in an edu-marketing campaign, we often position *the bait piece itself* as a solution (albeit, a partial solution) to the prospect's problem.

So, for instance, if the prospect is a web master struggling with the question of whether to spend a lot of his company's money on a content management system (CMS), a white paper on "How to Calculate ROI from Your CMS" may be just the thing he needs to make the decision.

Should your marketing materials focus on the product or the bait piece? It's not always clear. But here's a rule of thumb that direct marketers have been using for decades with good results:

> If you have an exceptionally strong offer, LEAD WITH THE OFFER in your direct mail package or other promotion.
>
> On the other hand, if the offer is not strong, lead with the PRODUCT, explain its advantages, and then close with the offer.

Therefore, let me suggest the following guidelines:

- If your bait piece is just average—meaning either the content is average, or not of compelling interest to the prospect, or there is already a lot of similar information on the topic available—do not stress it in your advertising.
- If your bait piece is superior—great quality content, valuable information, hard-to-get data, unique format or manner of presentation—consider stressing it early in your copy, perhaps even in the headline.
- If your product is similar to other products in its category, find an important aspect of the product that your competitors do not stress, and educate your prospects about this by offering them a free white paper explaining it.
- If your product is superior—more features, innovative technology, superior quality—devote a lot of your copy to making the case for its superiority, and then close with the offer of the bait piece as an added incentive to request more information on the product.

Step Four: Content

What is the topic of your white paper? We discussed the steps used to determine the topic in Chapter 2. Remember our rules:

- The narrower the topic, the better.
- Tailor the content to the specific reader (e.g., CEO, process engineer, plant manager).
- Design the content so it helps move readers to the next step in the buying process (see Exhibit 3.1).

What main points and secondary points should be covered? You can determine this by making a content outline. Different organizational methods used in making content outlines are outlined in Chapter 5. Or, you can use the list format or Q&A format described in the discussion of *Basis Documents* in Chapter 2.

Step Five: Media

Where and how can you reach potential buyers—your target audience? Edu-marketing depends on bringing the offer of a free bait piece to prospects, and that is usually accomplished through some form of direct marketing.

Direct marketing is not possible unless you can obtain a list of prospects in

Exhibit 3.1: The Role of the Bait Piece in the Sales Cycle

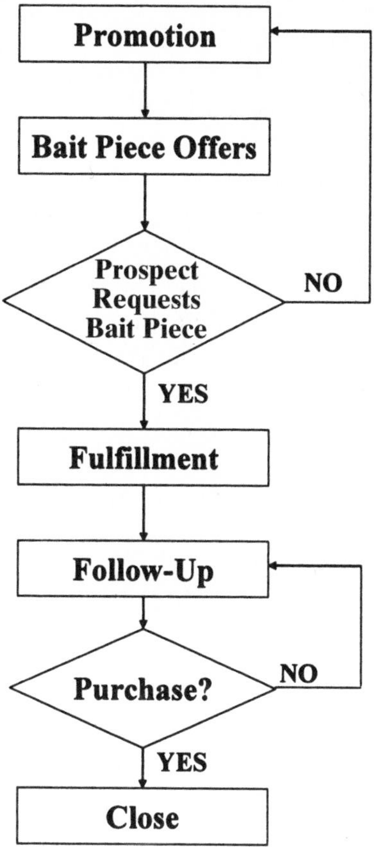

Where the bait piece fits into the selling process.

Source: Robert Bly

your target market. So you must identify such lists, determine whether they are available to you, and arrange for their use.

Look around to see what's available in your target market with regard to mailing lists, databases, publications, Web sites, trade shows, conventions, professional associations, newsletters, e-zines, and other media.

The more targeted your list, the greater the response rate to your marketing campaign.

On an episode of Donald Trump's reality TV program *The Apprentice*, Trump gave the same assignment to two competing groups: create a bridal shop and hold an evening sale; whichever team had the highest sales would win.

Team A's marketing strategy was to print up fliers on the sale and hand them out at Penn Station during rush hour. Trump questioned the wisdom of this strategy, asking, "How many people are thinking of getting married when they get off the train to go to work in the morning?"

Team B's marketing strategy was to obtain a large e-mail list of New Yorkers who are getting married and e-mail a notice about the sale to the list.

I think you can guess the outcome: Team A's store was virtually empty. They had only a handful of shoppers, and sold just two dresses, grossing $1,000.

Team B's more targeted e-mail marketing strategy was the winner: They had people waiting on line to get into the shop, sold 26 dresses, and grossed more than $12,000 in sales, outselling Team A by better than 12 to one. (Sure enough, Trump fired Team A's leader that week.)

The point: the more targeted your media—mailing lists, online lists, banner ads, magazine and newspaper ads, radio and TV commercials—the greater your response rates and ultimately, your sales.

Step Six: Tactics

Tactics are the means by which you will reach your prospects, i.e., direct mail, advertising, e-mail marketing, print advertising, radio spots, trade shows, and other marketing communications.

Part of your decision regarding tactics is governed by cost and availability. For instance, if there is no list you can rent of prospects with their e-mail addresses, you probably can't use e-mail marketing to reach them. Sometimes there is a mailing list priced at a reasonable rental cost of $100 per thousand e-mails. But if the list owner wants $1,000 per thousand, direct mail is not going to be economically feasible.

Another factor governing tactic selection is your prospects. E-mail marketing will not work if the majority of your prospects don't have access to the Internet.

Step Seven: Schedule

The schedule starts with a deadline or "drop date" (e.g., "We will mail 10,000 postcards on January 5" or "We will introduce our new product at XYZ Trade Show in December") and works backwards from there. A useful schedule has all project tasks and milestones (e.g., "first draft of white paper"), their due dates, and the person responsible.

Some marketing campaigns are simple, but most have multiple components and involve multiple contributors, reviewers, and approvers. Without a project schedule, including the tasks; steps involved in the task; the person responsible for each step; the date the step must be completed, the likelihood of timely completion is remote.

Step Eight: Budget

Budget is simply what the campaign will cost. To make a budget, you first make a list of the campaign deliverables. For an edu-marketing campaign offering a bait piece in a direct mail package, your expenditures would include the cost of the mailing and the cost of producing the bait piece. For a direct mail package, the two up-front costs are the copywriting and the graphic design.

The recurring costs are printing, letter shop fees (assembling the components of the mailing and preparing them for the post office), list rental, and postage. These costs are "recurring" because you pay them per piece mailed, as opposed to copywriting and design, both of which are one-time charges.

For the white paper, your costs are copywriting, design, and if it is a hard copy document, printing and binding. There is also the cost of inquiry fulfillment, which refers to sending prospects who respond to the mailing the bait piece and other materials they requested.

The cost of your marketing campaign is extremely important, because if the cost is excessive, the campaign is unlikely to be profitable. You can estimate whether the campaign has a chance of success based largely on the cost, likely response rate, and potential revenue.

For instance, say your direct mail piece costs a dollar to mail, which means mailing 10,000 pieces will cost you $10,000.

Now, suppose that the purpose of the letter is to generate sales leads by offering a free booklet. If you get a 1 percent response rate, mailing 10,000 pieces will produce 100 inquiries.

Further suppose that one out of four leads converts into a sale, and the average profit on each sale is $5,000. Based on these numbers, we will close 25 sales for total revenues of $125,000. On a $10,000 investment in direct mail, that's a 12.5 to one ROI. The campaign is clearly a winner.

On the other hand, say only 1 percent of our inquiries convert to a sale, and the profit on a sale is only $100. Just to break even on our 10,000-piece mailing, we now need a 10 percent response rate, which would produce 100 inquiries, one sale, and $100 in revenues.

Lead-generating mailings generally produce response rates in the range of a half percent to 3 percent, but very rarely do they return a 10 percent response. Therefore, based on costs, revenues, and response rates, such a campaign would be highly unlikely to be profitable.

Step Nine: Objectives

Determine your goals in terms of leads, cost per inquiry, revenues, profits, return on investment, number of sales closed, number of new clients acquired, or whatever other measurements you choose. The most common metrics are discussed in Chapter 10. The key point is that you cannot determine whether your marketing campaign was successful unless you first define what success is.

Be careful about selecting objectives that are difficult to measure quantitatively or are subjective in nature. "Building brand awareness" may be a valuable objective, but how will you know how well you have achieved it, if at all?

I recommend that if most of your objectives seem "soft" (e.g., "improve our image"), you add at least one hard objective as well (e.g., "generate 100 leads from potential new accounts"). This way you will be able to measure the results of your campaign, at least part way.

Step Ten: Measurement

In Chapter 10, we talk about how to measure and monitor the performance of our marketing campaigns, and the importance of doing so. The key to measurement is having a mechanism by which you can track which promotion generates which response. Be sure to design your promotions to incorporate this kind of tracking.

Your direct mail, for instance, should have key codes on the label so you know which mailing piece and list each reply came from. To track mail response by key code, you must somehow capture the key code when the reply comes in.

If you are mailing a direct mail package in a #10 envelope, affix the mailing label directly to the reply card. When it is returned, you can read the key code off the label. Use a window envelope so the label affixed to the reply card can show through the clear window.

If you are tracking online advertising, create a unique Uniform Resource Locator (URL) as the response device for each online ad or e-mail marketing message. Keep track of click-throughs to the URL as well as conversions to sale.

For promotions driving the prospect to call an 800 number, add a unique identifier to the number, such as "Extension 145" or "Ask for John," again, so you know where the response came from.

Tabulate and measure the responses, inquiries, and sales as explained in Chapter 10. You will know whether a particular edu-marketing tactic or campaign was a success or a flop. And you will also learn which sales letters, on-line ads, white paper titles, and bait piece offers pulled best.

Creating White Papers That Drive Sales

White papers can be extremely useful sales tools, especially for companies doing consultative and solutions selling. The white papers serve as education and decision-support materials for customers.

However, too often, white papers are developed in a corporate marketing vacuum, disconnected from real-world sales contexts, and inadvertently, they address topics that neither salespeople nor prospective buyers find useful.

How does this happen? Before developing a solution and creating marketing messages, companies usually conduct a market analysis to identify customer needs and "wants." And based on this information, marketing teams develop ideas for white papers.

While some papers may hit the mark, others fall short because they simply do not play a strategic role in the sales process. They might contain loads of information from very knowledgeable people, but not the specific information that helps move key stakeholders along in the sales process.

The source of the problem is lack of sales insight—experience-based knowledge about what real customers are thinking, doing, and asking during the sales process. Market analyses typically cannot help identify all the necessary nuances in messaging or fully anticipate where salespeople will run into roadblocks. These insights are often discovered only when salespeople start talking with real customers, and you can use these insights to create white papers that drive sales.

So how can you ensure that your next white paper is a powerful, targeted sales tool? First, take time to understand the complexities of the sales process for your particular offering.

Complicated, solution-oriented sales usually demand that salespeople "sell" to various stakeholders within a company, not just one person. Some stakeholders, such as CIOs and line-of-business VPs, have budgetary power.

Others champion the solution internally in order to be associated with a successful or high profile project. Still others influence key decision-makers, including IT managers who evaluate technology options and make recommendations, and purchasing agents who compare prices and recommend the "vendor of choice."

To close deals, salespeople must establish value in the minds of all stakeholders at just the right points in the sales process. White papers can play a critical role in communicating this value, particularly during intermediate sales stages when customers are considering their options and evaluating technologies. However, different stakeholders measure value in different ways and white paper topics, approaches, and information must be tailored accordingly.

For example, financial stakeholders (e.g., CFOs with discretionary budgets to spend) are usually responsible for achieving quantifiable business objectives, such as sustaining competitive advantage, reducing costs, and increasing business efficiency. They usually want to know how your solution fits into their overall strategy and vision, and they seek proof that its features and benefits will help them achieve important, long-term "wants" and goals.

In contrast, technical evaluators want detailed information about the solution's features, functionalities, and architecture because they are concerned about issues such as technical integration, security, and scalability.

At the same time, other influential stakeholders may not grasp that there is a problem to solve in the first place. They need to understand the latent pain or business problem that your solution solves before they can comprehend its value.

While mapping messages to audiences is usually a straightforward process, the challenge here is communicating with each of these purchasers and influencers in a unique way, with tailored value propositions and information appropriate to their responsibilities, concerns, and wants.

Given the complexities of the sales process, start by talking with your sales force to better understand which types of stakeholders would value a white paper, why, and what must be communicated in order to accelerate the sales process. In many cases, you may need to develop more than one white paper to adequately equip your sales force.

Key questions to ask include the following:

- Is this a key stakeholder during the sales process, and if so, what role does this stakeholder play during a typical sales process? Recommend? Specify? Authorize?

- What sales challenge would this white paper help you address? Why is a white paper the best sales tool in this case?
- At what point in the sales process do you anticipate using this paper, and what level or type of information is appropriate at this point?
- Ideally, what do you want the stakeholder to think, feel, and do after reading this paper?

You also may need to narrow the focus of your white paper to address the stakeholder's most important hot buttons or "wants." The key to narrowing your focus is to understand how your particular audience defines and measures value. Consider questions such as: What is this stakeholder's greatest concern or want? What does the stakeholder seek in a solution? How would the proposed solution address the stakeholder's greatest concern?

Some of the most common wants or hot buttons of key stakeholders include the following:

- Scalability, availability, and reliability.
- Resistance to obsolescence.
- Security.
- Performance.
- Cost effectiveness and TCO (total cost of ownership).
- Rapid (and long-term) ROI.
- Ease of use, implementation, and administration.
- Interoperability (ease of integration with existing systems).

After narrowing the focus of your paper, carefully consider the best type of white paper to accomplish your goals and appeal to the stakeholder. Each type of white paper educates your reader in a specific way, so the choice is important. Some of the most common white paper types include the following:

- *Technology briefings*, which explain new or underlying technologies, platforms, protocols, standards, or architectures.
- *Buyer's guides*, which may include a criteria list or a worksheet to assist customers during the evaluation process.
- *Planning and implementation guides*, which help customers plan for future industry or technology trends, or prepare for an implementation.
- *Application guides*, which explain how customers can apply a technology to solve different technical problems.
- *ROI guides*, which demonstrate the return on investment the customer can expect to get from owning the product.

- *Case studies* or example applications, which examine the success or failure of particular approaches, options, or technologies.
- *Business implication discussions*, which describe how technology decisions affect financial, operational, or other business issues.
- *Strategy discussions*, which explain how technology investments should be viewed as part of a business strategy.
- *Industry trend overviews*, which analyze market, operational, or technical trends.
- *Issues analyses*, which discuss key industry issues and offer recommendations on ways to respond in terms of strategy, technology investments, etc.

In some cases, selecting a single white paper type is most suitable. In other cases, combining white paper types into a single document may be appropriate.

Even with a sales-driven plan, a white paper is doomed to failure if your writer lacks the exceptional writing skills, technical savvy, and marketing experience that these documents require, as well as the ability to select and synthesize meaningful information from a variety of sources.

That's why many companies often hire short-term contractors who specialize in white paper development. A dedicated professional, particularly one who understands complex solution-selling processes, can devote full-time resources to your project so that it's completed quickly and efficiently, as well as offer fresh insights and experience to ensure the success of your white paper.

Coming Up with Ideas for Bait Pieces

Sometimes it's a challenge to keep your creative juices flowing and come up with a steady stream of new ideas for white papers, premiums, and other bait pieces. Copywriter Russ Phelps offers the following tips to stay sharp and creative:

1. Collect and study ads in your field and many others. Create a "swipe file" of ads, sales letters, white papers, booklets, free CDs, URLs of key Web sites. Refer to them when your brain needs a jump start. You, too, can stand on the shoulders of creative giants in marketing and advertising.
2. Read books and publications in your field, as well as general publications and even a few kooky ones. Russ recommends the tabloids, women's and men's magazines, financial news, health publications, self-improvement and how-to-stuff, expose and scandal pubs and

culture-sensitive magazines like *Vanity Fair, Cosmopolitan,* and *Rolling Stone.* For business-to-business and technology copywriters, I recommend *Information Week, Forbes, BusinessWeek,* and *Scientific American.*

3. Cruise the Internet. Start with a key-word search on search engines like Google, Yahoo, or Overture.com. Input key words related to your field and start cruising and book-marking sites. Do this regularly, as there are new sites coming online every day.

4. Visit and participate in discussion forums, blogs, and newsgroups in your areas of interest and a few that you have no interest in. It's amazing how one idea or approach in an odd field can be applied or modified to solve a challenge you face in your life and business. You can subscribe to an RSS (Really Simple Syndication) feed to get a constant stream of new contents from blogs. Also sign up for free e-zines on your topic.

5. Think outside the box, then bring those ideas into your existing box in order to enlarge it. Keep growing your box, and you'll grow too.

6. Take a hike literally, as in spending time in nature. "Nature is one of my greatest teachers," says Russ. "Not sure how to explain it, but if you spend enough time in nature, I don't have to explain it to you. It clears your head, renews you, and gives you fresh juice." You can't beat a walk around a lake on a crisp autumn day for getting rid of cobwebs.

7. Maintain a sense of child-like wonder. That's where you kind of wander around all day going, "Wow, look at that! What's going on over there? What's that? How does that work? Why did that happen? Why are they doing that? What is the meaning of this? What is emerging or unfolding regarding this or that?" And so on. Get involved with life by asking focused questions.

8. Stay crazy. Says Russ: "Most copywriters I know are at least a little eccentric, and some of them are downright crazy compared to most people who have 'real jobs' or wear suits all day. That's good. I guess it goes with being creative, but don't quote me on that or I'll go crazy."

9. "Laugh, sing and fool around a lot. Humor, music, and play somehow get the creative juices flowing and help disarm the left brain logic to let good ideas bubble up from the unconscious," advises Russ. If you are in a negative mood, smile: the physical act of forcing your mouth into a smile releases chemicals that elevate mood.

10. Get physical. Besides hiking, get fresh air, exercise, get a massage, dance, move your body. It keeps your brain fresh, fed with oxygen

and flowing with "happy chemicals." The mind-body connection, which was widely regarded as "New Age Hooey" in the 1970s, is now much more widely accepted.

11. If nothing else, cultivate the practice of what Russ calls "active compassion," which is simply finding what others need the most and giving it to them. This is a direct reflection of what smart marketers do, which is "find a need and fill it." As in life, so in business.

12. Immerse yourself in popular culture. Keep up on news, events, controversies, scandals, issues, people's problems, hopes, and dreams. It makes you better able to love and serve the market you are selling to. Eugene Schwartz recommended seeing all movies that gross $100 million or more, because these are what people like and reflect the tastes of the masses.

13. Get out of your ivory tower if you find yourself stuck in one for too long. Mix with people. All kinds of people. Ask them open-ended questions. Act like a journalist from time to time. Ask: Who? What? When? Where? Why? How?

14. Spend at least one day a week not writing copy or thinking about business. It helps you stay fresh and avoid burnout.

15. Travel. You will expand as a person and your creative capacities will expand at the same time.

16. Once in a while, break a habit or a routine and substitute a new one. Adopt a new way of doing something you normally do. Ultimately, be willing to change anything and everything about your life if you find it serves your "higher life purpose."[5]

Marketing to Technical Professionals

Although edu-marketing is widely used today for selling to both consumer and business audiences, white papers have their roots in selling to engineers, programmers, and other technical professionals.

This is an audience with which I have more than a passing familiarity: I am a chemical engineer and have been writing copy designed to sell products and services to engineers for 25 years. I have also been trained as a Certified Novell Administrator.

Here's what I know about appealing to this special audience:

1. *Engineers look down on advertising and advertising people, for the most part.* Engineers have a low opinion of advertising—and of people whose job it is to create advertising. The lesson for the business-to-

business marketer? Make your advertising and direct mail informational and professional, not gimmicky or promotional. Avoid writing that sounds like "ad copy." Don't use slick graphics that immediately identify a brochure or spec sheet as "advertising." The engineer will be quick to reject such material as "fluff."

Engineers want to believe they are not influenced by ad copy and that they make their decisions based on technical facts that are beyond a copywriter's understanding. Let them believe it—as long as they respond to our ads and buy our products.

2. *Engineers do not like a "consumer approach."* There is a raging debate about whether engineers respond better to a straight technical approach, clever consumer-style ads, or something in between. Those who prefer the creative approach argue, "The engineer is a human being first and an engineer second. He will respond to creativity and cleverness just like everyone else."

Unfortunately, there is much evidence to the contrary. In many tests of ads and direct mailings, I have seen straightforward, low-key, professional approaches equal or outpull "glitzy" ads and mailings repeatedly.

One of my clients tested two letters offering a financial book aimed at engineers. A straightforward, benefit-oriented letter clearly outpulled a "bells-and-whistles" creative package. And I see this result repeated time and time again.

Engineers respond well to communications that address them as knowledgeable, technical professionals in search of solutions to engineering problems. Hard-sell frequently falls on deaf ears here—especially if not backed by facts.

3. *The engineer's purchase decision is more logical than emotional.* Most books and articles on advertising stress that successful copy appeal to emotions first, reason second.

But with the engineering audience, it is often the opposite. The buying decision is what we call a "considered purchase" rather than an impulse buy. That is, the buyer carefully weighs the facts, makes comparisons, and buys based on what product best fulfills his requirement.

Certainly, there are emotional components to the engineer's buying decision. For instance, preference for one vendor over another is often based more on gut feeling that actual fact. But for the most part, an engineer buying a new piece of equipment will analyze the features and technical specifications in much greater depth than a consumer buying a stereo, VCR, or other sophisticated electronic device.

Copy aimed at engineers cannot be superficial. Clarity is essential. Do not disguise the nature of what you are selling in an effort to "tease" the reader into your copy, as you might do with a consumer mail-order offer. Instead, make it immediately clear what you are offering and how it meets the engineer's needs.

4. *Engineers want to know the features and specifications, not just the benefits.* In consumer advertising classes, we are taught that benefits are everything, and that features are unimportant. But engineers need to know the features of your product—performance characteristics, efficiency ratings, power requirements, and technical specifications—in order to make an intelligent buying decision.

   Features should especially be emphasized when selling to OEMs (original equipment manufacturers), VARs (value-added resellers), systems integrators, and others who purchase your product with an intention to incorporate it into their own product.

   Example: An engineer buying semiconductors to use in a device he is building doesn't need to be sold on the benefits of semiconductors. He already knows the benefits and is primarily concerned about whether *your* semiconductor can provide the necessary performance and reliability while meeting his specifications in terms of voltage, current, resistance, and so forth.

5. *Engineers are not turned off by jargon—in fact, they like it.* Consultants teaching business writing seminars tell us to avoid jargon because it interferes with clear communication. This certainly is true when trying to communicate technical concepts to lay audiences such as the general public or top management. But jargon can actually enhance communication when appealing to engineers, computer specialists, and other technical audiences.

   Why is jargon effective? Because it shows the reader that *you speak his language.* When you write direct response copy, you want the reader to get the impression you're like him, don't you? And doesn't speaking his language accomplish that?

   Actually, engineers are not unique in having their "secret language" for professional communication. People in all fields publicly denounce jargon but privately love it. For instance, who aside from direct marketers has any idea of what a "nixie" is? And why use that term, except to make our work seem special and important? (A nixie is a bad name on a mailing list; a label that is undeliverable because the person has moved.)

6. *Engineers have their own visual language.* What are the visual devices through which engineers communicate: Charts, graphs, tables, diagrams, blueprints, engineering drawings, and mathematical symbols and equations.

You should use these visual devices when writing to engineers—for two reasons. First, engineers are comfortable with them and understand them. Second, these visuals immediately say to the engineer, "This is solid technical information, not promotional fluff."

The best visuals are those specific to the engineer's specialty. Electrical engineers like circuit diagrams. Computer programmers feel comfortable looking at flow charts. Systems analysts use structured diagrams. Learn the visual language of your target audience and have your artist use these symbols and artwork throughout your ad, brochure, or mailer.

Marketing to Executives

When selling technology and other products to businesses, you often have to appeal to three different buying influences within each company:

1. Senior management—CEOs, CFOs, COOs, vice presidents.
2. End users—often middle managers or administrative staff.
3. IT—Information Technology professionals ranging from programmers to systems analysts.

The first two audiences consistent primarily of people who are not techies. And these nontechies care about different things, and respond differently, than the traditional IT technology buyer.

Nontechies are results-oriented, interested in the ends rather than the means, the bottom line rather than the process. They lack interest in the details, preferring to focus on the "big picture." Most nontechies simply want to resolve problems; engineers, scientists, and programmers enjoy actually working on problems.

The result is that nontechies are more interested in benefits, business results, and the reputation and credibility of the vendor. IT, by comparison, tends to focus on technical issues including platforms, scalability, interoperability with existing systems, reliability, specifications, limitations, and ease of implementation, operation, and maintenance.

When generating leads for big-ticket items (e.g., enterprise software), quote the price in the terms that seem most palatable—for instance, per user or per site license. Demonstrate, if it exists, the rapid return on investment.

For instance, a mailing for SurfControl, an application that monitors and controls employee Internet usage in organizations, informs the recipient that surfing the Internet for personal rather than business reasons costs $300 per employee per week. The letter then positions the license fee of a few dollars per user as a drop in the bucket compared to the savings SurfControl can generate.

When selling big-ticket items, the goal of marketing is often to get an appointment with the decision-maker. The offer then becomes, in essence, not the software, but rather the initial meeting—which is frequently positioned as a needs analysis or assessment, to be followed by recommendations. Of course, the seller's goal is to gain the information needed to provide a quote or proposal the buyer will accept.

For both lead generation and mail order, premiums are proven response-boosters. Premiums that have worked well for technology marketers include white papers, computer books, audio and videocassettes, free software, free support, free training, seminars, and electronic conferences that the user accesses via telephone (for voice) and, optionally, the Web (for visuals).

Another popular premium is a simple calculator that demonstrates the potential return on investment to the prospect if they purchase your product. This is typically an Excel® application on a disk. The prospect inputs his business scenario and instantly discovers whether your product will pay off for him.

Select a premium that is highly desirable and ties in with your product or service. A Web design firm, for instance, offered "four free digital photos of your key staff, postable on your Web site." When the rep visited the prospect, she carried a digital camera, took the photos, and immediately gave the disk to the prospect. Of course, the prospect wanted the photos posted on their Web site, something which could be done as part of the "Web site makeover" service the Web consulting firm offered for a fee.

There are four basic response mechanisms: paper reply forms (fax-backs, reply cards, and reply envelopes), online (e-mail or logging on to a Web site), phone, and fax. Since you never know which reply method a particular prospect prefers, why not offer them all? At a recent marketing conference, one software executive said, "Every software prospect is on the Internet today. It's a waste of time to offer any other response mechanism." A colleague from his company disagreed. "I don't want to log onto the Internet if I'm not already online just to respond to an ad or mailing," he said, insisting that for him, a toll-free number or reply card is more convenient.

While it's generally safe to assume IT professionals are comfortable responding by going to your Web site, don't make that assumption with non-techies. Some can access the Web but are not comfortable with it and prefer not to. Others, amazingly, don't even know how to get onto your site!

One tip: Always offer the Web as a response option when mailing to IT professionals—especially those involved with the Internet. Also, if you sell software, such as the latest antivirus or firewall, that prospects may want to try immediately, make it available for downloading from your Web site. You can let prospects download a demo version for free or the full program if they supply credit card information.

The key to success? Talk to businesspeople in their language, not yours. Show that if they give you a dollar, they'll get back two dollars. And test—sales appeals, offers, pricing, response mechanisms, copy, graphics, formats, and premiums. Don't assume you know which will work best. Instead, let your prospects tell you. Makes sense, doesn't it?

4

Creating White Paper Content

The major steps involved in creating a bait piece or free content offer include:

1. Processes for content development.
2. How marketing works with SMEs (subject matter experts).
3. Determining content topics, depth of complexity, and outlines.
4. Format selection, e.g., white papers, CD-ROMs, booklets, reports, articles, Web pages, audiotapes, videos, advertorials, software, books, webcasts, and others.
5. Production, e.g., writing, illustration, design and layout, editing, proofing, publishing, version control, updating, content management systems.

Of these, the first two can be the most problematic, and the problem centers around this question: who should write the white paper, the "techie"—the engineer, programmer, or analyst who understands the topic—or a marketing communications person, copywriter, content writer, or other professional writer of marketing materials? It seems like a simple question, but the debate of who should write materials of a technical nature—a techie or a professional communicator—has been raging for decades and shows no sign of ever being resolved.

Rather than get engaged in the debate, let's look at a process through which technical experts and marketing people, typically an engineer or programmer and a writer, can work together to produce the desired result: a white paper that is interesting, engaging, persuasive, yet technically accurate and full of useful content of interest to the target audience.

Assembling Your White Paper Team

Developing a high-quality white paper can be challenging. It's important to begin by clearly defining the roles of the team members and achieving consensus on goals and strategies.

Here are some typical roles in a development team. The same person may assume more than one set of responsibilities—for example, the project manager may also be a content provider—but no roles should be omitted.

- *Project manager.* As in any development process, the project manager is the "glue" that holds the project together. The project manager's responsibilities include setting the schedule; arranging meetings; locating and delivering background documents; coordinating document review, design, and production; helping resolve disputes among team members; and more.
- *Subject matter experts (SMEs).* These are engineers, programmers, designers, analysts, researchers, product managers, and brand managers who provide the technical and marketing content for the paper.

  Technical content providers should be willing to deliver existing documents (such as specifications or presentations), including internal documents, and should be available to answer questions that arise.

  Marketing content providers should be able to communicate key product messages as well as the business case for the product, including information about return on investment and other factors that influence decision-makers. They also should submit existing marketing documents or collateral related to the product to ensure messaging consistency.
- *Writer.* A white paper is doomed to failure if the writer is not experienced at writing the concise, convincing prose that this unique document requires. Ideally, the writer will possess exceptional writing skills, technical savvy, and marketing experience, as well as the ability to extract meaningful information from a variety of sources and translate it into coherent, compelling prose.
- *Copy editor.* Skilled copy editors almost always improve a white paper. They do more than check spelling and punctuation. They point out

flaws in logic, identify ineffectively developed concepts, and ensure clarity and continuity within the document.

- *Proofreader.* The proofreader checks the document to catch errors in spelling, punctuation, grammar, and style. Every white paper should be proofed by a professional proofreader prior to publication.
- *Illustration, design, and production staff.* Visual appeal is as crucial for white papers as for any other marketing document. Effective white papers employ illustrations and diagrams that simplify and communicate complex information in a way that complements the text. The visual design of the document as a whole should accurately reflect the company's brand and image, and adhere to any existing guidelines.

Developing white papers requires skilled resources. Consequently, companies often outsource some of the responsibilities to skilled contractors. With the exception of marketing and technical content providers, outside personnel can effectively perform all of the roles described.

By hiring short-term contractors skilled in developing white papers, companies reap the benefits of a highly qualified, dedicated professional who can devote full-time resources to the project without increasing headcount or red tape. As a result, companies can rapidly develop high-quality white papers that prove their products' technical validity and improve their chances for success.

Specialty writers can also ghostwrite articles that appear under a technical expert's name and the company name; reprints of these articles may be used as bait pieces in your edu-marketing campaign. It's an approach worth noting, because when specialty writers ghostwrite for a technical expert, they write very comfortably and specifically in the first person.

For example, instead of a technical expert writing, "The formulation was optimized through the utilization of a statistical software product," a ghostwriter states, "We improved the performance of the brake-lining formulation using XYZ software." The problem and solution are presented in clear and upbeat sentences, simplifying readability.

Ghostwritten white papers and articles provide readers with credible technical solutions that increase productivity, reduce costs, and improve quality. The stories tell how real technical experts solved real problems. The result is influence. A ghostwriter makes it possible for companies to communicate their work with one 30-minute phone call, and a few follow-up e-mails. This allows technical experts to quickly get back to what they do best—solving problems.

The bottom line: a ghostwriter/technical expert collaboration can generate more business for the company. "We get more calls from potential clients reading articles about us than we do from paid ads," says Don Muehlbaurer, president of Techworks, LLC in Milwaukee. "The articles definitely generate sales."[1]

If you're a technical expert who is understandably skittish about sharing proprietary information, simply mask it as "Formula A or Data set B." Don't give ghostwriters false data—just information that tells readers an accurate story, but doesn't reveal company secrets.

Trade publications and corporate marketing communications departments frequently look outside their staff for white papers and trade journal articles. Specialty writers may forge arrangements with trade publications, solidifying the process of getting articles seen by large numbers. This isn't a task to be viewed lightly, for it takes key writer-to-editor communications to attract editors, entice their willingness to run a story or case study, respond to their requests, and coordinate timely story appearances. That's why it's important to work closely with a competent writer who can mine and polish publishable stories.

How long does the white paper writing process take? From the initial interview between the technical expert and the writer, it usually takes several weeks. Slow reviews can cause significant delays: no matter how motivated an engineer is when interviewed, once it's time to review a draft, time seems to stand still. Extended approval periods can also hold up publication of your white paper.

Once the copy is approved, the white paper may get bottlenecked in the corporate graphic department or, if it is to be posted on the company Web site, in the web master's backlog of work.

The best white papers are produced when a professional writer is assigned the primary responsibility of writing the document and SMEs are assigned the responsibility of cooperating with the writer, both in providing content during the research and writing phase, and specific suggestions for changes and corrections during the review phrase. Obtaining signed releases from managers, lawyers, and marketing personnel within the expert's company is an important part of this process.

"A white paper that glosses over the details of how an offering helps solve a business problem is little more than a lengthy brochure," says Hoffman Marketing, a firm that writes white papers for many high-tech clients.[2]

You risk having your white paper fall into this category when the writer does not talk to SMEs or when the writer does not have sufficient technical background to grasp the subject matter.

Hoffman also says, "By contrast, a document that focuses solely on technical detail without placing the offering in a larger business context fails to make a persuasive case."[3]

You risk having your white paper fall into this category when it is written solely by engineers, programmers, or other technical experts who are not skilled in the subtle art of writing persuasive text—copy that appears informational but in fact helps sell the reader on why your product, method, or solution is best.

Finding the Right Writer for Your White Paper Project

Who is the best person to be assigned as principle writer on your white paper project? Ideally, it is a writer who:

- Has prior experience writing white papers, reports, booklets, and other bait pieces.
- Has written other informational and instructional material, e.g., books, monographs, articles, content-rich Web sites, e-zines, newsletters, training manuals, and videos.
- Has sufficient technical background to grasp the technology or business concepts to be covered in the white paper.
- Understands the difference between writing purely to educate or disseminate information (e.g., journalists, teachers, trainers) versus presenting information with an underlying purpose and sales objective.
- Understands the difference between pure hard sell and hype (e.g., an ad agency or freelance copywriter) versus writing to sell indirectly by presenting useful, educational content to the prospect.

The right candidate, whether on staff or independent, will have all or most of the above qualifications.

You can't judge solely by title. Someone calling herself a "copywriter" might be ideally suited to the project, as might someone else calling himself a "content writer" or "technical writer." The best way to determine suitability and qualifications is by asking the writer whether he meets the above list of criteria and reviewing his or her portfolio to determine same.

As for cost, most writers charge by the project. Stewart McKie, a writer specializing in white papers for business application vendors, charges somewhat under $5,000 to write a 10 to 20-page white paper. Other writers I have talked to charge anywhere from $2,000 to $5,000 for white papers that typically are five to 12 pages. If you hire a writer who is a known consultant and a recognized authority on the topic, the fee could go even higher. If the writer you hire charges by the word, figure anywhere from $1 to $2 a word.

Some writers also handle the design and give you the finished document as a PDF. They can either use their own template or flow their copy into yours, if you have one. Other writers give the client a Word file, which then must be put into a layout. Freelance desktop designers can design your white papers and generally charge an hourly rate ranging from $55 to $85, with some going as high as $100 an hour.

The White Paper Writing Process

The flow chart in Exhibit 4.1 shows how the white paper production team works together to produce the document.

Exhibit 4.1: The White Paper Writing Process

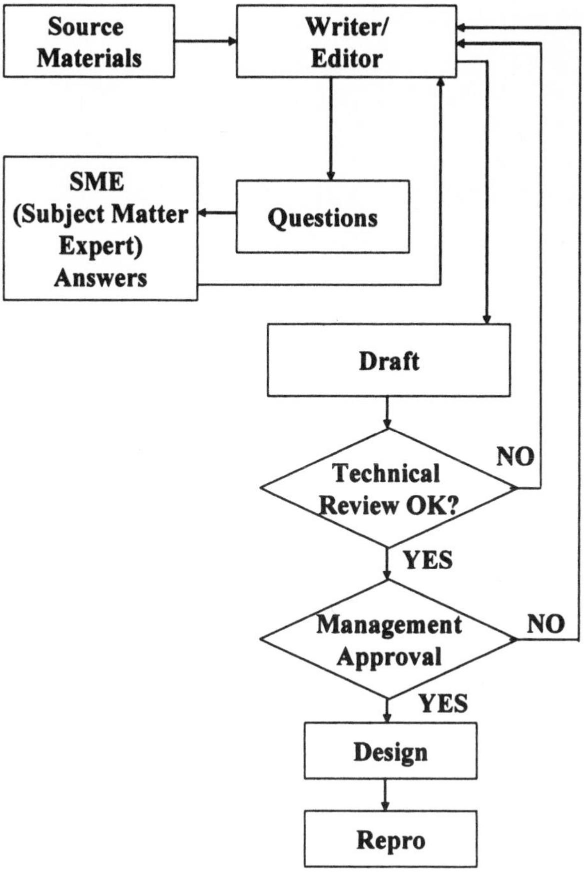

Flow chart showing the process for creating white papers.

Source: Robert Bly

The process of creating a white paper should begin with providing the writer with as much source material as possible on the topic of the white paper. This can include:

- Competitors' white papers on the same topic.
- Previous white papers from the client company.
- Tear-sheets of ads.
- Brochures.
- Catalogs.
- Data sheets.
- Case studies.
- Article reprints.
- PowerPoint® presentations.
- Technical papers.
- Copies of speeches.
- CD-ROMs.
- Manuals.
- Audio-visual scripts.
- Press kits.
- Swipe files of competitors' ads and literature.
- Internal memos.
- Letters of technical information.
- Product specifications.
- Engineering drawings.
- Business and marketing plans.
- Reports.
- Proposals.
- Past issues of e-zines.
- The company blogs.

By studying this material, the writer should have 80 percent of the information he needs to write the copy. The other 20 percent comes from interviewing subject matter experts.

These interviews may be done in person, over the phone, or via e-mail; each method has its pros and cons. The advantage of interviewing by e-mail is that it forces the SME to provide a complete answer and write it out; often the writer can cut and paste text directly from the SME's e-mail reply into the draft of the document.

The questions the writer asks the SME of course are specific to the topic of the white paper. For instance, if the white paper focuses on a specific product, these questions might include the following:

- What are the product's features and benefits? (Make a complete list.)
- Which benefit is the most important?
- How is the product different from the competition's? (Which features are exclusive? Which are better than the competition's?)
- If the product isn't different from its competitors, what attributes can be stressed that haven't been stressed by the competition?
- What technologies does the product compete against?
- What are the applications of the product?
- What industries can use the product?
- What problems does the product solve in the marketplace?
- How is the product positioned in the marketplace?
- How does the product work?
- How reliable is the product?
- How efficient is the product?
- How economical is the product?
- Who has bought the product and what do they say about it?
- In what materials, sizes, and models is the product available?
- How quickly does the manufacturer deliver the product?
- What service and support does the manufacturer offer?
- Is the product guaranteed?
- Who will buy the product? (What markets is it sold to?)
- What is the customer's main concern? (e.g., price, delivery, performance, reliability, service maintenance, quality efficiency)
- What is the character of the buyer?
- What motivates the buyer?
- To how many different buying influences must the copy appeal?

Next, the writer digests this material, and often augments it with his own research, which may include talking to other experts or doing a Google search.

When I first started writing white papers in the early 1980s (back then, we called them "technical papers"), the greatest problem the writer faced was lack of information. For many subjects, it was difficult to find enough information to produce a cogent paper.

In the Internet era, we have the opposite problem: too much information. The white paper writer must rely heavily on the subject matter expert, who has the in-depth topic knowledge, for guidance.

Be careful of picking up information on the Internet without verifying it with an expert. If you do use secondary sources, footnote them, so that the "client" (the person in charge of marketing or product management) can check your facts if challenged to do so.

Using my "Ten-Step Writing Process" outlined in the next section, create a solid draft of the white paper. Then, as shown in Exhibit 4.1, submit this draft to the technical reviewers (often these are the same SMEs who provided the content to you).

If the technical reviewers have changes (likely), they will send the draft back to you with comments and corrections. You may need to go back to them for clarification or additional information to implement their changes.

You resubmit the corrected draft, which goes through the process until it is approved by the technical reviewers. The copy then goes to executive or management reviewers, and once they give it their blessing, the document is sent to graphic design for layout and reproduction.

The 10-Step White Paper Writing Process

This section presents a ten-step writing process that I have been teaching in technical writing seminars for more than two decades. It will be especially useful to you if you are doing the actual writing of the white paper, rather than just serving as an SME, project manager, or reviewer.

1. *Do an SAP analysis.*

   SAP stands for Subject, Audience, Purpose. For a white paper, you should ask and answer three questions before moving to Step Two in the writing process:
   * What is the subject of this white paper?
   * Who is my audience?
   * What is the purpose of this white paper? What do we want the prospect to do, think, or believe after reading it?

2. *Outline.*

   Create a rough outline for your white paper. Write a preliminary table of contents. Indicate the major sections, and the main points to be covered in each.

3. *Gather research materials.*

   Collect all the documentation you can get from your SMEs. When in doubt, it is better to have too much rather than too little.

   Read or skim the source material quickly and make notes about anything you do not understand or need more information on. Make up a list of questions to ask the SMEs to get this material.

Interview the SMEs and take notes. Type up your notes. Search the Internet for additional facts you can use in your paper.

4. *Read and highlight your source documents.*

As you read the source material, highlight the useful information in each document using a yellow marker.

5. *Type your notes.*

Type the text from the highlighted portions of your source documents into a single-spaced Word (or comparable) file. This exercise can reduce mounds of source material to a manageable number of single-spaced pages.

6. *Reorder and annotate your notes.*

Rearrange the sections of your notes in roughly the same order as your outline. You can do this with your software's cut-and-paste feature or you can print out the raw notes, cut the pages apart, tape the sections to index cards (limiting the material on each card to one thought or idea), and then order the index cards according to your outline.

7. *Write.*

Transcribe the information from your cards or notes file into a first draft, rewriting the raw material to form coherent sentences. When you have done this, your first draft is complete. But you are not ready to submit a draft to the reviewers until you complete Steps Eight to Ten.

8. *Rewrite.*

Go through your draft. Work on achieving more conciseness and clarity in your sentences and paragraphs.

Replace big words with short, simple words wherever possible. Break long sentences into two or more shorter sentences.

Use the "Breath Test" to determine whether your sentences are short enough. How it works: without taking in a lungful of air, read the sentence aloud. If you run out of breath before you get to the end of the sentence, it is too long and should be divided into two or more sentences.

Break long paragraphs into two or more shorter paragraphs. Put the break wherever a new thought or idea begins. Use boldface subheads to break the text into sections. Ideally, you want to have one or two subheads per page.

9. *Edit.*

Go through the draft again and make it as clean as possible—clear writing, good flow, logical order, and correct in punctuation, spelling, and grammar. At the end of Step Nine, you want the draft to be good enough to submit for review, though you will not do that quite yet, because there is one more step. . . .

10. *Polish.*

Put your draft from Step Nine away and come back to it the next day. When you come in the next morning, turn on your computer, open the file, and read through it at a slow and leisurely pace one more time.

As you read, you will find little things—word choice, phrasing, a cumbersome sentence—you want to make simpler. This is the time to make them. After polishing your draft this one last time, you are now ready to release it into the review process.

Notice that we have broken the actual writing into four separate steps (write, rewrite, edit, and polish). This is deliberate and important. The number-one cause of writer's block is making the mistake of trying to edit yourself while you write. It just doesn't work!

Professional writers know that the important thing in the first draft (Step Seven) is just to write and get it all down on the screen, no matter how rough or raw the copy is. They know they will go back later and clean it up.

The amateur makes the mistake of trying to make each sentence perfect before going onto the next. Therefore, he never gets past the first page, the first paragraph, or even the first sentence, because he is never happy with what he writes.

One more tip: plan your schedule so you have at least one day each between Steps Seven through Ten. Reason: this allows you to put your draft away and "sleep on it" overnight. When you come back at the text the next day, you are fresher than when you attempt to edit your copy the same day you write it.

5

Writing Your Bait Piece

By now you understand how the edu-marketing strategy works: acquiring a sales lead means give to get. Your hoped-for lead provides you contact information—and perhaps answers qualifying questions—in exchange for something of value. And that "something of value" needs to be a qualifier in itself. Something only a person in your target audience would want. Something that shows you know a thing or two about the topics that matter to them.

In other words, give them free content. This can be a white paper, tip sheet, how-to guide, case study, special report, or any other information product. Yes, there are lots of bait pieces out there already. But people love them. They're tangible and have perceived value.

Now comes the intimidating part: Putting one together. Mike O'Sullivan provides the following guidelines on how to write an effective white paper.

1. *Take the right approach.* A good bait piece can:

   - Answer a pressing question.
   - Distill a fuzzy topic.
   - Clarify a misunderstood topic.
   - Explain a trend.
   - Give step-by-step advice to help the reader accomplish a specific task.
   - Illustrate how a larger business activity can be improved.

That's just a few examples. Whatever approach you choose, you want your target reader to come away thinking, "That was well worth reading. This company certainly 'gets' what I do."

Now you're probably not the first in your industry to produce a special report. So before you start, look at reports your competitors have put out. You'll undoubtedly see ads for them in publications you and your audience read. And you can also find them via directories such as *www.bitpipe.com*. (See Appendix A for a list of Web sites of white papers.)

Take notes. What do you like? What don't you like? What's missing? From the perspective of a member of your target audience, do you think you would have learned something? What you discover will help you write a report that stands above the pack.

2. *Don't be sales-y.* Beyond some "About Us" copy at the end, you don't need to promote your products or services at all. Here's why.

By definition, whatever topic you're talking about reflects what you do. After all, you wouldn't offer a tip sheet with "Ten Ways to Improve the ROI of Your Next Direct Mail Campaign" unless you sell direct marketing services. You wouldn't write a white paper about protecting a wireless LAN (local area network) unless you're in the wireless networking business. And so on.

Plus, your company's the one with its name on the report. Also, remember that most of your potential leads aren't ready to buy. And they may not be for awhile. So they're not looking for one vendor's sales pitch. They're looking for information that will help them do their jobs more effectively and make better decisions.

Give them what they want and your company's name will stick in their minds.

3. *Be brief.* As a general rule, subscribe to the "less is more" philosophy. Consider five to ten pages a good benchmark. You can cover a lot of ground in this amount of space, yet you're forced to focus.

When estimating word count, figure 400 to 500 words per published page of the white paper for pages without visuals. If the page has a large, prominent graphic or diagram, figure 200 to 250 words per page.

A tip sheet might be a few pages or less (given the name "tip sheet"). I've seen white papers that push 15 to 20 pages.

More important, you need to think long term. One report won't fulfill your needs—you're perpetually looking for new leads and so you'll need to offer new incentives. Plus, your content may have a limited shelf life, particularly if you're writing a technology-focused white paper. So don't cram everything into one report. Save ideas for future ones.

4. *Think visually.* Use visuals wherever appropriate. Whether it's a screen shot, graph, chart, or timeline, a good illustration will help your reader understand and absorb your material.

For the same reason, break up sections into subsections. (This of course may not apply to a tip sheet or other report shorter than five pages.)

Use lots of white space. Wide page margins and generous gaps between text and visuals will ensure your report is easy on the eyes.

5. *Make an outline.* Start by outlining your report in as much detail as possible. Write bullet points. Try to define your report's major sections. Don't worry about whether anything "sounds right." Most of it won't. But you'll get there. At this point you're just trying to put down raw ideas and organize them.

Do this as long as you need to and eventually your rough notes will evolve into sentences, paragraphs, and completed sections.

6. *Allow enough time to produce a quality document.* The amount of time you will need depends on (1) the type of report and (2) whether you're starting from scratch.

Regarding point two, you probably aren't. If you haven't already, look at content you already have, from PowerPoint® presentations to internal e-mail discussions. Maybe there's material you can reuse or repurpose.

But generally speaking, give yourself two to four weeks minimum. Sound like a lot of time? You'll need it.

For one, your first draft will take longer than you think (it always does). Then you'll want to solicit detailed feedback from colleagues inside and outside your company. And even if your first draft achieves the thrust of what you want, you'll still go through a few more before you're satisfied. Plus extra rounds of feedback in between.

After you reach that point, you'll need to incorporate everything into an appealing PDF design template. And before you know it, you've hit your deadline.

7. *Solicit reader feedback.* If you're giving away valuable information, it's appropriate—even respectful—to initiate a dialogue with your reader. Ask for her take on your topic. Offer an easy way for her to give it to you (a fax number, a phone number, a form on your Web site, an easy-to-spell e-mail address). And before you know it, you've created a relationship with a potential customer.[1]

9 Characteristics of Effective White Papers

Nick Copley of *www.bitpipe.com* presents the following checklist for writing an effective white paper:

1. *A sexy title.* "Readers typically select white papers from a long list of papers on a single topic, so the title is very much the most important element in attracting readership," says Copley. A good title "unambiguously" identifies the subject of the paper, he says; in addition, the title should also suggest who the target reader is and should convey a compelling "what's in it for me" benefit.
2. *An executive summary.* Like the title, the summary is essentially marketing copy that persuades readers to download the full white paper. "This is where you lay out your key message, and it's a good idea to write this copy even before you write the paper itself, just to make sure it's done well."

    A good summary should be "meaty"—at least several paragraphs long, with enough detail to suggest what the paper covers in more depth. "If the paper is more than about ten pages, you should also include a table of contents here."
3. *A clear story line.* "Many white papers are choppy and hard to follow," Copley notes. "That's usually a sign of a disorganized editorial process, not bad writing. The project is given to a junior member of the marketing group, and then everyone throws in ideas about what the paper should cover. The right approach is to decide upfront what one goal you're trying to achieve with this document. Save all the other nuggets of ideas for other white papers."
4. *Competitive positioning.* "It's pointless to pretend that you have the only solution in the market—the people who download white papers are usually doing research and will probably look at several papers at the same time," says Copley. "Instead, start by reviewing competing white papers and make sure that your own document addresses major issues that competitors raise. You want to say, 'Here's

our solution to this problem, and here's how it maps against the competition.'"

5. *Charts and diagrams.* "If you're trying to get across a complex message, good visual elements always help," Copley says. "But be sure the diagrams actually tie into the text and say something meaningful. If the reader has to figure out the context, then you're just interrupting the flow of your discussion."

6. *Third-party references.* "This is something many people leave out," says Copley. "But in fact it helps when you can bring in outside authorities—standards bodies, research firms, experts on best practices, and so forth. These references show that you know what's going on in the market and they make the paper more credible."

7. *Case studies.* White papers tend to address fairly abstract technology issues, but Copley argues that one or two case studies or user profiles (perhaps presented as sidebars) "can bring the paper back to reality." Case studies "also show that you have at least a few customers who are happy to endorse your solution."

8. *The author's biography.* Another simple way to add credibility is to include a short profile of the white paper's author, says Copley: "This is always good, especially if the writer is well-known in the field. It helps make the publication look more like an editorial document and less like marketing copy. "

9. *A call to action.* "What is the reader supposed to do after reading the paper?" Copley asks. "'Presumably, you've educated and persuaded the reader, so now you should spell out the next step." White paper readers are generally at a very early stage in the sales cycle, he adds, so trying to move them straight to a sale may not practical. "But you can certainly suggest they get additional information from you—by requesting a personal sales call, signing up for a newsletter, attending a seminar, or even downloading additional white papers. Never leave the reader dangling."[2]

White papers contain at least some of these items:

1. Current industry problems/trends: Begin with a description of the broadest issues and trends in the industry that will introduce the reader to the topic. Then move on to discussing the specific attributes of the solution.

2. Technology: Description of the technology if necessary.
3. How the service offered or the new technology or business model works.
4. Benefits/application/ROI/case studies.
5. Visual appeal: Add graphics, charts, and images to break the monotony of reading text and also serve as tools to understand the topic better.
6. How to choose a solution/vendor, if applicable.
7. Summary.

The 12 Most Common Technical Writing Mistakes

The average engineer, programmer, or manager in industry cannot write clear, lucid prose. He or she may know the basics—sentence structure, grammar, punctuation, exposition. But most have a few poor stylistic habits that mar their technical writing, making it dull and difficult to read.

Why do engineers and corporate people write so poorly? Many feel that writing is time consuming, unimportant, and unpleasant. Others lack confidence in their ability to communicate or simply don't know how to get started. A third group has the desire to write well, but lacks the proper training.

In seminars given at New York University, American Chemical Society, Society of Technical Communication, American Institute of Chemical Engineers, and numerous corporations, I have surveyed hundreds of engineers to discover which problems occur most frequently in their writing. Below are the 12 most common problems in technical writing, along with tips on how to recognize them and how to solve them.

1. *Poor organization.* According to the survey, poor organization is the number one problem in engineering writing. As technical writer Jerry Bacchetti points out, "If the reader believes the content has some importance to him, he can plow through a report even if it is dull or has lengthy sentences and big words. But if it's poorly organized—forget it. There's no way to make sense of what is written."[3]

   Poor organization stems from poor planning. While a computer programmer would never think of writing a complex program without first drawing a flow chart, he'd probably knock out a draft of a user's manual without making notes or an outline. In the same way, a builder who requires detailed blueprints before he lays the first brick will write a letter without really considering his message, audience, or purpose.

Before you write, plan. Create a rough outline that spells out the contents and organization of your paper or report. The outline need not be formal. A simple list, doodles, or rough notes will do—use whatever form suits you.

By the time you finish writing, some things in the final draft might be different from the outline. That's okay. The outline is a tool to aid in organization, not a commandment cast in stone. If you want to change it as you go along—fine. The outline helps you divide the writing project into many smaller, easy-to-handle pieces and parts. The organization of these parts depends on the type of document you're writing.

In general, it's best to stick with standard formats. A laboratory report, for example, has an abstract, a table of contents, a summary, an introduction, a main body (theory, apparatus and procedures, results, and discussions), conclusions and recommendations, nomenclature, references, and appendices.

An operating manual includes a summary; an introduction; a description of the equipment; instructions for routine operation, troubleshooting, maintenance, and emergency operation; and an appendix containing a parts list, spare-parts list, drawings, figures, and manufacturer's literature.

If the format isn't strictly defined by the type of document you are writing, select the organizational scheme that best fits the material. Some common formats include:

- *Order of location.* An article on the planets of the solar system might begin with Mercury (the planet nearest the sun) and end with Pluto (the planet farthest out).
- *Order of increasing difficulty.* Computer manuals often start with the easiest material and, as the user masters basic principles, move on to more complex operations.
- *Alphabetical order.* This is a logical way to arrange a booklet on vitamins (A, B-3, B-12, C, D, E, and so on) or a directory of company employees.
- *Chronological order.* Here you present the facts in the order in which they happened. History books are written this way. So are many case histories, feature stories, and corporate biographies.
- *Problem/solution.* Another format appropriate to case histories and many types of reports, the problem/solution organizational scheme begins with "Here's what the problem was" and ends with "Here's how we solved it."

- *Inverted pyramid.* This is the newspaper style of news reporting where the lead paragraph summarizes the story and the following paragraphs present the facts in order of decreasing importance. You can use this format in journal articles, letters, memos, and reports.
- *Deductive order.* You can start with a generalization, and then support it with particulars. Scientists use this format in research papers that begin with the findings and then state the supporting evidence.
- *Inductive order.* Another approach is to begin with specific instances, and then lead the reader to the idea or general principles the instances suggest. This is an excellent way to approach trade journal feature stories.
- *List.* The text you're now reading is a list because it describes, in list form, the most common problems in technical writing. A technical list article might be titled "Six Tips for Designing Wet Scrubbers" or "Seven Ways to Reduce Your Plant's Electric Bill."

2. *Misreading the reader.* When I admit to doing some direct-mail copywriting as part of my consulting work, people turn up their noses. "I always throw that junk in the garbage," they say. "Who would ever buy something from a letter addressed to 'Dear Occupant'?"

They're right, of course. Written communications are most effective when they are targeted and *personal.* Your writing should be built around the needs, interests, and desires of the reader.

With most technical documents—articles, papers, manuals, reports, brochures—you are writing for many readers, not an individual. Even though we don't know the names of our readers, we need to develop a picture of who they are, their job title, education, industry, and interests.

- *Job title.* Engineers are interested in your compressor's reliability and performance, while the purchasing agent is more concerned with cost. A person's job influences his perspective of your product, service, or idea. Are you writing for plant engineers? Office managers? CEOs? Machinists? Make the tone and content of your writing compatible with the professional interests of your readers.
- *Education.* Is your reader a Ph.D. or a high-school drop-out? Is he a chemical engineer? Does he understand computer pro-

gramming, thermodynamics, physical chemistry, and the calculus of variations? Write simply enough so that even the least technical of your readers can understand what you are saying.

- *Industry.* When engineers buy a reverse-osmosis water purification system for a chemical plant, they want to know every technical detail down to the last pipe, pump, fan, and filter. Marine buyers, on the other hand, have only two basic questions: "What does it cost?" and "How reliable is it?" Especially in promotional writing, know what features of your product appeal to the various markets.

- *Level of interest.* A technical expert who has responded to your ad is more likely to be receptive to a salesman's call than someone who the salesman calls on cold. Is your reader interested or disinterested? Friendly or hostile? Receptive or resistant? Understanding his state of mind helps you tailor your message to meet his needs.

If you don't know enough about your reader, there are ways to find out. If you are writing an article for a trade journal, for example, get several copies of the magazine and study it before you write. If you are presenting a paper at a conference, look at the conference brochure to get a feel for the audience who will be attending your session. If you are contributing text to product descriptions, ask the marketing or publications department the format in which the material will be published, how it will be distributed, and who will be reading it.

3. *Writing in "technicalese."* Anyone who reads technical documents knows the danger of "technicalese"—the pompous, overblown style that leaves your writing sounding as if it were written by a computer or a corporation instead of a human being.

"Technicalese," by my definition, is language more complex than the concepts it serves to communicate. By loading up their writings with unnecessary jargon, clichés, antiquated phrases, passive sentences, and an excess of adjectives, technicians and bureaucrats hide behind a jumble of incomprehensible memos and reports.

To help you recognize "technicalese" (also known as "corporitis"), I've assembled a few samples from diverse sources. Note how the authors seem to be writing to impress rather than to express. All of these excerpts are real.

"Will you please advise me at your earliest convenience of the correct status of this product?"

—-Memo from an advertising manager

"All of the bonds in the above described account having been heretofore disposed of, we are this day terminating same. We accordingly enclose herein check in the amount of $30,050 same being your share realized therein, as per statement attached."

—-Letter from a stockbroker

"This procedure enables users to document data fields described in master files that were parsed and analyzed by the program dictionary."

—Software user's manual

"This article presents some findings from surveys conducted in Haiti in 1977 that provide retrospective data on the age at menarche of women between the ages of 15 and 49 years. It considers the demographic and nutritional situation in Haiti, the cultural meaning of menarche and the source of data."

—-Article abstract

How do you eliminate "technicalese" from your writing? Start by avoiding unnecessary jargon. Don't use a technical term unless it communicates your meaning precisely. Never write "mobile dentition" when "loose teeth" will do just as well. When you avoid jargon, your writing can be easily read by novices and experienced professionals alike.

Use contractions. Avoid clichés and antiquated phrases. Write simply. Prefer the active voice. In the active voice, action is expressed directly: "John performed the experiment." In the passive voice, the action is indirect: "The experiment was performed by John."

When you use the active voice, your writing will be more direct and vigorous; your sentences, more concise. As you can see in the samples below, the passive voice seems puny and stiff by comparison:

Passive Voice	Active Voice
Control of the bearing-oil supply is provided by the shutoff valves.	Shutoff valves control the bearing-oil supply.
Leaking of the seals is prevented by the use of O-rings.	O-rings keep the seals from leaking.
Fuel-cost savings were realized through the installation of thermal insulation.	The installation of thermal insulation cut fuel costs.

4. *Lengthy sentences.* Lengthy sentences tire the reader and make your writing hard to read. A survey by Harvard professor D.H. Menzel indicates that in technical papers the sentences become difficult to understand when they exceed 34 words in length.[4]

One measure of writing clarity, the Fog Index, takes into account sentence length *and* word length. Here's how it works:

First, determine the average sentence length in a short (100 to 200 words) writing sample. To do this, divide the number of words in the sample by the number of sentences. If parts of a sentence are separated by a semicolon (;), count each part as a separate sentence.

Next, calculate the number of big words (words with three or more syllables) per 100 words of sample. Do not include capitalized words, combinations of short words (butterfly, moreover) or verbs made three syllables by adding *ed* or *es* (accepted, responses).

Finally, add the average sentence length to the number of big words per hundred words and multiply by 0.4. This gives you the Fog Index for the sample.

The Fog Index corresponds to the years of schooling you need to read and understand the sample. A score of 8 or 9 indicates high-school level; 13, a college freshman; 17, a college graduate.

Popular magazines have Fog Indexes ranging from 8 to 13. Technical journals should rate no higher than 17.

Obviously, the higher the Fog Index, the more difficult the writing is to read. In his book *Gene Control in the Living Cell,* J.A.V. Butler leads off with a single 79-word sentence.

> In this book I have attempted an accurate but at the same time readable account of recent work on the subject of how gene controls operate, a large subject which is rapidly acquiring a central position in the biology of today and which will inevitably become even more prominent in the future, in the efforts of scientists of numerous different specialists to explain how a single organism can contain cells of many different kinds developed from a common origin.[5]

With 17 big words, this sample has a Fog Index of 40—equivalent to a reading level of 28 years of college education! Obviously, this sentence is way too long. Here's a rewrite I came up with:

> This book is about how gene controls operate—a subject of growing importance in modern biology.

This gets the message across with a Fog Index of only 14.

Give your writing the Fog Index test. If you score in the upper teens or higher, it's time to trim sentence length. Go over your text, and break long sentences into two or more separate sentences. To further reduce average sentence length and add variety to your writing, you can occasionally use an extremely short sentence or sentence fragments of only three to four words or so. Like this one.

Short sentences are easier to grasp than long ones. As I mentioned in Chapter 4, a good guide for keeping sentence length under control is to write sentences that can be spoken aloud without losing your breath (do not take a deep breath before doing this test).

5. *Big words.* Technical experts sometimes prefer to use big, important-sounding words instead of short, simple words. This is a mistake; fancy language just frustrates the reader. Write in plain, ordinary English and your readers will love you for it.

Here are a few big words that occur frequently in technical literature; the column on the right presents a shorter—and preferable—substitution:

Big Word	Substitution
Terminate	End
Utilize	Use
Incombustible	Fireproof
Substantiate	Prove
Parsimonious	Cheap

Example: I am a chemical engineer, so I know that chemical engineering has a special language all its own. Technical terms are a helpful shorthand when one is communicating within the profession, but they may confuse readers who do not have your special background.

Take the word, "yield," for example. To a chemical engineer, yield is a measure of how much product a reaction produces. But, to car drivers, yield means slowing down (and stopping, if necessary) at an intersection.

Other words that have special meaning to chemical engineers but have a different definition in everyday use include: vacuum, pressure, batch, bypass, recycle, concentration, mole, purge, saturation, catalyst.

Use legitimate technical terms when they communicate your ideas precisely, but avoid using jargon just because the words sound impressive. Do not write that material is "gravimetrically conveyed" when it is simply dumped.

Technical readers are interested in detailed technical information—facts, figures, conclusions, recommendations. Do not be content to say something is good, bad, fast, or slow when you can say *how* good, *how* bad, *how* fast, or *how* slow. Be specific whenever possible.

General	Specific
A tall spray dryer	A 40-foot-tall spray dryer
Facility	Warehouse
Plant	Oil refinery
Unit	Evaporator
Unfavorable weather conditions	Rain
Structural degradation	A leaky roof
High performance	95% efficiency

The key to success in technical writing is to *keep it simple*. Write to express—not to impress. A relaxed, conversational style can add vigor and clarity to your work.

Formal Technical Style	Informal Conversational Style
The data provided by direct examination of samples under the lens of the microscope are insufficient for the purpose of making a proper identification of the components of the substance.	We can't tell what it is made of by looking at it under the microscope.
We have found during conversations with customers that even the most experienced of extruder specialists have a tendency to avoid the extrusion of silicone profiles or hoses.	Our customers tell us that experienced extruder specialists avoid extruding silicone profiles or hoses.
The corporation terminated the employment of Mr. Joseph Smith.	Joe was fired.

6. *Writer's block.* Writer's block isn't just for professional writers; it can afflict technical experts and managers, too. Writer's block is the inability to start putting words on paper or computer screen, and it stems from anxiety and fear of writing.

When technical people write, they're afraid to make mistakes, and so they edit themselves word by word, inhibiting the natural flow of ideas and sentences. But professional writers know that writing is a process consisting of numerous drafts, rewrites, deletions, and revisions. Rarely does a writer produce a perfect manuscript on the first try.

Here are a few tips to help you overcome writer's block:

- *Break the writing up into short sections, and write one section at a time.* Tackling many little writing assignments seems less formidable a task than taking a large project all at once. This also benefits the reader. Writing is most readable when it deals with one simple idea rather than multiple complex ideas. Your entire paper can't be simple or restricted to one idea, but each section of it can.

- *Write the easy sections first.* If you can't get a handle on the main argument of your report or paper, begin with something routine, such as the section on "Apparatus" or "Procedures." This will get you started and help build momentum.

- *Write abstracts, introductions, and summaries last.* Although they come first in the final document, it doesn't make sense to try to sum up a paper that hasn't been written yet.

- *Avoid grammar-book rules that inhibit writers.* One such rule says every paragraph must begin with a topic sentence (a first sentence that states the central idea of the paragraph). By insisting on topic sentences, teachers and editors throw up a block that prevents people from putting their thoughts on paper. Professional writers don't worry about topic sentences (or sentence diagrams or ending a sentence with a preposition). Neither should you. Instead, just make sure that whenever you begin to write about a new idea, you start a new paragraph.

- *Sleep on it.* Put your manuscript away and come back to it the next morning—or even several days later. Refreshed, you'll be able to edit and rewrite effectively and easily.

7. *Poorly defined topic.* Effective writing begins with a clear definition of the specific topic you want to write about. The big mistake many

engineers make is to tackle a topic that's too broad. For example, the title "Project Management" is too all encompassing for a technical paper. You could write a whole book on the subject. But by narrowing the scope, say, with the title "Managing Chemical Plant Construction Projects With Budgets Under $500,000," you get a clearer definition and a more manageable topic.

It's also important to know the purpose of the document. You may say, "That's easy; the purpose is to give technical information." But think again. Do you want the reader to buy a product? Change methods of working? Look for the hidden agenda beyond the mere transmission of facts.

8. *Inadequate content.* OK. You've defined your topic, audience, and purpose. The next step is to do some homework, and to gather information on the topic at hand. Most technical experts I know don't do this. When they're writing a trade journal article, for example, their attitude is, "I'm the expert here. So I'll just rely on my own experience and know-how."

And that's a mistake. Even though you're an expert, your knowledge may be limited, your viewpoint lopsided. Gathering information from other sources helps round out your knowledge or, at the very least, verify your own thinking. And there's another benefit: backing up your claims with facts is a real credibility builder.

Once you've crammed a file folder full of reprints and clippings, take notes on index cards or a computer. Not only does note taking put the key facts at your fingertips in condensed form, but reprocessing the research information through your fingers and brain puts you in closer touch with your material.

9. *Stopping after the first draft.* Once you gather facts and decide how to organize the piece, the next step is to sit down and write. When you do, keep in mind that the secret to successful writing is rewriting.

You don't have to get it right on the first draft. The pros rarely do. E.B. White, essayist and co-author of the writer's resource book *The Elements of Style*, was said to have rewritten every piece nine times. Maybe you don't need nine drafts, but you probably need more than one. Use a simple three-step procedure that I call SPP—Spit, Prune, and Polish.

When you sit down to write, just spit it out. Don't worry about how it sounds, or whether the grammar's right, or if it fits your outline. Just let the words flow. If you make a mistake, leave it. You can always go back and fix it later. You may find it helpful to talk into a tape recorder or dictate to an assistant. If you can type and have a personal computer, great. Some old-fashioned folks even use a pencil and paper.

In the next step, pruning, print out your first draft (double-spaced, for easy editing) and give it major surgery. Take a red pen to the draft and slash out all unnecessary words and phrases. Rewrite any awkward passages to make them smoother, but if you get stuck, leave it and go on; come back to it later.

Use your word processing program's cut and paste feature to cut the draft apart and reorganize it to fit your outline or to improve on that outline. Then print out a clean draft. Repeat the pruning step, if necessary, as many times as you want.

In the final stage, polish your manuscript by checking such points as equations, units of measure, references, grammar, spelling, and punctuation. Again use the red pen and print out a fresh copy with corrections.

10. *Inconsistent usage.* "A foolish consistency," wrote Ralph Waldo Emerson, "is the hobgoblin of little minds." This may be so. But, on the other hand, inconsistencies in technical writing will confuse your readers and convince them that your work and reasoning are as sloppy and unorganized as your prose.

Good writers strive for consistency in the use of numbers, hyphens, units of measure, punctuation, equations, grammar, symbols, capitalization, technical terms, and abbreviations.

For example, many writers are inconsistent in the use of hyphens. The rule is: two words that form an adjective are hyphenated. Thus, write: first-order reaction, fluidized-bed combustion, high-sulfur coal, space-time continuum.

The U.S. Government Printing Office Style Manual, Strunk and White's *The Elements of Style,* and your organization's writing manual can guide you in the basics of grammar, punctuation, abbreviation, and capitalization.

11. *Dull, wordy prose.* Professionals are busy people. Make your writing less time-consuming for them to read by telling the whole story in the fewest possible words.

How can you make your writing more concise? One way is to avoid redundancies—a form of wordiness in which a modifier repeats an idea already contained within the word being modified.

For example, a recent trade ad described a product as a "new innovation." Could there be such a thing as an *old* innovation? The ad also said the product was "very unique." Unique means "one of a kind," so it is impossible for anything to be *very* unique.

By now, you probably get the picture. Some other redundancies that have come up in technical and business literature are listed below, along with the correct way to rewrite them:

Redundancy	Rewrite as:
Advance plan	Plan
Actual experience	Experience
Two cubic feet in volume	Two cubic feet
Cylindrical in shape	Cylindrical
Uniformly homogeneous	Homogeneous
Armed gunmen	Gunmen
Living survivors	Survivors
Free gift	Gift

Many writers are fond of overblown expressions such as "the fact that," "it is well known that," and "it is the purpose of this writer to show that." These take up space but add little to meaning or clarity.

The following list includes some of the wordy phrases that appear frequently in technical and business literature. The column on the right offers suggested substitute words:

Wordy Phrase	Suggested Substitute
During the course of	During
In the form of	As
In many cases	Often
In the event of	If
Exhibits the ability to	Can

12. *Poor page layout.* To enhance readability, break your writing into short sections. Long, unbroken blocks of text are stumbling blocks that

intimidate and bore readers. Breaking your writing into short sections and short paragraphs makes it easier to read.

Use visuals. Drawings, graphs, and other visuals can reinforce your text. In fact, pictures often communicate better than words; we remember 10 percent of what we read, but 30 percent of what we see.

Visuals can make your technical communications more effective. The different types of visuals and what they can show are listed below:

Type of Visual	This shows...
Photograph or illustration	. . . what something looks like
Map	. . . where it is located
Exploded view	. . . how it is put together
Schematic diagram	. . . how it works or is organized
Graph	. . . how much there is (quantity); how one thing varies as a function of another
Pie chart	. . . proportions and percentages
Bar chart	. . . comparisons between quantities
Table	. . . a body of related data

These tips should help eliminate some of the fear and anxiety you may have about writing, as well as make the whole task easier and more productive. Finally, keep in mind that success in writing, or any form of communication, is largely a matter of attitude: If you don't think writing is important enough to take the time to do it right, and you don't really care about improving, you probably won't. But if you believe that writing is important and you want to improve, you will.

Writing Compelling Bait Piece Titles

Whether prospects eagerly send for your white paper or pass it by is determined largely by the title. If you have followed the advice in Chapter 2 and chosen an appealing topic, writing the title is relatively easy: it must communicate the topic in a clear, exciting, and engaging way.

Here are a few ways to create white paper titles that sell:

1. *Use a list title.* If your white paper is organized as a list or in sections, use a title that reflects the number of items in the list or sections in the white paper.

   For instance:

   "7 Steps to Implementing a Successful _____"
   "8 Reasons to Switch to _____ Now"
   "6 Ways to Save Money on _____"
   "5 Tips for Better _____"
   "11 Commonly Asked Questions About _____—and One Good Answer to Each."

   Why this works: the number makes people curious. In their minds, they guess at what the seven steps or eight reasons are, and feel compelled to send for your white paper to see whether they guessed correctly. For instance:

   "The Top 7 Security Problems of 802.11 Wireless Networks"

   The list technique can work even if there is only one item on the list or topic in the white paper. *Example:* "The One Filtering Technology Every Network Administrator Should Implement Today to Prevent Spam."

2. *How-to.* How-to is a staple of marketing. It continues to work today in ad headlines, book titles, subject lines, articles, and white papers. *Example:* "How to Stop Teeth in Your Plastic Gears from Breaking."

   If you are tired of how-to, you can use "a guide to" as an alternative, e.g., "A Guide to Preventing Teeth in Plastic Gears from Breaking."

3. *Begin with an active "ing" verb.* Beginning with a verb is known as the "imperative" voice; it's both lively and active. Examples:

   "Implementing RFID for Rapid ROI and Long-Term Success"
   "Managing Large UNIX Data Centers"
   "Filtering Unwanted Internet Content"
   "Securing Financing for Undercapitalized Public Companies"

4. *Why.* Students in journalism classes are taught that newspaper articles must answer the following questions: who, what, when, where, why, and how.

   We have already seen that *how* (as in how-to) makes an effective white paper title. "Why" titles can be similarly effective. By adding why to an ordinary title, you instantly arouse curiosity, because the reader wants to know the answer to the question "why?" For instance, instead of "Large Companies Need Effective Content Management," write "Why Large Companies Need Effective Content Management."

5. *Add a benefit.* You can spice up a flat title by adding a benefit. For instance, instead of "Personal Information Managers," write "How to Save at Least an Hour a Day With a Personal Information Manager." Or instead of "Operator's Workstation Basics," write "How to Control Processes in Your Plant Better and Faster Using the Operator Workstation."

6. *Use a colon title.* A colon title is a combination headline and subhead separated by a colon (the separation can also be done graphically by putting the subhead under the headline and setting in two point sizes smaller than the headline). Examples of colon headlines:

> "Sarbanes-Oxley: Challenges and Opportunities in the New Regulatory Environment"
> "Defending the Remote Office: Which VPN Technology is Best?"
> "Practical Security and Risk Management: The Good Guys Fight Back."

When you have written a working title for your bait piece, ask yourself if it passes the "3 U's" test. According to the 3 U's formula, a strong title should be (a) ultra-specific, (b) unique (you haven't heard it before), and (c) useful (it states a benefit or reward for reading the paper). *Example:* "How to Reduce Emissions by 95% at Half the Energy Costs of Conventional Venturi Scrubbers."

This title is:

A. Ultra-specific—it references 95 percent reduction in emissions and 50 percent savings in energy costs.

B. Unique—the other systems use something called "Venturi scrubbers," and this clearly is something else.

C. Useful—there are two clear benefits: reducing emissions and saving energy.

Writing the Case Study

A specialized type of bait piece, the case study, can be an effective alternative to conventional white papers and other "how-to" content. A case study is a "product success story," showing how a customer used your product, services, or methods to solve a problem.

Here is an outline you can use to organize any case study you may want to write:

A. *The customer.* In the lead paragraph, focus on your customer, not on your product or company. Gain attention with an interesting lead.

B. *The challenge.* Next, introduce the problem. What condition was your customer trying to change or improve? If possible, use the customer's own words in the form of a quotation.

C. *The journey.* What steps were taken to solve the problem? What other products or services were investigated? Why didn't these work out? Many case study writers skip this section. Don't *you* skip it. This is the place in the story where the reader begins to identify and *empathize.*

D. *The discovery.* How did the customer find out about you? In an ad? At a trade show? Through a media interview? This section often acts as a bridge to the remainder of the case study.

E. *The solution.* This is where you have unbridled freedom to pitch your product or service without fear of sounding too promotional. The earlier sections have earned you this right.

F. *The implementation.* How was your product or service implemented? Was there any downtime or disruption involved? How long was it before it was up and running full steam? Be honest about any problems that arose and how they were resolved. Highlight instances where you went "the extra mile" to satisfy the customer.

G. *The results.* How well did your product or service solve your customer's problem? Be as specific as you can here. If possible, use hard numbers such as savings, revenue gains, sales growth, and return on investment. This is another good spot to include a customer quotation. And a great place to summarize and close your story.

6

Graphics and Production

M ost corporate white papers are over-designed. The companies put a lot of thought into the design of their white paper, but from the wrong perspective. There are two primary flaws I see with the design and layout of white papers today. Avoid these sins and you are already halfway toward a superior design.

The first mistake is over-elaborate design: deliberate ornateness and complexity. Just because your software offers an almost infinite variety of fonts, graphics, and page layouts doesn't mean you should use them. In fact, you should not.

Simplicity is a virtue, not just in graphic design, but in almost every endeavor known to humankind. Keep your design simple. Pick a layout, a format, a typeface and stick with it. Do not waste endless hours experimenting; there is no ROI in such activity.

The second mistake is too much concern and attention focused on standardized white paper "templates." Graphic consistency is usually a desirable characteristic when creating a series of white papers, brochures, or data sheets; but at the end of the day, the reader doesn't care that much.

So don't agonize over finding the perfect white paper design template. You can simply use the template in Exhibit 6.1 as is or modify it as you see fit.

So, what *do* readers respond to in white paper design? There are only three concerns they really have:

1. A bold, visually arresting cover that grabs their eye and gets their attention—usually accomplished by putting the white paper title in large, bold type.

Exhibit 6.1: White Paper Design Template

'WPC' set in Arial Black 48 pt. type

'INTERNATIONAL' set in Arial Black 14 pt. type

Headline set in Arial Black 48 pt. type

WPC

WPC Technical White Paper

Subhead set in Arial 20 pt. type

Subhead set in Arial 16 pt. type

Enabling Lorem Ipsum Worldwide
A Business and Technology Review of WPC

Subhead set in Arial 12 pt. type

Date set in Palatino Linotype 14 pt. type

March 24, 2004

Address set in Palatino Linotype 12 pt. type

Copyright set in Palatino Linotype 12 pt. italic type

WPC • 123 New St. • Your City, AK • 12345-1234
Phone: 123.456.7890 • Fax: 123.456.0987

Copyright © 2000-2004 by WPC International All Rights Reserved

Exhibit 6.1 (Continued)

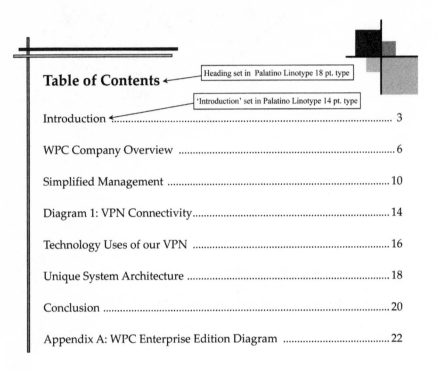

Table of Contents

Heading set in Palatino Linotype 18 pt. type

'Introduction' set in Palatino Linotype 14 pt. type

Footer set in Palatino Linotype 10 pt. type

Exhibit 6.1 (Continued)

Header set in Arial Black 14 pt. type

INTRODUCTION

Body text set in Palatino Linotype 12 pt. type

Lorem ipsum dolor sit amet, consectetuer adipiscing elit. Morbi gravida ullamcorper diam. Mauris fermentum, quam at varius ullamcorper, magna augue malesuada justo, pulvinar euismod neque ipsum quis lorem. Sed sit amet lacus sit amet dolor elementum dignissim. Quisque euismod turpis in lectus. Nam aliquet, purus id ornare nonummy, elit erat vestibulum ipsum, quis commodo pede nunc rutrum odio.

Paragraph line spacing is 1.5 lines

Mauris a tortor. Nunc a wisi. Proin quis augue a purus imperdiet dictum. Donec tempus, nunc sit amet congue scelerisque, nunc mi pharetra orci, eget congue augue arcu vel massa. Vestibulum velit. Pellentesque est. Maecenas sagittis libero non lorem. Aliquam id sapien eget purus fringilla tincidunt. In hac habitasse platea dictumst. Vestibulum id ipsum. Maecenas non turpis sit amet magna porttitor pharetra.

Nunc ut dui. Vestibulum pharetra diam ut eros. Cras non massa non augue tristique aliquam. Donec vehicula. Cras eget arcu vitae tellus elementum nonummy. Vestibulum mollis, quam at volutpat cursus, mauris leo pulvinar sem, in porttitor sapien leo ut arcu. In mattis pede sit amet odio. Vivamus vehicula scelerisque metus. Pellentesque quam elit, egestas sed, auctor vitae, tempor eget, libero. Donec ut augue vitae leo vestibulum rutrum. Cras sit amet tellus quis sapien ullamcorper placerat. Sed luctus lectus vel quam. Nulla non magna malesuada dolor egestas tincidunt. Lorem ipsum dolor sit amet, consectetuer adipiscing elit.

Class aptent taciti sociosqu ad litora torquent per conubia nostra, per inceptos hymenaeos. Duis urna magna, lacinia sed, consequat non, pulvinar sit amet, elit. Nam erat nisl, hendrerit ut, accumsan ut, vehicula non, nisl. Phasellus eros elit, volutpat a, pretium eu, dictum at, dui. Sed eget nunc. Vestibulum egestas imperdiet mauris. Viva-

Footer set in Palatino Linotype 10 pt. type

You can create your own standard template for white papers or use this one.
Source: Robert Bly

2. A layout—column width, type size and style, fonts—that makes the copy easy to read. No micro-type, for example, and no reverse (white on black) type.
3. Valuable content—your design should make the white paper look like important information, not advertising or marketing hype. That means a low-key, clean layout; black text on white paper; simple design. Avoid slick four-color artwork and high-concept graphics; both say "advertising here" loudly.

The Ultimate Secret to Successful White Paper Design

The most powerful graphic design technique for making your white paper credible and acceptable to the reader, and generating his interest in reading it, is to make it look like valuable information instead of marketing material. In fact, making advertising look like information, known as the "editorial" approach, is effective in nearly every medium, including:

- Infomercials that look like TV programs instead of the paid TV advertising that they are.
- E-zines that look like informational newsletters but are actually e-mail marketing promotions.
- Print ads that look like articles except for the word "Advertisement" at the top.
- Advertorials that look like special sections of a magazine but whose content is wholly dictated by the advertisers paying for those pages.

One of the biggest advocates of editorial-style design in marketing is master copywriter Gary Bencivenga. He recently shared with me his thoughts on the power and effectiveness of editorial style layouts:

As you well know, you need strong copy to sell anything, and that's always a given.

But once I started writing my packages as magalogs, bookalogs, and surveys, I found that a good rule of thumb was my "ABA" rule. I only half-jokingly told my clients that my copywriting style had become to write packages that resemble "Anything But Advertising."

I came to this "rule" because I had always made it a practice to write two versions of a package, or at least try two radically different designs.

Every time I wrote a package in a magalog, bookalog or "newsletter" look-alike format (i.e., resembling and actually containing valuable editorial matter), that package would trounce the same exact copy in a traditional #10 package.

I didn't record my clients' exact percentages, but I recall the typical difference was anywhere from 25 to 75 percent and sometimes over 100 percent, always in favor of the editorial-looking piece.

So in time I stopped writing #10 and 6 x 9-inch packages (since they always lost). Yet I still wanted to test two different packages on each major test, as this was my usual practice and always gives the client greater "response insurance."

So instead of writing packages in two different formats, I stuck with editorial formats only, and started testing radically different headlines within the same editorial-style design.

And this yielded an amazing revelation. Over at least a dozen packages, maybe more, radically different headlines (but with the same interior body copy) made no difference at all.

And my clients (most notably Phillips) told me that similar tests on other writers' work yielded the same surprising result. Well written but radically different headlines on magalogs almost never made any appreciable difference in response.

This completely called into question the Ogilvy dictum that "your headline is 80 percent of the sale" (though he said that referring to space ads in magazines and newspapers).

In direct mail, all our tests have shown that with these editorial-style formats (of course assuming strong body copy), the format, not the headline, drives the sale.

I came to realize this: in direct mail, your format *is* your headline. If your format is editorial-looking, it communicates value, so it doesn't get tossed.

An editorial-looking cover, leading to valuable information inside, buys you a reading. It enables your package to survive the initial "toss it" screening, as a person first sorts his or her mail (usually standing over a waste basket). It gets into the "A" pile, to be read.

But what's so interesting is that this is nothing new. Both Ogilvy and Caples strongly advised copywriters to write their ads in an editorial style, which later became known as the "advertorial."

Ogilvy, for example, cited research that editorial style space ads scored 50 percent higher on readership. (Many of Ogilvy's clients were general advertisers, so there were no response rates to measure. Readership was the closest he could get to scientific measurement.)

For his part, John Caples cited a *Reader's Digest* test where the editorial-style layout boosted actual response by 80 percent over the exact same copy in a standard "advertising" layout.

My friend, Yanik Silver, a young and very gifted online copywriter, puts it this way, "Readership studies prove five times as many people read editorial matter as they did advertisements. So it follows if you want to gain 500 percent more readers, you should try employing an editorial look."[1]

The 14 Biggest Graphic Design Mistakes

Design plays an important role in the success of your white paper. Design pre-sells the importance of your words. Long before your words are read, readers will begin judging the value of your publication by its appearance.

Design influences reader satisfaction. Satisfaction goes up when your white paper is easy to read and its design projects an optimistic, professional image. Quality design differentiates your white papers from the competition and builds equity in your brand.

Here, according to desktop design guru Roger C. Parker, are the most common graphic design mistakes and how to avoid them:

1. *Overuse of color.* The overuse of color does a disservice to readers who print white papers on ink-jet printers. Avoid solid colored backgrounds behind the text. Such pages can cost several dollars each in ink jet supplies.

   The overuse of color can send the wrong message. Readers know that color is often used to camouflage a lack of content. In addition, bright colors can create distractions that make adjacent text hard to read. Finally, text set in color is often harder to read than black text against a white background.

   When in doubt, play it safe. Use the minimum amount of color needed to brighten, but not dominate, your pages.

2. *Missing page numbers.* Many white papers lack page numbers. Pages without numbers present several problems. First, readers depend on page numbers to track their progress through a publication. Readers also rely on page numbers to refer back to previously read information.

   Worse, if you print a white paper and drop the pages before stapling or placing in a binder, readers have to waste time reassembling them in the proper order.

3. *Boring similarity.* The front cover is the first thing your readers will notice about your white paper. It's hard to project a unique image if the cover of your white paper resembles the covers of hundreds of other white papers the reader has encountered.

   The interior pages of many white papers look the same because they were created using the templates built into Microsoft® Word, the most popular word processing software program. As a result, typeface, type size, line spacing, and text alignment choices are the same, regardless who published the white paper.

This similarity prevents your white papers from projecting a unique image. Layout, type, and color should project a strong "family resemblance" that not only sets your white papers apart, but also relates them to your firm's marketing materials including business card, letterhead, newsletter, and Web site.

4. *Long lines of type.* Many white papers are hard to read because text extends in an unbroken line across the page from the left-hand margin of the page to the right-hand margin.

   Long lines of type present two problems. One is that the resulting left and right margins are very narrow. White space along the edges of pages provides a resting spot for your reader's eyes and emphasizes the adjacent text. Margins also provide space for your reader's fingers to hold each page without obscuring any of the words.

   In addition, long lines of type are difficult and tiresome to read. It's very easy for readers to get lost making the transition from the end of one line of text to the beginning of the next. Doubling (rereading the same line) can occur, or readers may inadvertently skip a line of text.

5. *Inappropriate typeface.* There are three main classifications of type: decorative, serif, and sans serif:

   - Decorative typefaces—like Papyrus or Broadway—are heavily stylized and great for attracting attention or projecting an atmosphere or image. The use of these typefaces should be restricted to logos and packaging, however, where image is more important than readability.
   - Serif typefaces—like Times New Roman or Garamond—are ideal for extended reading. The serifs, or finishing strokes at the edges of each character, help define the unique shape of each letter and lead the reader's eyes from letter to letter.
   - Sans serif typefaces, like Arial or Verdana, are very legible. Their clean, simple design helps readers recognize words from a long distance away, which is why they are used for highway signage. Sans serif typefaces are often used for headlines and subheads combined with serif body copy.

The historic analogy has been that type is similar to a wineglass. You should notice the wine inside the glass, rather than the wineglass holding it. You can easily extend that analogy to all of graphic design: you should focus on the copy in the document, not the page layout containing it.

6. *Wrong type size.* Type is often set too large—i.e., 14 points—out of habit. (There are approximately 72 points to an inch.) Type set too large is as hard to read as type set too small. When type is set too large, there is not enough space for enough words on each line for readers to comfortably skim the line.

   The details that help readers identify each character become lost when type is set too small and readers have to squint. Type set too small also requires too many left-to-right eye movements on each line.

   Remember: in most cases, those who buy your white paper are not scanners: people scanning groups of words and recognizing their shapes, rather than phonetically "sounding out" each word. Skimming works best when each line contains about an alphabet and a half—40 to 45 characters.

7. *Improper line and paragraph spacing.* Few white paper publishers take the time to carefully adjust line and paragraph spacing. Correct line spacing—called leading—depends on typeface, type size, and line length. White space between lines acts like "rails" guiding your reader's eyes from word to word along each line.

   Very seldom is your software program's default or "automatic" line spacing measurement right for easy reading. Correct line spacing depends on:

   - *Line length*: as the line length increases, you will probably want to add more white space, or leading, between lines.
   - *Typeface*: sans serif typefaces like Verdana require more leading than serif typefaces like Times New Roman.
   - *Type size*: line spacing should increase as type size increases.

Correct paragraph spacing is equally important. Avoid the temptation to press the Enter (or Return) key twice at the end of each paragraph. This creates far too much space between paragraphs. New paragraphs should be separated by noticeably more space than line spacing within paragraphs, but not so much space that it isolates each paragraph. Paragraph spacing should equal one and one half lines of space.

8. *Awkward gaps between sentences.* Never press the space bar twice following the period at the end of a sentence. This is especially true when working with paragraphs of justified text, i.e., lines of equal length.

    When word spacing is adjusted to create lines of equal length, each space will expand, often creating a very noticeable gap between sentences. Sometimes, these gaps will be located in adjacent lines, creating distracting rivers of white space running through your text.

9. *Difficult-to-read headlines.* Headlines should form a strong contrast with the text they introduce. Readers should have no trouble locating or reading them.

    Never set headlines entirely in uppercase, i.e., capital letters. Headlines set entirely in upper-case characters are harder to read than headlines set in a combination of upper and lower case type. This is because words set entirely in uppercase characters lack the distinctive shapes that words set in lower case characters create.

    Headlines set entirely in upper case type also occupy up to a third more space than headlines set in both upper and lower case letters.

10. *Failure to chunk content.* Chunking refers to making white papers easier to read by breaking them into manageable, bite-sized pieces. The best way to chunk content is to insert frequent subheads through the text. Subheads convert "skimmers" into readers by "advertising" the text that follows.

    Before committing to spend time on each page, readers quickly skim each page for clues indicating whether or not it will be worth reading the page. Subheads attract your reader's eyes and "advertise" the paragraphs that follow. Each subhead thus provides an additional entry point into the text.

    Subheads avoid visual boredom created by page after page of nearly identical paragraphs.

11. *Poor subhead formatting.* To succeed, subheads must form a strong visual contrast with the adjacent paragraphs. It's not enough to simply set subheads in the italicized version of the same typeface used for body copy. Subheads should be noticeably larger and/or bolder than adjacent text.

    A few more subhead formatting tips:

- *Type face*: one of the safest formulas is to combine sans serif bold subheads with serif body copy. To unify your publication, use the same type face for both headlines and subheads.
- *Underlining*: never underline subheads to "make them more noticeable." Underlining makes them harder to read. This is because underlining interferes with the descenders—or portions of letters like g, p, and y—that extend below the invisible line the subheads rest on.
- *Length*: limit subheads to one or two key words. Avoid full sentences. Subheads work best when limited to a single line.

Subheads should also be set off by generous amounts of white space. Avoid "floating" subheads, i.e., subheads equally spaced between the previous paragraph and the next paragraph. Ideally, there should be twice as much space above a subhead as there is below the subhead and the paragraph it introduces.

12. *Inappropriate hyphenation*. There are different hyphenation rules for headlines, subheads, and body copy. Never hyphenate headlines or subheads, but always hyphenate text paragraphs. A failure to hyphenate body copy is very noticeable.

    Failing to hyphenate justified text can cause awkward word spacing problems. There will be huge gaps between words in lines containing a few long words. Word spacing in lines containing several short words is apt to be noticeably cramped. The differing in word spacing will be very obvious in adjacent lines.

    When our copy is set flush left, ragged right, failure to hyphenate text can cause lines containing a few long words to be very short, while lines containing several short words will be very long. These differing line lengths will be very noticeable.

    Be on the lookout for excessive hyphenation. Avoid hyphenating more than two lines in a row. If your text shows excessive hyphenation, the type size you have chosen may be too large for the line length you are working with.

13. *Distracting headers, footers, and borders*. Headers and footers refer to text or graphic accents repeated at the top or bottom of each page.

    Often, white paper publishers use the same typeface and type size for both body copy and header and footer information. Page numbers, copyright information, and the publisher's address should be smaller and less noticeable than the text on each page.

Compounding the problem: often headers and footers contain Web site hyperlinks set in blue. This creates another distraction which pulls the reader's eyes away from the primary message.

Few white papers help readers keep track of their location in the paper and their progress through it. Without section and chapter numbers and titles, it is hard for readers to locate, or relocate specific chapters, and specific topics.

Often the author or company's e-mail address appears in a header or footer as a bright blue hyperlink—sometimes the only color on each page. The bright blue link attracts attention far out of proportion to its importance.

Large, colored logos on each page can also be very distracting, without adding meaningful information.

As for borders, white papers pages are often boxed with lines of equal length and thickness at the top, bottom and sides. Boxed pages project a conservative, old-fashioned look. A more contemporary image can be created using rules—or lines—of different thickness at just the tops and bottoms of each page.

14. *Widows and orphans.* Widows and orphans occur when a word, a portion of a word, or part of a line of text is isolated at the bottom of a page (or column) or at the top of the next of the next page or column.

The worst-case scenario occurs when a subhead appears by itself at the bottom of a page, isolated from the paragraph it introduces which appears at the top of the next page Although most software programs permit you to automatically "lock" subheads to the text they introduce, this feature is rarely used.[2]

When someone downloads a white paper from you, within seconds they will either feel a glow of pleasure or a feeling of disappointment. Readers check out the cover and glance at inside pages, then either say "Aw gee, just another hard-to-read, look-alike white paper" or "Wow! This looks really great!"

Whether your white paper receives the attention it deserves and paves the way for future sales, or—worst case scenario—is instantly deleted or round-filed—depends to a great extent on the design of your white paper.

7

White Paper Alternatives

The title of this book is *The White Paper Marketing Handbook,* but it is really about taking an educational approach to marketing by giving away free information to potential customers. White papers are just one format for our bait pieces, but there are many others. Let's take a look at our format options in this chapter.

White Papers

White papers are informational documents that are designed to look like special reports, opinion papers, or other important information.

The page size is typically 8½ by 11 inches, and white papers may be distributed both as hard copy documents or downloadable Adobe® Acrobat® PDFs.

Hard-copy white papers are either run off on a laser printer, high-quality photocopier, or on an offset printing press. They may be color, although the majority are black and white.

Most are produced either in a Word template or with desktop publishing software. Text can be set in one, two, or three columns.

Typical length for a white paper is four to ten pages, though a few are shorter and some can run longer. Tables, graphs, charts, diagrams, tables of contents, bibliographies, and appendices are optional but desirable features that can add value and cause the recipient to retain the white paper longer. For more details on how to write white papers, see Chapter 5.

Tips and Tip Sheets

Tip sheets are short, to-the-point fact sheets on a particular subject. They are usually printed on one or two sides of an 8½ by 11-inch sheet of paper.

Advice or information is typically (but not necessarily) presented as a series of short, numbered items or tips. You can write tip sheets as electronic files, then run them off one at a time on your laser printer as orders come in.

You can also e-mail tip sheets or individual tips to clients who prefer an electronic file. The e-mail format lends itself to sending single tips, and a number of marketers, including Ilise Benun and Markus Allan, send out e-mails with just one tip per message.

Here are Ilise's guidelines for writing effective tips:

1. Think of yourself as a conduit. Your job is to pass useful information along to those who can use it.
2. Pay close attention to questions, problems, and ideas that come up when you're doing your work or interacting with clients.
3. Distill the lesson (or lessons) into a tip that you can share with your network, via e-mail or snail mail or even in simple conversation.
4. State the problem or situation as an introduction to your tip. Distill it down into its essence.
5. Give the solution. Tips are action-oriented. So make sure you give a couple of action steps to take.
6. Describe the result or benefit of using these tips to provide some incentive to take the action.
7. Include tools the reader can use without doing any work, phrases they can use verbatim, boilerplate clauses, checklists, forms, and so on.
8. List Web sites and other resources where readers can go for more info.

Ilise also offers the following suggestion for writing tip sheets: for the strongest impact, put your best tip first, in case people don't read the whole thing—because sometimes even really short tips are too much.[1]

Booklets and Pamphlets

These are, in essence, expanded versions of tip sheets. They contain similar information except in more detail: In a booklet, there's space to flesh out each point more fully.

Booklets are generally 4 by 9 inches, so they can be mailed in a standard #10 business envelope. Or, you can fold sheets of 8½ by 11-inch paper once horizontally and then turn them on their side to form a booklet with a 5½ by 8½-inch page size; this format is often referred to as a "digest."

A booklet is constructed by printing and folding the pages and then saddle-stitching them together (saddle-stitching is binding by stapling through the fold). Booklets typically run anywhere from eight to 16 pages although they can be longer.

On the upper right-hand front cover of your booklet, put a price; I recommend $7. Reason: the price creates the perception that the free gift you are giving has real value.

Special Reports

This format is typically longer than a booklet, and so can be even more detailed. Special reports, like tip sheets, are printed on 8½ by 11-inch sheets of paper, but are multiple pages instead of one page.

The larger page format allows for bigger illustrations, tables, and charts than you can put in a booklet. A special report can run anywhere from five pages to 100 or more, although typically they are six to 12 pages.

The easiest way to produce special reports is to use Word or desktop publishing software to design the pages, then run off copies of the report on your copier, collate, and staple them. For large special reports (say, 15 pages or longer), you may want to bind them in a report cover.

As with booklets, put a price on the front cover in the upper right corner—anywhere from $7 to $29, depending on length.

Monographs

A monograph is an essay or article on a single subject. They are similar in look and feel to special reports, but often on the lengthy side (20 to 30 pages) and written in more formal professional language.

The medical products industry frequently uses monographs written by doctors to promote a drug, material, instrument, or a piece of equipment. They give monographs away free as bait pieces and sales literature.

Note: If the audience for your monograph is physicians, the monograph should carry the byline of an M.D.

Resource Guides

These are mini-directories of information resources in a particular field—for example, Web sites for quality control professionals. A resource guide does not have to be thick or list a lot of resources to be useful; even two or three pages listing one or two dozen resources can be of enormous appeal to a prospect looking for what these resources offer.

Example: Fern Reiss, a consultant who specializes in personal branding, gives away a "Hot Contact" sheet with the names and addresses of talk show hosts, editors of major magazines, syndicated columnists, and other publicity outlets.

"This Hot Contact sheet promotion has been tremendously successful," says Fern. "I use it as both an e-mail address capture and a hard copy tease that I hand out at conferences, workshops, and trade shows. My mailing list is over 10,000 names, almost all directly attributable to my Hot Contact sheet."[2]

Manuals

Reference manuals are long, comprehensive special reports, usually placed in a binder or notebook and organized into sections. Manuals can range from 30 to 150 pages or more.

When I worked as the advertising manager for Koch Engineering, a manufacturer of chemical process equipment, we produced a technical manual, called the "Tray Design Guide," on how to size, design, and select trays for distillation towers. It was our most popular piece of literature, and we could barely keep it on the shelves.

Even though it was expensive to produce (I seem to remember a cost of $5 or more a copy, and this was back in 1980), giving it away gave us our best return on investment in marketing—far greater ROI than slick sales brochures and trade ads.

Because it was expensive to print, we did not prominently feature the free design guide in our advertising. As a result, we generated far fewer inquiries than we might have.

Audiotapes

By producing your bait piece content as an audiotape, you can dramatically increase readership, response, and the time people spend with your message. There are several reasons for the effectiveness of audiocassettes.

Audiocassettes are the medium of choice when your message can be communicated solely in words. When graphics are required as well as text, you can use a videotape, CD, or DVD.

Electronic media are attention-getting because, even in the electronic age, they are underused. Most white papers and other bait pieces are either print documents or electronic documents (PDFs) that can be downloaded from a Web site. Offering an audiotape, videocassette, CD, or DVD makes your bait piece different and helps it stand out. Also, electronic media have a higher perceived value than print, creating a sense that you are giving away something really valuable. Cassettes have several specific characteristics:

- *They are bulky.* "One of the major challenges of designing direct mail packages is to get them opened," says Paul Cook, advertising manager of Eva Tone, a large cassette duplicator. "The cassette is dimensional, so the package gets opened."[3]
- *They are tangible.* Your prospect is flooded with paper mailings. A cassette stands out from the rest of the package. Prospects notice it.
- *They are not overused.* Personalized sales letter, laser-addressed envelopes, yes-no-maybe stickers, 800 numbers, buck slips, lift letters, and other attention and involvement devices are all overused to some degree. But not one inquiry fulfillment package in a hundred contains an cassette. This uniqueness adds to the cassette's attention grabbing powers.
- *They have high perceived value.* The retail price of a single C-60 spoken word cassette ranges from $10 to $15. Because their perceived value is higher than a paper brochure or sales letter, secretaries are less likely to screen mail containing cassettes, and prospects are not likely to throw them away.
- *They address the time problem.* Business prospects complain of overflowing in-baskets and having too much to read. But a cassette can be listened to when the prospect has nothing else to do—in the car on the way home from the office, when taking a walk with a Walkman.
- *They address the reading problem.* We're told that the young entrepreneurs and executives of today's generation, brought up on TV, don't like to read long copy. But they do listen to cassettes. By including a tape with your letter and brochure, you can reach those prospects who don't read direct mail as well as those who do.

A single C-60 or C-90 cassette in a soft poly box with label weighs about two ounces, so when you are mailing a thick envelope with multiple brochures and white papers as your inquiry fulfillment package, the added weight of the cassette is negligible in terms of postage costs.

Another advantage of mailing cassettes is their low production costs. An audiocassette can be produced on an extremely low budget. Professional studio recording and editing isn't as necessary with audio as it is with video; excellent results can be achieved by renting a good quality tape recorder and narrating your own program in your office, or recording a live presentation at a meeting or seminar.

Purists in the audio business will argue that such a method is amateurish and produces low-quality tapes that present a poor image of the advertiser, but I disagree. There is something vibrant and energetic about most live recordings of seminars and speeches that is a pleasant contrast with the stilted dullness and lack of enthusiasm found in many professional, "slick" audio productions. I have gotten excellent sales results using live recordings of presentations, seminars, demos, and similar events as inserts.

You don't need to be a professional actor to narrate your own audiocassettes, but you must have a clear, pleasant, and resonant speaking voice. If you have a strong accent, mumble, or are otherwise difficult to understand, consider finding someone else to narrate your audiocassette for you.

Audiocassettes are a popular medium for disseminating spoken-word business and how-to-information. A single audiocassette is easy to produce. Just get a speaking engagement and tape your talk.

Vendors who can tape and duplicate talks for you are listed on the Vendors page of my Web site www.bly.com. Also look in your local Yellow Pages under Audio or Sound Recording Studios. In addition, some organizations that sponsor conferences and meetings routinely tape speaker presentations and sell them to their members. You should make it a condition that you retain the rights to the tape and get a free master copy. This eliminates the cost of paying a professional or buying your own taping equipment.

Cassettes are inexpensive to duplicate. They have a lower cost per unit than videos and, unlike printed materials, can be duplicated economically in small quantities.

For example, I recently produced a 16-page booklet to be mailed in a #10 envelope. Although the cost per unit was low (only 39 cents each), to make the promotion economical I had to print a minimum of 1,000 booklets.

By comparison, for a series of 90-minute audiocassettes I use as promotional items, the duplication cost—including cassette, laser-printed label, and soft poly box—is about $1.25 per cassette. But there is no minimum order: I pay this price whether I order 50 or five. For a comparison of production costs for various electronic media, see Exhibit 7.1.

Exhibit 7.1: Electronic Media Comparison Guide

Medium	Presentation length (minutes)	Complexity/ degree of difficulty to produce	Percent of recipients able to view (business audience, at office)	Duplication cost per unit (in quantities of 100)
Audiocassette	60	Low	High	$1.35
Videotape	30	Medium-high	Medium	$4.50
CD	60	Medium-high	High	$1.60
DVD	30	Medium-high	Medium	$3.10

Audio Albums

Once you have done eight, six, or even two tapes on related topics, you can package them in a vinyl album and offer them as an audiocassette program. Albums are a couple of dollars each, and available from any tape duplication service.

Power Packs

A power pack is a multimedia information product. Typically, it's a combination of tapes, reports, and perhaps a book or CD-ROM, all in a nice package. Power packs have a high perceived value ($50 to $150 or more), and therefore are a highly attractive premium.

Videotapes

You can videotape your presentation, duplicate it, and offer the videos as bait pieces.

The viewer expects your video to have production quality equivalent to what he sees on TV every evening. Therefore, the video should be edited professionally in a video studio.

Add graphics, special effects, charts, and other footage for a varied presentation that's more than just you talking behind a lectern. Have a nice label or package. Even though you are giving the video away, put a price on the package indicating that the video retails for $29 to $59 or more.

The average business video today runs approximately eight to 10 minutes. More complex products (e.g., mainframe software) may require 12 to 15 minutes or more. Never exceed 20 to 25 minutes—the maximum people seem to be able to watch without tuning out.

Figure your narration at 100 words per minute. A 10-minute script would then have 1,000 words—the equivalent of four double-spaced typed pages. As for content, the best guideline is, "One presentation—one topic." Your video should only talk about one product, one idea, or one offer. After all, you have only 1,000 words or so in which to tell your story. So you have to be selective.

Video is at its very best when used to demonstrate a product or system. Because videos offer the added element of motion, they are far more effective for demonstration than print brochures.

Video is an ideal medium for industrial products that are either too big to be carried by a salesperson or too complex to demonstrate in print. One good approach is to put a product demonstration on video and accompany the tape with a printed data sheet or brochure listing all the features, benefits, and specifications.

According to Craig R. Evans, director of marketing for Minneapolis-based Computer Video Productions, consumer studies show that more than half of consumers now have VCRs. "In business, we don't have such precise statistics," says Evans, "but our experience shows that at companies with more than 50 employees, the recipient of your video brochure is likely to have access to a VCR, either at work or at home."[4]

Cost for producing your video from start to finish can range from $800 to $2,500 a minute. For a 10-minute video, this translates into $8,000 to $25,000.

The two factors that add the most to costs are extensive on-location shooting requiring travel to multiple sites and elaborate special effects. Shooting the entire presentation at one local site can save you a bundle.

Sometimes you can get a tape done for less. One client told me they found a camera-man at a local TV station that would produce their entire presentation for $2,000. The fact that he had free use of the station's editing facilities and camera helped him offer this bargain price.

A number of firms have used video presentations as direct mail. One major computer manufacturer, for example, mailed videos to thousands of firms that used a specific type of computer the company had manufactured years earlier. The tape explained how these companies could trade in their old computer for substantial savings on a newer model. In addition to the tape, the package contained a letter, brochure, and reply element.

Computer Video Productions used video direct mail to promote its own capabilities as a producer of "video brochures" (marketing presentations on videotape). The company's first video mailing went to 70 prospects. "Only one was thrown away, and that was by accident," says Evans.

Eventually, Computer Video Productions mailed 300 video brochures to potential clients—with impressive results. Ninety-five percent of the recipients watched the tape—half the day they received it. The response rate was 30 percent.

"We learned that the corporate manager does not throw away a tape when he receives it," Evans says. "Rather, he will search out a machine to watch it on, or go to extra pains to pass it along to the right person." One of Evans' videotapes was passed along 16 times before ending up in the right prospect's VCR.[5]

In addition to being used as a cold mailing piece, a video can be used as a presentation aid, bait piece, or a leave-behind by a salesperson. Videotapes can also be offered as a response piece in advertising or direct mail campaigns. Some firms charge $10 to defray the cost of the tape; some request that the tape be returned; most offer it free with no strings attached.

In my estimation, currently fewer than one company in 100 is using video in direct mail or as sales literature. This represents an opportunity for you to stand out from the crowd. In an age when direct marketers are searching for something new and different, video is one medium that can add an irresistible attention-getting quality to a direct mail piece or a marketing presentation.

CD-ROMs and DVDs

Once you've produced your video you can transfer it to CD-ROM and DVD and have it available in those formats as well as video. That way, you can offer your prospects their choice of media.

Most people in large corporations have easy access to a VCR, but many small businesses do not have a VCR and monitor at the office. It's much easier for them if you give them a CD-ROM they can view right at their desktop.

One benefit of a CD-ROM or DVD over a videotape is their greater storage capacity. If you transfer your video about plant safety to a CD-ROM, that disc can also include your entire product catalog, which the videotape cannot.

An additional benefit of CD-ROMs is their interactivity: You can give the viewer choices, including the ability to select specific presentations or modules, take an interactive quiz, even click onto a Web site for more detailed information.

Newsletters

Some marketers produce a quarterly promotional newsletter of two to eight pages they distribute free to prospects and clients.

Coming up with good story ideas is one of the toughest tasks in publishing a company newsletter. Here's a checklist of story sources to stimulate editorial thinking and help identify topics with high reader interest that help to promote the company.

1. *Product stories*: New products; improvements to existing products; new models; new accessories; new options; and new applications.
2. *News*: Joint ventures; mergers and acquisitions; new divisions formed; new departments; other company news. Also, industry news and analyses of events and trends.
3. *Tips*: Tips on product selection, installation, maintenance, repair, and troubleshooting.
4. *How-to articles*: Similar to tips, but with more detailed instructions. Examples: How to use the product; how to design a system; how to select the right type or model.
5. *Previews and reports*: Write-ups of special events such as trade shows, conferences, sales meetings, seminars, presentations, and press conferences.
6. *Case histories*: Either in-depth or brief, reporting product application success stories, service successes, etc.
7. *People*: Company promotions, new hires, transfers, awards, anniversaries, employee profiles, customer profiles, human interest stories (unusual jobs, hobbies, etc.).
8. *Milestones*: e.g., "1,000th unit shipped," "Sales reach $1 million mark," "Division celebrates 10th anniversary," etc.
9. *Sales news*: New customers; bids accepted; contracts renewed; satisfied customer reports.
10. *Research and development*: New products; new technologies; new patents; technology awards; inventions; innovations; and breakthroughs.
11. *Publications*: New brochures available; new ad campaigns; technical papers presented; reprints available; new or updated manuals; announcements of other recently published literature.
12. *Explanatory articles*: How a product works; industry overviews; background information on applications and technologies.
13. *Customer stories*: Interviews with customers; photos; customer news and

profiles; guest articles by customers about their industries, applications, and positive experiences with the vendor's product or service.

14. *Financial news*: Quarterly and annual report highlights; presentations to financial analysts; earnings and dividend news; etc.

15. *Photos with captions*: People; facilities; products; events.

16. *Columns*: President's letter; letters to the editor; guest columns; regular features such as "Q&A" or "Tech Talk."

17. *Excerpts, reprints, or condensed versions of*: Press releases; executive speeches; journal articles; technical papers; company seminars; etc.

18. *Quality control stories*: Quality circles; employee suggestion programs; new quality assurance methods; success rates; case histories.

19. *Productivity stories*: New programs; methods and systems to cut waste and boost efficiency.

20. *Manufacturing stories*: New techniques; equipment; raw materials; production line successes; detailed explanations of manufacturing processes; etc.

21. *Community affairs*: Fund raisers; special events; support for the arts; scholarship programs; social responsibility programs; environmental programs; employee and corporate participation in local/regional/national events.

22. *Data processing stories*: New computer hardware and software systems; improved data processing and its benefits to customers; new data processing applications; explanations of how systems serve customers.

23. *Overseas activities*: Reports on the company's international activities; profiles of facilities, people, markets, etc.

24. *Service*: Background on company service facilities; case histories of outstanding service activities; new services for customers; new hotlines; etc.

25. *History*: Articles of company, industry, product, community history.

26. *Human resources*: Company benefits program; announcement of new benefits and training and how they improve service to customers; explanations of company policies.

27. *Interviews*: With company key employees, engineers, service personnel, etc.; with customers; with suppliers (to illustrate the quality of materials going into your company's products).

28. *Forums*: Top managers answer customer complaints and concerns; service managers discuss customer needs; customers share their favorable experiences with company products/services.

29. *Gimmicks*: Contents; quizzes; puzzles; games; cartoons.

Today more and more companies are abandoning their print customer newsletters and company magazines (once known as "house organs") and instead publish their newsletters online only, as "e-zines" (electronic newsletters). E-zines are discussed in detail in Chapter 9.

Software

If some of the processes you teach can be automated using software, consider working with a software developer to create custom software that you can sell to your clients and attendees.

One consultant who gives workshops on how to write documentation for ISO (International Standards Organization) compliance sells a disk containing boilerplate text and outlines for all the necessary documents she helps attendees create in her class.

Studebaker-Worthington Leasing (see case study in Chapter 10) produced a private-label contact management software product, "LeasePower," that they distributed free to computer resellers who are their clients and potential clients.

Seminars

Many marketers believe that offering a "free seminar" to their prospects will boost sagging direct mail response rates and make their company stand out from the crowd.

"Organize seminars that involve your products to encourage people to buy more of them," advises consultant Michael Phillips.[6] For example, a woman's clothing store can offer color analysis and wardrobe design. A locksmith can offer a free seminar on how to improve home security.

But beware. The free seminar strategy is not as simple and easy as it appears and is fraught with peril. If you are considering offering a free seminar to your prospects, here are some of the questions you should ask—along with the answers.

Obviously, your purpose in presenting the seminar is to convince people to buy your product. But if the seminar is a blatant promotional pitch, people become annoyed—even disgusted.

On the other hand, if you present information of genuine value, attendees will think well of your firm and be more inclined to do business with you. Attendees know they will be sold, but want to learn something, too.

Free seminars work well when introducing new products or technologies.

They are also ideal for products that require an in-person demonstration, such as software or computer systems. Also, if your product solves or addresses a major business problem or issue (e.g., computer security), a seminar is a good place to educate your prospects on the subject.

Be warned: the mere fact that the seminar is free is not going to get people to come running to your door. Executives, managers, and professionals in business are flooded with invitations to attend free seminars and don't have time to go to even a fraction of them. Response rates for free seminars in fields where the free seminar offer is common (e.g., software, computers, telecommunications, office equipment) are generally not much higher than for paid seminars. Your response will probably be anywhere from 1 percent to 3 percent.

You might get a higher response when giving free seminars on a topic not usually available in such seminars. Gary Blake, a corporate trainer specializing in writing seminars, recently gave a free three-hour seminar on "Effective Business Writing" and got a 10 percent response.[7]

Another way to increase response is to have a celebrity as your featured speaker. One software vendor recently packed a large ballroom by announcing that Bill Gates, chairman of Microsoft, was the speaker. (The invitation didn't even mention the topic or contents.)

The title of your seminar is very important as it connotes value. "Product demonstration" is least desirable and should only be used when the event is indeed a pure and straightforward demonstration of a system. "Seminar" implies that the attendee will gain useful knowledge. "Workshop" implies hands-on participation and should not be used for most free seminars.

Copywriter David Yale suggests calling the seminar a "forum" and has gotten good results doing so.[8] I also like "briefing" for a session aimed at executives and managerial types.

You can invite people to your seminar using a combination of e-mail marketing (usually to your customer list) and direct mail (DM) (to both your customer list and rented lists). The most effective DM invitation contains a personalized letter of invitation combined with a brochure outlining the seminar contents and the benefits of attendance. I recommend adding a business reply card (BRC) or other reply element, even though most people will register by fax or telephone. You can use a #10 envelope, a 9 by 12-inch size, or mailings that look like formal invitations (similar in size to wedding invitations).

Remember, the mere fact that the seminar is free is not, by itself, enough to persuade the busy reader to attend. You should write copy that will make the reader say, "This sounds wonderful; I would really love to go. How much does it cost?" Then, tell him or her it's free.

You don't have to sell your free seminar as hard as a paid seminar—but you do have to sell it almost as hard. The copy might not be as long as that for a paid seminar promotion, but it should still tell the reader what he or she will learn at your session. You must convince readers they will learn amazingly valuable information—or else they will not give up their time to attend.

Articles

"Over the past few years, I've conducted a series of successful direct mail campaigns consisting of a two-page sales letter accompanied by professionally produced reprints of published articles," says Steve Yoder. "I also included a fax-back form offering a free consultation.

"Each time I mailed the package, I got a good response. I gave a handful of free phone consultations that converted prospects into paying clients."[9]

Sales trainer Jeffrey Gittomer has written a newspaper column on selling, "Sales Moves," since 1992. Says Jeff, "Any penny I have ever made over the last 12 years I can attribute to writing. The column has positioned me and created the opportunity to brand myself in a way that I could have neither learned about nor done had I gone to school to learn about branding or marketing."[10]

Article reprints are versatile tools in an edu-marketing campaign. Just one article in a trade journal can bring a company hundreds of leads and thousands of dollars in sales. And with more than 6,000 magazines from which to choose, it's a safe bet there's at least one that could accommodate a story from your company.

In addition, the reprints have enormous marketing value. You can offer them as bait pieces, or use them as enclosures in direct mail and inquiry fulfillment packages.

But, while nearly all business people know the value of placing trade journal stories, they don't always know how to approach an editor. What's the best way to pitch an idea? Should you present more than one idea at a time? Is it wise to present the same story to more than one editor? Should you call or write first?

Following are some tips that answer those questions, and more. They can give you an edge in placing an article in the right journal for your company and reaping the rewards of increased recognition.

Chances are that you already know which journals you'd like to approach.

The magazines that cross your desk every week are strong candidates, because they're likely to deal with you and your competition.

But if you have an idea for an article that is outside your industry, or if you're just not sure which magazine would be most appropriate, here are two excellent resources: *Bacon's Publicity Checker*, from Bacon's Publishing Co., Chicago; and *Writer's Market*, from Writer's Digest Books, Cincinnati.

Bacon's is the bible of the public relations industry. It lists thousands of magazines and newsletters according to business or industry category, and also provides an alphabetical index. Beside giving the basics of magazine titles, addresses, phone numbers, and editor's names, *Bacon's* notes circulation and the types of articles published by each journal.

Writer's Market, by comparison, lists fewer publications, but describes their editorial requirements in far greater detail. Since *Writer's Market* is published primarily to help freelance writers find suitable markets for their work, it is more helpful than *Bacon's* when it comes to finding a home for a full-length feature story.

If you are not familiar with a magazine that sounds as if it may be appropriate for your article, be sure to read a few issues before contacting an editor there.

Many trade journals will send a sample issue and set of editorial guidelines to prospective authors upon request. These can provide valuable clues as to style, format, and appropriate topics. They often tell how to contact the magazine, give hints on writing an article, describe the manuscript review process and discuss any payment/reprint arrangements.

The quickest way to turn off an editor is to offer an idea that has nothing to do with his or her magazine. "My pet peeve with people calling or writing to pitch an idea is that they often haven't studied the magazine," says Rick Dunn, editor of *Plant Engineering*. "If they haven't read several issues and gotten a handle on who we are and who our audience is, they won't be able to pitch an idea effectively."[11]

There's no substitute for knowing the audience and the various departments within a magazine," adds Jim Russo, editor of *Packaging*. "I'm more impressed by someone who has an idea for a particular section than by someone who obviously doesn't know anything about our format."[12]

Every magazine is different in some way from its competitors and from other magazine in general. Tone, style, content, and the quality of a journal's writing and illustrations should all be studied to increase your chances of making a "sale."

Offer an editor the type of article that the magazine seems to prefer—

frequency and length are good indicators of preferred subjects—and the odds are more in your favor.

Companies can easily increase their chances for coverage by requesting a magazine's editorial calendar and scanning it for planned articles that might mesh with their products or activities.

"If people respond to our editorial calendar with ideas for specific issues, great!" says Mr. Dunn. "Or if they can provide background for a story we want to do, they'll have an edge in getting into the magazine."

You may even want to suggest feature story ideas for next year's calendar. The trick is to do that tactfully. "Don't come across as pushy or demanding," warns Mr. Dunn. "Stay away from saying things like, 'This is important to your readers' or, 'You should run this story.' If someone knows our business better than we do, we'll hire him or we'll go back to school."[13]

However, if you spot a new trend in, say, packaging food in plastic containers versus glass jars, and you can provide statistics and information to back up your claim, go ahead and contact the appropriate editor. He or she will probably appreciate your interest and effort.

Should you call or should you write? Most editors won't object to either method of pitching an idea, but they usually have a preference for one or the other. It's simply a matter of personal choice and time constraints. If you don't know how a particular editor feels on the subject, call and ask. An appropriate opening might be: "This is Joe Jones from XYZ Corp. and I have a story idea you might be interested in. Do you have a few minutes right now, or should we set up a time to discuss it later in the week?"

An editor who prefers a query letter (See Appendix B) or written outline will no doubt take this opportunity to tell you so. Editors who prefer a quick description over the phone will appreciate your respect for their time, whether they take the call or ask you to phone back later.

Do not send an attached file via e-mail to an editor you do not know. Most will delete it without opening it. Do not e-mail your query to an editor unless the editor has said that he or she will accept article proposals by e-mail.

Some editors, such as Mr. Russo, favor a phone call to zero in on an idea. "If I know someone and have confidence in their work, I'll often say go ahead and submit an article. Otherwise, I like to see an outline first," he says.[14]

Mark Rosenzweig, editor at *Chemical Engineering*, agrees. "With a phone call, I can tell someone right away he's on the right track. But a letter summarizing the idea is OK, too. In any case, if I like an idea, I'll then request a detailed outline describing the proposed article."[15]

A written query with a detailed outline appeals to Mr. Dunn because, he says, "A phone call is all right, but I can't make an editorial decision until I see a query letter."

At *Modern Materials Handling*, Assistant Editor Barbara Spencer suggests writers send in a letter of introduction, followed by a phone call a week or two later. "We look for someone who knows his field and products, and the letter helps us gauge that expertise," she explains. "But call the magazine first and find out which editor handles the type of article you have in mind."[16]

That's good advice for dealing with any journal. A two-minute phone call to find the right editor, get the correct spelling of his or her name and check the address where the query letter should be sent can save time and aggravation later.

All letters should be addressed to a specific editor. A letter that begins "Dear Editor" not only could end up in the wrong hands, but it's also unlikely to impress the editor with the writer's research abilities.

Follow-up calls are almost always a good idea, too. The editor's reaction to your call will determine whether you should call again later. If an editor flat out rejects an idea, accept the verdict gracefully and try another publication.

If you're told an idea has "merit" but needs further explanation or a different approach, you may be able to get a go-ahead by answering the editor's questions or suggesting a new angle over the phone.

On the other hand, you may need to supply more information in writing and call again a couple of weeks later. Of course, if the editor gives you a go ahead, great. You've cleared the major hurdle to getting an article in print.

What if you have more than one great story idea you want to pitch? Most editors are willing to listen to two or even three at once, but don't overdo it. Each idea should be fully developed ahead of time, not "pulled out of a hat" in desperation if an original idea is turned down.

It's a good idea to ask editors what kind of stories or applications they're looking for. Perhaps you'll find out they're interested in new ways to use one of your company's products, or how a new government regulation is affecting your industry's production operations. They may well have an interest in something that ties in with your company and which you are qualified to write about.

Mentioning certain elements in your initial query—whether over the phone or in writing—can sway an editor toward accepting your proposal. For instance, many magazines seek practical information that shows their readers how to save money, time, labor, or improve on-the-job performances. Statistics, benefits, examples, and how-to tips can strengthen your case substantially.

Specifics are what sell a story: You're much more likely to grab an editor's attention if you say, "Our newly developed Dry Scrubber pollution control device saved the Smithson Paper Plant $4,400 a day in fuel costs" than if you say, "Our new product can save paper plants a lot of money." Then go on to explain just how the company has saved money. And be prepared to back up your claim with documented facts.

"If someone tells us something is more efficient than something else, we want to know how much more efficient," says Mr. Russo. "Superlatives should be backed up with percentages and explanations."

The more help your idea promises readers, the more likely it is to interest an editor. "We're interested in articles that help our readers solve specific problems," says Mr. Dunn. "We want technical, engineering-oriented but down-to-earth articles that address common problems. A good question to ask before coming to us is, 'Will this provide readers with information they can apply to their jobs?'"

Put yourself in the readers' shoes, analyze their problems, and you will have a better perception of what kind of articles an editor wants. If you happen to read the magazine regularly, you may well have a head start in coming up with useful ideas. Also, any knowledge and technical expertise you have will help you "sell yourself" to an editor as an authoritative source.

"We prefer bylines by technical experts or plant engineers, since that is our audience," Mr. Dunn says. "If they've got a good subject, we'll go as far as necessary to accommodate them."

Adds Ms. Spencer: "We value technical ability above writing ability. Know your field and its products; if you are 'visible' in your field for giving speeches or being active in a professional organization, so much the better."

But don't despair if you are not a technical whiz or industry "name": Plenty of trade journal authors, including legions of public relations executives, aren't either. They are published because they take the time to study a subject they want to write about. That doesn't mean they acquire nearly the amount of knowledge a technical expert would have; they are simply able to delve into a subject enough to write clearly, concisely, and logically about it. For many trade journals, that's all that's required.

Take *Packaging*. Says Mr. Russo, "We have both outstanding journalists and excellent technical people on staff, so we can consider articles that are short on either end." What counts for him and scores of other editors is the newsworthiness of an article.

"I'm particularly interested in new ways of doing things, whether someone has found a better way to package products, or new and significant developments that are practical."

Mr. Rosenzweig looks for "heavy duty nuts and bolts articles, not puff or promotional pieces. Title or position isn't that important to use—it's whether there's any 'meat' in an idea," he says. Impartiality is another "must" with many editors. Remember, they're not there to praise your company's products—although being published can be as good as if they were; they're there to give readers an objective overview of goings-on in their industry. This can be a particular sticking point in dealing with public relations personnel, although most editors recognize the "one-hand-feeds-the other" usefulness of such contacts.

"We're certainly not prejudiced against articles from PR firms," says Mr. Rosenzweig. "We just generally have to make more revisions to eliminate their tendency toward one-sidedness. We want all the disadvantages spelled out, as well as the advantages."

Adds Mr. Dunn: "If an article is about storage methods, we want to see all 15 methods discussed, not just the ones used by the writer's company or client."

Still, the fact that public relations people are generally eager to give editors information and can be trusted to produce articles on target and on time helps endear them to many editors. "We don't have to chase after them," explains Mr. Dunn. "They understand our role a little better than most people, they know how we operate, and they tend to give us good service."

So, follow the public relations agencies' example and make yourself available to editors when they call, follow their guidelines, and deliver written copy as promised. You'll put yourself in good stead with people who are in a position to exert considerable influence on your company's fortunes.

Some magazines will kill a feature story simply for lack of photos or illustrations. Many others weigh heavily the availability of appropriate graphics. Those visual "extras" can be a deciding factor in choosing one story idea over another. Even though the larger journals may have illustrators on staff to produce high-quality finished drawings, they often work from original sketches supplied by an author.

You can get a good idea of how important visuals are to a particular magazine, before you make your pitch, by scanning a couple of issues. Note whether photos or drawings are used. If photos, are they black-and-white or color? Is at least one illustration used with every story of one page or more? If so, you should be prepared to provide the same. Otherwise, your article may move to the reject pile, regardless of its other merits.

Professional photographs, while nice, are not necessary for most trade journals. Straightforward, good-quality 35mm color slides satisfy most trade editors. Some magazines will also take black-and-white glossies or color-prints—an editor will be happy to tell you what's acceptable.

Never submit the same idea or story to more than one competing magazine at a time. Only if the idea is rejected should you approach another editor. This is one point nearly all editors agree on: They want exclusive material—especially for feature articles.

If a story is particularly timely or newsworthy, and has run in a magazine not directly competing with the one you're approaching, you may be able to get around the problem by working with the editor to expand or rewrite the piece. But be up-front about it or you will risk losing an editor's confidence and goodwill.

"I'd like everything to be exclusive," says Mr. Russo. "That increases its value to us and can sway us toward acceptance if it's a 'borderline' story." Offering "world exclusives" can also make an article more appealing to an editor. That means you promise not to submit the article to any other magazine, even if it's in a completely different field.

Whether you are willing to do that depends on how much you want a story in a particular magazine. You may decide you'd rather try to get more mileage out of a story by submitting it to a number of unrelated magazines or newspapers.

As Mr. Dunn points out: "Exclusivity is a quality consideration for a feature article. Editors don't want their readers to pick up their magazine and see something that they've already read elsewhere."

Often the exceptions to this rule are column items or case histories—for example, a problem/solution/result story describing how a particular customer successfully used a company's product. However, even those items should not be submitted to a magazine that competes with one that has already accepted them.

Submitting unsolicited manuscripts is always a risky proposition—again, with the exception of case histories and short news pieces. Some editors never want to see an unsolicited manuscript; others are willing to review them and may even publish a few. *Chemical Engineering* falls into that category.

"We get hundreds of unsolicited manuscripts every year, but we have the resources to do a heavy amount of rewriting for the ones we use," says Mr. Rosenzweig.

On the other hand, Ms. Spencer says she never uses unsolicited feature manuscripts, and Mr. Russo can't remember the last time his magazine used an unsolicited piece as a major story.

What it boils down to is this: Most editors prefer to be asked about story ideas before an author writes the article. It saves them the substantial amount of time required to read a lengthy manuscript to determine whether the subject is right for the magazine. And it saves the author the time and trouble of researching and writing an article that might never get accepted anywhere.

Even if you have a manuscript already in hand, by submitting it "blind" you may lead an editor to suspect you're submitting it to nine other magazines at the same time. That's not what an editor wants to see. It's far better to query first, then send the story only if the editor expresses interest.

Once you've gotten your idea accepted, which is always tentative until final review of the manuscript, you'll need to know any length and deadline requirements. If the editor doesn't volunteer this information, by all means ask. The answers may help avoid misunderstanding later.

As a rule, be generous with length. Include everything you think is—or may be—relevant, and don't skimp on examples. Editors would rather cut material than have to request more.

A few magazines, such as *Chemical Engineering*, are very flexible on length. "We run articles anywhere from three paragraphs to 40 to 50 pages long," says Mr. Rosenweig. Most other magazines give authors more specific limits. Check with your editor for the specific range.

Deadlines, too, can vary considerably among journals. Some don't like to impose any deadlines at all, especially if they work far enough ahead that they're not pressed for material. But if the article is intended for publication in a special issue, the editors will probably want the finished manuscript in hand at least two months prior to publication. That allows time for final revisions, assembling photos or illustrations, and production.

Chemical Engineering, for example, has a six to 12 month lead time on many of the articles it assigns. In at least one case, the magazine waited for six years before receiving a promised manuscript. Not surprisingly, the editor had completely forgotten about the story.

Some magazines may send a follow-up letter to remind delinquent authors about expected articles, but, as Mr. Dunn says: "We won't chase after someone. If we don't hear from a writer in about six months, we figure the article is never going to materialize."

Don't put an editor's patience to the test. You may gain a reputation as being undependable, which can hurt your future chances of getting ink.

Stay tuned to editors' needs by keeping up with information in their field, as well as your own; staying up to date with any changes—in format or content—of their publications; heeding their suggestions; being considerate of their time; and, above all, delivering articles as promised. "The best way to cultivate an editor's friendship is to produce results," advises Mr. Dunn, "because the people who are sincerely interested in helping us out are the ones we go back to."

Books

A free book is a highly desirable premium and an effective bait piece. Even in this Internet era, many people value books (even though they say they don't have time to read them!) and like getting them.

I tell virtually every self-employed professional, as well as many small-business owners, who asks me for advice on how to promote themselves to define their niche specialty, write a book about it, and get it published.

Here are just a few of the ways you can benefit from writing your own book and having it published:

1. In writing a book on a subject, you are forced to do additional research to flesh out gaps in your knowledge. Your knowledge therefore increases, making you a better authority to your clients.
2. Writing a book also requires you to organize your material in logical sequence. Doing so increases clarity of presentation in all your communications, including individual consultations with clients.
3. A book can serve as the basis for a profitable seminar or workshop. The chapters of the book become modules of the seminar.
4. Potential clients reading your book will call you to inquire about the services you offer, and will be predisposed to hire you.
5. Associations will ask you to speak at their conferences for handsome fees if you are the author of a book that interests their members.
6. Listing yourself as the author of a book is an impressive credential on your Web site, brochure, and other marketing materials. It increases your status.
7. You can give copies of your book to potential clients to familiarize them with your methodology and convince them that you are an expert in your field.
8. You may be called upon to serve as an expert witness on your topic in court cases, at a handsome day rate.
9. Editors will ask you to contribute articles to their publications.
10. The media will want to interview you as an expert in your field. This can lead to appearances as a guest on radio and TV shows.

A developer in Florida held receptions for groups of real estate investors. To entice the investors to come to the presentation, the developer offered a free book, *Ten Tips on Buying and Enjoying Vacation Property*. The author, Christopher Cain, was even on hand to autograph the books!

"Books make an outstanding premium for developers who sell vacation property," says Cain. "In four consecutive one-day receptions, we targeted 88 highly qualified buyers, and the developer sold out the first phase of his resort project in record time."[17]

Books have been proven so effective as bait pieces in edu-marketing campaigns that IDG, publisher of the *Dummies* series of books, formed a group devoted to publishing books specifically as bait pieces.

Ken Ball, a former executive with the group, comments: "I started a custom publishing group at IDG Books and we regularly created short books and booklets to be used as premiums. We'd sell a client a minimum of 25,000 pieces for $1 or less apiece, making such a tool real affordable as a bait piece in a DM campaign."[18] Of course, that represents an up-front investment of $25,000, which is a bit pricey for smaller companies.

Conventional books published by trade publishers are typically too expensive to use as bait pieces. If you are an author and your hardcover book sells for $25, even with a 50 percent author's discount, copies cost you $12.50 apiece.

Therefore, if you are going to use a book as a bait piece, self-publishing is a better option; a self-published book might only cost $1 or $2 a copy if it's relatively modest in length (100 pages for a self-published bait piece book is ideal), paperback, and you print at least 3,000 copies.

However, if your cost is $2 a book, a 3,000-copy print run requires an up-front investment of $6,000. If the book proves not to be an effective bait piece, you may be stuck with thousands of copies.

An alternative is to produce your book using print on demand (POD) technology. The cost per book is higher, but there's no minimum quantity; you can print one book at a time.

If you prefer to go the conventional route and publish your book with a traditional publishing house, here are the steps involved:

- *Step 1: Come Up with a Good Idea for Your Book.* If you already have a good idea, move on to Step 2. If not, analyze your knowledge base, consulting specialties, client base, and service offerings. Which topic is broad enough that thousands of people will buy a book on the topic?

  Some first-time authors are intimidated by this step. They feel they lack the creativity to come up with good ideas. My experience is that all of us are capable of coming up with good ideas, including ideas for books. The hard work is not coming up with the idea; it's writing the book.

- *Step 2: Evaluate Your Book Idea.* There are many ideas and titles that sound good, but once evaluated with a critical eye, must be rejected because they are not commercially viable and would not appeal to a publisher.

When I ask potential authors why they think a publisher would want to publish their book—and why a reader would want to buy and read it—a lot of them answer, "Because it's a good book" or "The subject is important."

In today's marketplace, that's not enough. Remember: According to a recent Gallup survey, people read nonfiction books either for information or entertainment. Your book has to entertain or inform them. A book that does neither is going to be extremely difficult to sell.

- *Step 3: Create the Content Outline.* Once you decide on a topic for your book, I recommend that you develop a content outline. A content outline is similar to the table of contents you find in any nonfiction book, except it is more detailed and fleshed out.

  Developing the content outline has three purposes. First, it helps you determine whether you can produce enough text on the subject to fill a book. Second, it is perhaps the single most powerful tool for convincing publishers that your book idea has merit. Third, it will save you an enormous amount of time when you sit down to write your book proposal and the book itself.

  I always make my content outlines detailed rather than sketchy. I am convinced this is important in selling the book to a publisher.

- *Step 4: Write Your Book Proposal.* The book proposal is often the most mysterious part of the book publishing process, especially to beginners. The reason: You know what books look like, because you've seen hundreds of them. But chances are you don't know what a book proposal looks or sounds like, because you have never seen one.

  A book proposal typically contains the following elements:

  - ❖ *Title Page*—The book's title and the name of the author are centered in the middle of the page. In the upper left corner, type Book Proposal. In the bottom right, type your name, address and phone number (or, if you have one, your agent's).

  - ❖ *Overview*—One to two pages summarizing what your book is about: the topic, who will read it, why it's important or interesting to your intended audience, and what makes your book different from others in the field.

  - ❖ *Format*—Specify approximate word length, number of chapters, types of illustrations or graphics to be included, and any unique organizational schemes or formats. (For example, is your book divided into major sections or do you use sidebars?)

❖ *Market*—Tell the editor who will buy your book, how many of these people exist, and why they need it or will want to read it. Use statistics to dramatize the size of the market. For example, if your book is about infertility, mention that one in six couples in the U.S. is infertile.

❖ *Promotion*—Is your book a natural for talk radio or *Oprah* (be realistic)? Can it be promoted through seminars or speeches to associations and clubs? Give the publisher some of your ideas on how the book can be marketed. (*Note:* Phrase these as suggestions, not demands. The publisher will be interested in your ideas but probably won't use most of them.)

❖ *Competition*—List books that compare with yours. Include the title, author, publisher, year of publication, number of pages, price, and format (hardcover, trade paperback or mass market paperback). Describe each book briefly, pointing out weaknesses and areas in which your book is different and superior.

❖ *Author's Bio*—A brief biography listing your writing credentials (books and articles published), qualifications to write about the book's topic (for instance, for a book on popular psychology, it helps if you're a therapist), and your media experience (previous appearances on TV and radio).

❖ *Table of Contents/Outline*—A chapter-by-chapter outline showing the contents of your proposed book. Many editors tell me that a detailed, well thought-out table of contents in a proposal helps sway them in favor of a book.

• *Step 5: Get an Agent.* Although it's possible to sell directly to the publishers, I recommend you get a literary agent. *Literary Market Place,* (R. R. Bowker) available in bookstores or the reference room of your local library, lists agents you can contact.

• *Step 6: Send Your Proposal to Publishers and Get an Offer.* If you have an agent, the agent will approach publishers for you. If you choose to go without an agent, you can approach publishers directly. Many large publishing houses do not look at unagented manuscripts. But small and mid-size publishers are open to doing so, and some small publishers actually prefer authors who do not have an agent.

• *Step 7: Negotiate Your Contract.* If you have an agent, the agent negotiates the contract on your behalf, with your input and approval. If you don't have an agent, you handle the negotiations yourself. Key contract terms include advances, royalties, first and second serial rights, termination, and copyright. If you intend to use the book as a bait piece, negotiate the largest author's discount you can get, and ask if the publisher can give an even larger discount if you buy multiple copies at one time.

- *Step 8: Write and Deliver the Manuscript.* Follow the outline the publisher bought when accepting your proposal. And be on time.

Teleconferences and Webinars

A relatively new way to package information, free or paid, is the teleconference. A teleconference or "teleseminar" is a live event, usually 60 to 90 minutes, where you invite your prospects to listen to a presentation given over the phone in a group conference call.

With the help of a specialized vendor (see below), you can set up a teleconference that can accommodate anywhere from 10 to 1,000 listeners or more. Each listener calls into a special number and enters a pass code from his or her touch-tone telephone. You confirm the time and date, and distribute the phone number and pass code, via e-mail.

Depending on which vendor you use and which options you select, the participants can either listen passively while you lecture, or participate interactively. As the moderator, you control the call. Typically, in a one-hour teleconference, you would speak for 50 minutes, and allow 10 minutes at the end for Q&A.

The participants are muted during the call, meaning they can listen but not speak. When you take calls, the participants can press a number on their phone to indicate they'd like to ask a question. You can unmute them one at a time to let them ask the question, then mute them after you've answered and take the next call.

A "Webinar" is a teleconference call in which the attendees can follow a visual presentation being simultaneously shown on the Internet at a private URL only they can access.

The Webinar participants need both a touch-tone phone and a PC with an Internet connection. If it's a dial-up, it must be on a separate phone line. Participants listen to you lecture on the phone, and watch your presentation visuals on their PC. The presentation visuals are stored on a server at a location for which you have given them a URL link. You have the ability to control the presentation; the participant can watch but not manipulate the visuals.

For instance, Intuit® invites financial professionals to a free teleseminar on tax planning to introduce them to the capabilities of their Lacerte tax planning software. They also offer a free Evaluation Kit that includes a demo of the software (actually a fully operational version of the prior year's program; the software is updated annually to account for changes in the tax code) and a database of sample client tax files.

There are companies that specialize in producing teleconferences and Webinars for corporate clients wishing to use these formats for marketing, training, and employee communications. They will be able to guide you through the technical aspects and provide all of the phone line capacity and technology you need to produce such an event. All you have to do is write the content and present the material. You can find several of these firms on the Vendors page of my Web site, *www.bly.com*.

Content-Rich Web Sites

If your Web site is packed with free content, you can offer this content as a kind of bait piece in your promotions.

One option is to make part of your Web site open for public access, while restricting access to other segments containing valuable free content. To access the restricted sections, the prospect has to give you his e-mail address.

You can add value to your site with an ask-the-expert forum, which is a Q&A page where customers go to post questions and get answers from company experts. You can try out Bulletin Board packages at the Free Bulletin Board Software Directory (*www.emailaddresses.com/email_bb.htm*).

Blogs

"A blog is an online journal," explains blogging expert Deb Weil in her Business Blogging Starter Kit (*www.wordbiz.com*). "It's called a journal because every entry is time and date stamped and always presented in reverse chronological order."[19] A blog has a unique URL. It can stand alone, or be a section of your main Web site. My Web site is *www.bly.com* and my blog is located at *http://www.bly.com/blog/index.php*.

The theory is that if you are an information marketer—or, if you publish information to establish your expertise in a niche industry or field—blogging should be part of your publishing arsenal.

According to Deb, a business blog is "a platform from which to lobby, network, and influence sales. It's a way to circumvent traditional media and analysts. And blogging can be done instantly, in real time, at a fraction of the cost of using traditional channels."

One big advantage of blogs, according to Paul Chaney, is that having a blog can help pull traffic to your Web site.

"The search engines, especially Google, love blogs," says Paul. "You'd be amazed at how many of your posts will end up in the top ten returns. If search engine optimization is a concern to you, blogs are the best way I know to move up the ladder as well as increase your page rank."[20]

"I confidently predict that blogs will soon be a key piece of an effective on-line marketing strategy," says Deb Weil. "Ultimately, they're nothing more than an instant publishing tool, one that makes posting fresh content to the Web within anyone's reach. No tech skill or knowledge required."

"It's all about the conversation," writes Marc Orchant. "That's the point of the blog space. As a lifelong marketer myself, I find the DM industry behind the curve, generally speaking, when it comes to embracing disruptive technologies."[21] B. L. Ochman says, "Blogs help develop a conversation between a company and its customers [and] have become an important part of the marketing mix."[22]

"My argument is that blogging is more likely to raise brand awareness, but that the impact on direct sales will be more difficult to assess," says Max Blumberg. "Therefore, I don't think it is appropriate to look for a close relationship between blogging and direct sales."[23]

Jennifer Rice adds, "Blogging is not a direct response vehicle. It's an awareness, visibility, and promotion vehicle that happens to be terrific for those of us selling intellectual capital. It's also extremely useful for corporations to use as a means to connect with customers and get feedback."[24]

In my blog, I post comments on topics that interest me and presumably also interest the people who read my blog. To incorporate your blog as part of an edu-marketing campaign, your blog must focus on the same topics as your bait pieces, e.g., content management, hazardous materials handling, or whatever it is that you are promoting.

But even more so than a bait piece, a blog must be educational and informative, and not a sales piece. Readers will only stick with your blog if they feel you are telling the truth and educating them. If you start selling your product on a blog, they will be turned off unless you keep product talk to a minimum.

Case Studies

Case studies are a specialized type of marketing literature. It may be self-published or published as an article in a trade magazine. A case history is a product success story; it tells how a particular customer solves a problem using a particular product.

"Readers love a good story," says copywriter Steve Slaunwhite. "That's why prospects, customers and editors have such an insatiable appetite for the best ones they can find."[25] So if you've been racking your brains thinking of new ways to get the word out about your products and services, then consider producing a case study. It's easily the best kind of story you can tell.

If you're not familiar with the modern case study, rest assured it's not the dry, technical tome of yesteryear. Case studies, also known as customer profiles or case histories, are essentially success stories about your products and the customers who use them. Typically, a case study is written in standard feature article format, just like you'd read in a trade or business magazine.

What makes a case study so effective?

- It moves your marketing communications several notches up the credibility ladder. Think about it. What is more powerful than enabling prospects and customers to see how your product or service is working in the real world?
- It breaks through the clutter. Especially if it is reasonably unbiased and timely, a case study will almost always gain the attention of readers. Just flip through the pages of any trade or professional magazine. You'll find a significant percentage of articles based on case study material.
- It enjoys a high readership. Readers want to know what their colleagues in other organizations are doing to solve similar problems. A case study allows them to be a fly on the wall.

Customers and prospects are inundated by ads, e-mail, direct mail, and especially brochures. A case study, by contrast, is rarer and conjures visual images of your product or service in action. It's told (at least in part) from the perspective of a happy customer. And that's the kind of story that people find hard to resist.

The outline for a case study almost always follows the same format:

1. Describe the customer who is featured in the case study.
2. Describe the customer's problem.

3. Tell about the various solutions the customer considered and what led him to ultimately choose the one he bought.
4. Outline the steps required to implement the solution.
5. Discuss the specific results the customer achieved by using the product, e.g., energy savings, money savings, improvements in productivity, greater efficiency.
6. Ask the customer whether the product solves his problem, how well, and whether he would recommend it to others facing a similar problem.

Most case studies can be published on one or two sides of a single sheet of 8½ by 11-inch paper; greater detail is rarely required. Typical length: 800 to 1,500 words.

8 Ways to Recycle Case Studies

"Few marketing tools are more effective than an anecdotal customer success story," says Casey Hibbard of Compelling Cases, a marketing firm that develops case study materials for technology companies. "Yet companies usually multiply the value of a good customer story by using it in many different ways." Her advice:

1. *First, treat case studies as fresh news.* "Before a case study is republished on your Web site or distributed to sales reps, pitch it to the trade press," Hibbard advises. "In fact, many publications now have sections called 'Case Studies' or 'Technology in Action' specifically for this purpose—and many readers regularly troll these publications for real-world business and technology solutions.

2. *Next, post cases on your Web site.* "Web sites are an obvious place to post case studies," Hibbard notes. "But it pays to put some thought into where and how you present them. The best approach is to feature product-specific cases among other product information on your site, along with white papers and brochures that highlight each product. You can even go a step further by allowing visitors to search for case studies by industry to find one that best matches their situation."

3. *Add a short version to the company newsletter.* Case studies are popular content for e-mail newsletters; in fact, Hibbard says one large software company with more than 300 products publishes a newsletter that contains nothing but customer stories. "Newsletter stories

educate customers and prospects about the many ways that other people are using the product successfully."

4. *Create slides for sales presentations.* "To punch up sales presentations, give the sales team slides with highlights from successful client implementations," says Hibbard. "That's more effective than using printed case studies as leave-behinds [handouts you leave on the table after a presentation or meeting]."

5. *Enter your case studies in awards events.* "One CRM software vendor submitted a particularly compelling case study for Aberdeen Group's annual 'Top Ten CRM Implementations' list," Hibbard recalled. "The company was honored as one of the top ten and was then mentioned in at least a dozen follow-up stories."

6. *Use case studies as customer references.* If reference customers get too many calls, they're likely to get irritated. "To give your references a break, hand out case studies. While it's not as informative as a person-to-person discussion, a case study can often provide enough specifics to make a call unnecessary."

7. *Build a searchable CD.* Especially when a company has lots of case studies, it may make sense to load them all on a leave-behind CD that's easily searchable by product or industry. "This puts the case studies right in the hands of your prospects," says Hibbard. "Sometimes that's even better than asking people to go online."

8. *Add testimonial quotes to your sales materials.* "Make sure that quotes within the case study can stand by themselves if you chose to pull them as testimonials on your Web site or in collateral materials. I've also seen sales materials that feature 'snapshots' of success stories, and that's very powerful."[26]

Copywriter Steve Slaunwhite offers these additional suggestions for getting the most mileage out of your case studies:

- *Use it in a press release.* A case study can quickly be abridged and reformatted into a press release. Be sure to note that a longer, more complete case study version is available. Editors might pick it up.
- *Mail it to prospects and customers.* This is a terrific way to keep in touch, raise awareness about a new product or service, and even convert prospects into customers.
- *Give it to your salespeople.* Salespeople love case studies. They use them in presentations, to illustrate key points, and as testimonials. A case study is often more convincing than a brochure.

- *As a speaking topic.* If your executives speak at meetings and conferences, a case study makes an excellent presentation. The content can easily be converted into PowerPoint® slides. The printed case study itself can be used as a handout.
- *In lead-generation programs.* A case study makes a terrific "free giveaway" in an ad, e-mail, direct mailer, and on a Web site.
- *As a trade show handout.* Case studies are a great way to break through the clutter of flyers and brochures that permeate trade shows. One of my clients even had a case study enlarged and printed on a trade show exhibit wall![27]

Tips on Using Testimonials

Using testimonials—quotations from satisfied customers and clients—is one of the simplest and most effective ways of adding punch and power to brochure, ad, and direct mail copy. Here are some guidelines for effective use of testimonials:

1. *Always use real testimonials instead of made-up ones.* Even the most skilled copywriter can rarely make up a testimonial that can match the sincerity and credibility of genuine words of praise from a real customer or client.

   If you ask a customer to give you a testimonial, and he or she says, "Sure, just write something and I'll sign it," politely reply: "Gee, I appreciate that, but would you mind just giving me your opinions of our product—in your own words?" Fabricated or self-authored testimonials (those written by the advertiser or their copywriter) usually sound phony; genuine testimonials invariably have the ring of truth.

2. *Prefer long testimonials to short ones.* Many advertisers are hooked on using very short testimonials. For instance:

   ". . . fabulous! . . . " "truly funny . . . thought-provoking . . . " ". . . excellent . . . wonderful . . . "

I believe that when people see these ultra short testimonials, they suspect that a skillful editing job has masked a comment that was not as favorable as the writer makes it appear. Longer testimonials— say, two or three sentences versus a single word or phrase—come across as more believable:

"Frankly, I was nervous about using an outside consultant. But your excellent service has made me a believer! You can be sure that we'll be calling on your firm to organize all our major sales conferences and other meetings for us. Thanks for a job well done!"

Sure, it's longer, but it somehow seems more sincere than a one-word superlative.

3. *Prefer specific, detailed testimonials to general or superlative testimonials.* Upon receiving a letter of praise from a customer, our initial reaction is to read the letter and find the single sentence that directly praises our company or our product. With a blue pencil, we extract the words we think are kindest about us, producing a bland bit of puffery such as:

"We are very pleased with your product."

Actually, most testimonials would be stronger if we included more of the specific, detailed comments our client has made about how our product or service helped him. After all, the prospects we are trying to sell to may have problems similar to the one our current customer solved using our product. If we let Mr. Customer tell Mr. Prospect how our company came to his rescue, he'll be helping us make the sale:

"We have installed your new ChemiCoat system in each of our bottling lines and have already experienced a 25 percent savings in energy and material costs. Thanks to your system, we have now added an additional production line with no increase in energy costs. This has increased profits 15 percent and already paid back the investment in your product. We are very pleased with your product."

Again, don't try to polish the customer's words so it sounds like professional ad copy. Testimonials are usually much more convincing when they are not edited for style.

4. *Use full attribution.* We've all opened direct mail packages that contained testimonials from "J.B. in Arizona" or "Jim S., Self-Made Millionaire." I suspect that many people laugh at such testimonials and think they are phony.

To increase the believability for your testimonials, attribute each quotation. Include the person's name, city and state, and (if a business customer) their job title and company (e.g., "Jim K. Redding, vice president of manufacturing, Divmet Corporation, Fairfield, NJ").

People are more likely to believe this sort of full disclosure than testimonials which seem to conceal the identity of the speaker.

5. *Group your testimonials.* There are two basic ways to present testimonials: You can group them together in one area of your brochure or ad, or you can scatter them throughout the copy. (A third alternative is to combine the two techniques, having many testimonials in a box or buck slip and a smattering of other testimonials throughout the rest of your copy.)

I've seen both approaches work well, and the success of the presentation depends, in part, on the skill of the writer and the specific nature of the piece. But, all else being equal, I prefer the first approach: to group all your testimonials and present them as a single block of copy. This can be done in a box, on a separate page, or on a separate sheet. My feeling is that when the prospect reads a half dozen or so testimonials, one right after another, they have more impact and power than when the testimonials are separated and scattered throughout the piece.

6. *Get permission.* Make sure you get permission from your customer to reprint his words before including his testimonial in your copy.

I suggest that you send a letter quoting the lines you want to reprint and ask permission to include them in ads, direct mail, brochures, and other materials used to promote your firm.

Notice I'm asking for a general release that gives me permission to use the customer's quotation in all current and future promotions, not just a specific ad or letter. This lets me get more mileage out of his favorable comment and eliminates the need to ask permission every time I want to use the quote in a new ad or letter.

Brochures

Although brochures are usually thought of as blatant sales vehicles rather than "content," a well-written, well-designed brochure containing useful data, graphs, tables, and illustrations can serve as a bait piece in an edu-marketing campaign.

When I was the advertising manager for a process equipment manufacturer, one of my responsibilities was to serve as liaison between the advertising agency we hired to write our ads and product brochures and our staff engineers.

The engineers, because of their technical expertise in the subject matter, were responsible for reviewing the agency's work.

As is often the case in our industry, the engineers complained that those "ad types" at the agency didn't understand the product or the audience—and that their copy was way off base.

The agency countered that engineers may know technology but don't know writing, marketing, design, or selling—and that they wanted to cram the brochures with too much unnecessary detail that would dilute the sales message.

Who was right? The fact is, both arguments have some merit.

On the agency side, ad agency folk often have a flair for creative, colorful communication, which can help a brochure gain attention and be noticed.

On the other hand, clients—especially the engineers who review the agency's brochure copy—often complain, sometimes correctly, that the agency's brochure copy is superficial.

Laziness is often the cause. The writer did not do sufficient research to understand both the technology and the needs, concerns, and interests of the target audience. The copy he writes reflects this lack of understanding. When you read it, you immediately think, "This person doesn't know what he is talking about"—and you are probably right.

Another problem with professional or agency-written product literature is a tendency toward cleverness for the sake of being clever. "Be creative!" the client instructs the agency. But the reader often doesn't get the joke, pun, or reference in the headline, the creativity goes over her head, and she is turned off rather than engaged.

Engineers who write their own brochure copy are rarely superficial; they usually have a solid understanding of the products and its technology. However, engineers tend to assume that the reader knows as much as the writer, speaks the same jargon, and has the same level of interest in the technology. And often this is not the case.

Take jargon. People today frequently use the term "open systems architecture" in sales literature. But do they really know what this means? Write down your own definition, ask five colleagues to do the same, and compare. I guarantee they will not be the same. Engineers who write often don't strive for clarity. So they fall back on buzzwords and clichés that, unfortunately, don't get across the messages they wish to convey.

Given these conditions, how can you—as an engineer or manager who either writes brochure copy, edits copy, approves copy, or provides input for ad agencies or freelance industrial copywriters—do your job better so the finished brochure is the best one possible?

Here are some simple guidelines to follow:

1. *Define the topic.* Is your brochure about a solution? A system? A product line? A product? A specific model of that product? A specific industry use or application of that product? The support services you offer for that product? The accessories?

   Define what the piece is about. The narrower the topic, the more focused, specific, and effective your brochure can be within the limited space available.

   Tip: Your brochure doesn't have to cover everything. You can always decide to have other pieces of sales literature that go into more depth on certain aspects of the product.

   For instance, you can talk about satisfied users in case histories. You can expand on specifications in a spec sheet. Some marketers use application briefs to focus on a specific application or industry. Others develop separate sell sheets on each key feature, allowing more in-depth technical discussion than is possible in a general product brochure.

2. *Know your audience.* Are you writing to engineers or managers? The former may be interested in technical and performance specifications. The latter may want to know about support, service, ease of use, scalability, user benefits, or return on investment.

   If you are writing to engineers, are they well-versed in this particular technology? Or do you have to bring them up to speed? Just because someone is a chemical engineer does not mean they know nearly as much about industrial knives, turbine blades, corrosion-resistant metals, ball valves, or your particular specialty as you do. Indeed, they probably don't.

   When in doubt, it is better to explain so everyone understands than to assume that everyone already understands. No engineer has ever complained to me that a brochure I wrote was too clear.

3. *Write with your objective in mind.* Unlike a Victoria's Secrets catalog, which gives the buyer all the information she needs to place an order, most technical product brochures support the selling process but are not designed to complete it on their own.

   Is the objective of the brochure to convince the prospect that your technical design is superior to your competition? Or show that you have more features at a better price? Or demonstrate that your system will pay back its cost in less than six months?

Establish a communication objective for the brochure and write with that goal in mind. For instance, if the objective is to get a meeting for you to sell consulting services to the client, you only need to include enough to convince them that the meeting is worth their time. Anything more is probably overkill.

4. *Include the two things every brochure should contain.* These simply are (a) the things your prospects need and want to know about your product to make their buying decision and (b) what you think you should say to persuade them that your product is the best product choice—and your company is the best vendor.

   The things a prospect wants to know about an industrial product might include weight, dimensions, power requirements, operating temperature, and whether it can perform certain functions.

   Things you might want to tell them include how the performance compares with competitive systems in benchmark tests (if you were the winner, of course) or the fact that it was cited as "Best Product" by an industry publication, or won an award from a trade association, or is the most popular product in its category with an installed base of more than 10,000 units.

5. *Be selective.* While ad agency copy is sometimes too light and tells the reader too little, engineer copy often makes the opposite error, attempting to cram every last technical fact and feature into a four or eight page brochure.

   Keep in mind that your prospect is bombarded by more information than he can handle on a daily basis. Everyone has too much to read and not enough time to read it. So, while thoroughness and detail are important, don't give your reader "too much of a good thing" by going into excruciating detail or using unnecessary repetition.

   Be selective in your presentation. Copywriter Herschell Gordon Lewis has a formula, $E^2 = 0$. Or as Lewis says, "When you emphasize everything, you emphasize nothing."[28] If every fact about your product is given equal weight in the brochure, the key facts that make the most persuasive case for buying the product will not stand out.

6. *Understand the selling environment.* There are three basic selling situations for selling products. You must know what situation your product falls into, so you can market it effectively.

   The first situation is that the prospect is not acutely aware of the problem he has that your product can solve. Or he is aware of it but does not consider it a priority. In this situation, to get your prospect's attention, your brochure must dramatize the problem and its severity, then position your product as the solution.

Example: Mainframe computer operators did not realize that certain operations accidentally overrode and erased files stored on magnetic tapes. A brochure for a utility that prevented this operation from occurring began, "Did you know that your storage devices may be accidentally wiping out important files even as you read this sentence?" It alerted them to the problem in a dramatic way.

Once alerted to a problem they didn't know existed, the readers were eager to find a solution, which the utility handily provided. Sales were brisk.

The second situation is that the prospect is aware of the problem or need your product addresses, but is not at all convinced that your type of product is the best solution.

Example: A chemical manufacturer warned wastewater treatment plants that their current activated charcoal bed systems were too costly.

The plant managers believed that, but didn't believe that the manufacturer's alternative filter technology was a viable solution. A paper reprinting lab test results plus the offer of a free trial overcame the disbelief and got firms to use the new filter system.

The third situation is when the prospect knows what his problem is, believes your type of product is the right solution, but needs to be convinced that your product is the best choice in the category, and better than similar products offered by your competitors.

One way to demonstrate superiority is with a table comparing your product with the others on a feature by feature basis. If you have a more complete feature set than they do, such a table makes you look like the best choice.

Another technique is to give specifications that prove your performance is superior. If this cannot be quantitatively measured, talk about any unique functionality, technology, or design feature that might create an impression of superiority in the prospect's mind.

There are many other copywriting techniques available to produce a superior technical product brochure in any of these three situations; this is why I've devoted the past 20 years, my entire professional life, to practicing and studying copywriting—just like a technical expert practices and studies his or her specialty.

But if you follow the basics in this section and do nothing else, I guarantee an improvement in your brochures that you, your sales reps, and your customers will appreciate. You might even some day receive that rare compliment: "You know, I actually read your brochure. It wasn't boring, and it told me what I needed to know!"

8

Using Direct Mail, Ads, and Other Lead-Generating Communications

Direct marketing—sales letters, self-mailers, postcards and postcard decks, ads, and TV and radio commercials—can be one of the most effective methods for generating sales leads. And in my experience, today it is absolutely essential to offer a bait piece as an enticement for the recipient to reply.

People are bombarded by advertising materials. And they are busy, with too much to read, and not enough time to read it. Which is why they toss out most direct mail without a second glance.

By offering a bait piece, you can generate inquiries from many more prospects than would otherwise respond. A bait piece offer can easily double or triple the response versus the same direct mail promotion without a bait piece offer.

For instance, an associate of mine works in medical advertising aimed at doctors. The offer is an invitation to a half-day seminar on a disease topic, the purpose of which is to educate doctors so they will prescribe the drug of the company sponsoring the event.

On a whim, he decided to split test his mailing. Test mailing "A" was the standard invitation to the free event. Testing mailing "B" was the exact same invitation but with the added enticement of a "free pocket diary" that would be given to the recipient when he arrived at the event.

Remember, the audience was doctors, and the pocket diaries cost about a dollar a piece. Can you guess the results? Test mailing "B" offering the free pocket diary generates six times the response of mailing "A," which did not offer the free bonus.

Witness the incredible power of a bait piece. Here was a professional, highly educated audience, all earning six figures. By being offered a pocket diary worth about a dollar, six times more of these physicians were persuaded to give up half a day of their billable time to hear a sales pitch!

5 Ways to Design Your White Paper So That Your Prospects Want to Get It

Do you plan on generating leads through a direct mail or e-mail campaign? Will you be offering a fulfillment piece that can be downloaded from your Web site or sent via snail-mail?

"Then you had better use a little imagination and creativity," advises copywriter Ivan Levison. "The days of simply telling the prospect that they can get a free 'white paper' are over." Here are Ivan's five suggestions for making your next fulfillment piece so enticing that prospects will just have to request it:

1. *Give it a compelling title.*
   For starters, instead of calling your document a "white paper," make the offer more exclusive, exciting, and lively. "The goal is to make prospects feel that they MUST read what you've got waiting for them!" says Ivan.

2. *Tell the prospect what they'll learn.*
   Be sure to let the reader know what specific information they'll find in the fulfillment piece. Go to town and tell them, in detail, all about the "must read" information that's waiting for them.

   For example, if you're offering a free brochure titled "Unlocking the Power of Contact Management Software," you could use descriptive bullets like these:

   - How to turn the business cards in your drawer into a winning sales campaign. It's worth requesting your free brochure for this section alone! (Page 2.)
   - Five ways to get a flood of great new leads coming down the pipeline! (Page 4.)
   - Three techniques for closing sales in half the time! (Page 5.)
   - How to launch a money-making, non-spamming, e-mail sales campaign with just three clicks of your mouse. (Page 6.)

WRONG:	RIGHT:
Free White Paper on Network Security	Free Guide: How to Stop Hackers, Crackers, Snoops, and Kooks from Bringing Down Your Network (They're Trying to Do It Right Now!).
Free White Paper: "Improving Warehouse Productivity"	Free for warehouse managers: "Seven Proven Ways to Manage Your Warehouse Better!"
Free White Paper: "Reducing Medical Malpractice Exposure"	Being Sued for Malpractice Can Damage Your Livelihood, Your Family, and Your Reputation. Our "Free Guide for Concerned Physicians" Can Show You How to Stay Out of Court and Out of Trouble!

- The four biggest mistakes salespeople make—and how you can avoid them! (Page 8.)
- How five real-life salespeople used our software to increase their income by 35 percent—and how you can too! (Page 11.)

3. *Design the cover for maximum impact.*
Use large type on the cover of your fulfillment piece. That way, when you reproduce it on an envelope, letter, or html e-mail, it will be easy to read.

Also avoid front covers where the title is black type against a dark background. These don't reproduce well, and if you show a small picture of the bait piece cover in your mailer or ad, prospects won't be able to read the title.

4. *Use call-outs or captions to highlight reasons for requesting your fulfillment piece.*
Link these call-outs or captions to a photo of the fulfillment piece. In a direct mail letter offering a free white paper on ERP and SCM (enterprise resource planning and supply chain management), some of these call-outs read as follows:

- How to unlock the full power of your ERP system.
- The manufacturing "wave of the future" and how you can ride it now.
- How to turn your supply chain into a competitive advantage.
- Five ways to speed up the ROI on ERP.

5. *Emphasize that there's no cost or obligation.*
Be sure to state that your fulfillment piece is absolutely free. "There's no cost. No obligation. Nothing to buy."[1]
   The point is this: it isn't just what's in your fulfillment piece that counts. How well you motivate the prospect to request it in the first place is also vitally important!

33 Ways to Get More Bait Piece Inquiries from Your Space Ads

A space ad can be an effective marketing tool for generating inquiries for a white paper or other bait piece. Here are 33 ways to write and design a bait-piece-offer ad for maximum response:

1. Ask for action. Tell the reader to phone, write, contact his sales rep, request a free brochure or booklet, or place an order.
2. Offer *free* information, such as a special report or catalog.
3. Describe your report or catalog. Tell about its special features, such as a selection chart, planning guide, installation tips or other useful information it contains.
4. Show a picture of your free report or catalog.
5. Give your literature a title that implies value. "Product Guide" is better than "catalog." "Planning Kit" is better than "sales brochure."
6. Include your address in the last paragraph of copy and beneath your logo, in type that is easy to read (also place it inside the coupon, if you use one).
7. Include a toll-free number in your ad.
8. Print the toll-free number in extra-large type.
9. Put a small sketch of a telephone next to the phone number. Also use the phrase, "Call toll-free."
10. Create a hot line. For example, a filter manufacturer might have a toll-free hot line with the numbers 1-800-FILTERS. Customers can call the hot line to place an order or get more information on the manufacturer's products.
11. For a full-page ad, use a coupon. It will increase response 25 to 100 percent.
12. Make the coupon large enough that readers have plenty of room to write in their name and address.

13. Give the coupon a headline that affirms positive action—"Yes, I'd like to cut my energy costs by 50% or more."

14. Give the reader multiple response options: "I'd like to see a demonstration," "Have a salesperson call," "Send me a free planning kit by return mail."

15. For a fractional ad—one-half page or less—put a heavy dashed border around the ad. This creates the feel and appearance of a coupon, which in turn stimulates response.

16. In the closing copy for your fractional ad, say, "To receive more information, clip this ad and mail it to us with your business card."

17. A bound-in BRC, appearing opposite your ad, can increase response by a factor or two or more.

18. Use a direct headline—one that promises a benefit or stresses the offer of free information—rather than a headline that is cute or clever.

19. Put your offer of a free booklet, report, selection guide, or other publication in the headline of your ad (see Exhibit 8.1).

20. Offer a free gift, such a slide rule, metric conversion table, pocket ruler, etc.

21. Offer a free product sample.

22. Offer a free consultation, analysis, recommendation, study, cost estimate, computer printout, etc.

23. Talk about the value and benefits of your free offer. The more you stress the offer, the better your response.

24. Highlight the free offer in a copy subhead. The last subhead of your ad could read, "Get the facts—FREE."

25. In a two-page ad, run copy describing your offer in a separate sidebar.

26. Be sure the magazine includes a reader service number in your ad.

27. Use copy and graphics that specifically point the reader toward using the reader service number. For example, an arrow pointing to the number and copy that says, "For more information circle reader service number below."

28. Consider using more than one reader service number. For example, one number for people who want literature, another for immediate response from a salesperson.

29. In a full-page ad for multiple products, have a separate reader service number for each product or piece of literature featured in the ad.

30. Test different ads. Keep track of how many inquiries each ad pulls. Then run only those ads that pull the best.

Exhibit 8.1: Small Space Ad Offering a Free Report.

This ad has not one but eight free offers.

Source: Robert Bly

31. Look for a sales appeal, key benefit, or theme that may be common to all of your best-pulling ads. Highlight that theme in subsequent ads.
32. Send readers to the URL of a specific page on the Web where they can download your free report or booklet as a PDF.
33. Create a specific landing page that highlights the free bait piece offer and its benefits. Send readers to this page, not to your home page.

Here are some additional characteristics shared by successful direct response print ads:

- *They stress a benefit.* The main selling proposition is not cleverly hidden but is made immediately clear. *Example:* "How to Win Friends and Influence People."
- *They arouse curiosity and invite readership.* The key here is not to be outrageous but to address the strongest interests and concerns of your target audience. *Example:* "Do You Make These Mistakes in English?" appeals to the reader's desire to avoid embarrassment and write and speak properly.
- *They provide information.* The headline "How to Stop Emission Problems—at Half the Cost of Conventional Air Pollution Control Devices" lures the reader because it promises useful information. Prospects today seek specific, usable information on highly specialized topics. Ads that provide information the reader wants get higher readership and better response. Another example is this ad for a cake mix: "The Secret to Moister, Richer Chocolate Cake."
- *They are knowledgeable.* Successful ad copy reflects a high level of knowledge and understanding of the product and the problem it solves. An effective technique is to tell the reader something he already knows, proving that you, the advertiser, are well-versed in his industry, application, or requirement.
- *They have a strong free offer.* Good ads contain a stronger offer. They tell the reader the next step in the buying process and encourage him to take it NOW. All ads should have an offer, because the offer generates immediate response and business from prospects who are ready to buy now or at least thinking about buying. Without an offer, these "urgent" prospects are not encouraged to reach out to you, and you lose many potential customers. In addition, strong offers increase readership, because people like ads that offer them something— especially if it is free and has high perceived value.

- *They are designed to emphasize the offer.* Graphic techniques such as "kickers" or eyebrows (copy lines above the headline), bold headlines, liberal use of subheads, bulleted or numbered copy points, coupons, sketches of telephones, toll-free numbers set in large type, Web site URL in boldface, pictures of response booklets and brochures, dashed borders, asterisks, and marginal notes make your ads more eye-catching and response-oriented, increasing readership.

  Why? My theory is that when people see a non-direct response ad, they know it's just a reminder-type ad and figure they don't have to read it. But when they see response-type graphic devices, these visuals say to the reader, "Stop! This is a response ad! Read it so you can find out what we are offering. And mail the coupon—so you can get it NOW!"

- *They are clearly illustrated.* Good advertising does not use abstract art concepts that force the reader to puzzle out what is being sold. Ideally, you should be able to understand *exactly* what the advertiser's proposition is within five seconds of looking at the ad. As John Caples observed a long time ago, the best visual for an ad for a record club is probably a picture of records.[2]

Using Direct Mail to Generate Sales Leads

Direct mail (DM) is one of the most effective methods of generating large quantities of high-quality sales leads. Aside from public relations and postcard decks, few promotional methods can even come close to matching direct mail's effectiveness for lead generation.

A good lead-generating direct-mail letter will generate response rates of between 1 and 5 percent—and sometimes higher—when mailed cold to a rented mailing list or directory of prospect names. This response rate produces quality leads with a genuine and serious interest in your product or service—or at least in the problem your product or service solves. It can be achieved using copy with a strong sales appeal and an attractive offer that is free and without obligation.

Can response rates be higher? Yes. Some lead-generating mailings have achieved response rates of 10 to 50 percent or more, although this is rare. Response rates are generally two to five times higher when mailing to existing customers versus cold mailing to rented prospect lists.

Response rates can also increase when offering expensive free gifts or other "bribes" to prospects in return for their reply. The more costly and desirable the bribe, the more inquiries produced. But when prospects respond just for the bribe rather than a genuine interest in the product or service, conversion of leads to sales becomes poor. With lead generation, you must always balance quantity with quality of inquiries.

The most effective format for lead-generating direct mail seems to be a one- or two-page letter in an envelope with a BRC and perhaps one insert, such as a brochure, flyer, or article reprint.

Self-mailers (see Exhibit 8.2) can also be effective. The most successful self- mailer format for lead generation is the tri-fold. This is made by taking a piece of paper and folding it two or three times horizontally so you form sections or panels (the same way you fold a business letter for insertion into a #10 business envelope).

Of all the lead-generating direct-mail formats, simple sales letters mailed with reply cards and tri-fold self-mailers have the longest track record of success and are, therefore, your safest bets. There are numerous variations, but these two simple formats seem to work best and are inexpensive to produce. Try them before spending money on something more elaborate that may not get any better response (and may very well get less).

Profits from Postcards

Because of their low cost, a third DM format, postcards (see Exhibit 8.3), is growing in popularity. Aside from low cost, their major advantage is that, unlike direct-mail packages and tri-fold mailers, postcards do not require opening or unfolding: The message is completely visible as soon as you pick it up. Another advantage of postcards is that they are easy and inexpensive to produce. The postage is also lower than that of a first-class letter in an envelope.

The disadvantage of a standard postcard is that there is no reply element. Mailers have found several solutions to this. One company instructs prospects to return the entire postcard as-is in an envelope to receive a free sample copy of its product (the postcard does not have to be filled in since the front panel already contains a label with the recipient's name and address).

Other postcards stress response through e-mail, the Web, 800, 888, and 900 numbers, and phone numbers that dial up recorded hot lines with more detailed promotional messages and product information on tape. Fax seems a logical response option, but smaller postcards do not fax well (they do not feed through many machines smoothly).

A variation on regular postcards is the double postcard, in which two post- cards are attached via a perforated border. One postcard carries the promo- tional message; the other is the reply element. While used with considerable

Exhibit 8.2: Self-Mailer

FREE
JAM basket

JAM Information Kit Request:
Complete the information below,
and drop in the mail today! Or visit,
www.jamagency.com/dmresults to register.

☐ **Yes**, I'm interested in learning
how JAM's talented team can help me
achieve breakthrough results on my
direct marketing campaigns. Please
send me the JAM Communications
Information Kit, outlining strategic
approches to maximize the impact of
your web-based marketing, the FREE
White Paper, and a FREE JAM Basket.
I understand I'm under no obligation
whatsoever.

NAME

TITLE / ORGANIZATION

STREET ADDRESS / SUITE

CITY / STATE / ZIP

PHONE / FAX

E-MAIL

Self-mailer used to offer a free white paper.

Reproduced with permission of the JAM Agency.

success in selling magazine subscriptions, double postcards have not found widespread use in other applications as of yet.

Because of limited space for graphics and copy, and lack of a response form, postcards work best when the following conditions exist:

1. The product is familiar to the reader or, if not familiar, simple in nature and easy to explain.
2. The marketing objective is to generate a lead or inquiry, rather than to generate mail orders accompanied by checks and credit card payments.
3. The offer features a premium or other free item the prospect can send for, such as a demo disk, CD, catalog, or brochure.

Why use postcards instead of a traditional DM package, tri-fold self-mailer, or other formats?

- "Postcards offer immediate impact," says Perry Frank of Modern Postcards. The message is immediately visible, with no envelopes to open. "Postcards stand out in the mail with a brief, to-the-point message. Even when someone is sorting incoming mail over the trash can, the

Exhibit 8.3: Direct Mail Postcard

 MJ & Associates

RETURN SERVICE REQUESTED

S.O.S.
In these rough economic seas, you need effective marketing solutions. A professional writing and communications consultancy that understands your business, not highfalutin, high-fee agencies. Discover the marketing results on your horizon with MJ & Associates.

marketing planning • media relations • press releases web content • case studies • white papers

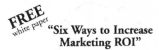 **FREE** white paper "Six Ways to Increase Marketing ROI"
Now available for download at www.marciajedd.com

MJ & Associates
smart writing & marketing communications services

Contact Marcia Jedd, MJ & Associates

Postcard offering a free white paper.
Reproduced with permission of MJ & Associates.

postcard will get noticed and read—even if it's on its way to get tossed."[3]

- You can bypass lingering concerns about anthrax. "With the post-911 anthrax scare, people are leery of opening envelopes from businesses they don't recognize," writes Sean Lyden on Entrepreneur.com. Furthermore, he notes, the envelope is a barrier to your message because you need to convince the recipient to open it and read the letter inside.[4]
- Creative and printing costs for postcards are much less than for a full-blown direct mail package, because there are no envelopes, letters, brochures, buck slips, or other inserts. The cost to mail a standard size

(4¼ by 6-inch) postcard first class is 23 cents versus 37 cents for a 1-ounce first class letter. That's a postage savings of $140 per thousand.

- Ease of production. With no folding, bindery, or packaging, postcards have only two sides—the front and the back.
- Postcards offer an affordable option for testing offers and creative prior to launching a more costly campaign. They can also be used to qualify prospects prior to mailing catalogs and other, more expensive DM packages. A postcard announcing that a new catalog will be mailing gives the recipient a chance to opt out from future mailings, saving the marketer production and mailing costs by updating their list.
- Many postcards wind up on the refrigerator or walls of cubicles in the office, giving them greater visibility and "shelf life" than regular DM. "Mail someone a postcard that really grabbed their attention, and chances are they'll hang onto it," says Frank. Copywriter Roscoe Barnes adds: "Some postcards are collector's items. They are designed to be kept and praised. To work, however, they must have a striking drawing, painting, or photograph. Using the works of a famous artist helps."[5]
- Postcards are extremely versatile. They can be used for coupons, invitations, announcements, save-the-date reminders, thank-you cards, follow-ups, special offers, inserts in magazines, admission tickets, mini-newsletters, bookmarks, and quick-reference guides.
- Postcards can drive response to a Web site URL or toll-free phone number. Add a perforation with a tear-off BRC to create a "double postcard," and you can generate mail response as well.
- Postcards also offer a quick, affordable way to create clever campaigns with a consistent theme. "We see many of these mailings on a regular basis to the same audience with trivia questions, creating anticipation for the next mailing," says Frank.

What marketers have used postcards with success? One, Haag Engineering Company, specializes in failure and damage consulting—the analysis of why a structure, such as a bridge or building, collapsed. Clients include manufacturers, insurance companies, and law firms.

Accredited in several states to provide continuing education, Haag recently mailed 20,000 postcards to promote their seminars. Recipients of the card are driven to their Web site to view course offerings and locations.

The card can also be kept as a reminder: while visiting a client, one of Haag's engineers saw that the client had the postcard pinned to their wall.

Response rates, according to Cheryl Markstahler, marketing manager, average between 10 and 25 percent.[6]

The USA Rice Federation, a trade association promoting the eating of rice, mailed a postcard promoting September as National Rice Month to 6,800 food professionals. The postcard offers free brochures, posters, recipes, and other materials, driving response to a phone number or e-mail address.

Because the federation is in the business of promoting rice, they have an extensive library of beautiful food photographs in stock, allowing them to produce high-quality postcards inexpensively. With limited staff and budget, postcards are both cost-effective and time-efficient.

"Postcards work extremely well in establishing or maintaining relationships and keeping rice top-of-mind among our target audience," says Kimberly Park, Director of National Consumer Education.[7] The postcards generated a response rate of almost 3 percent.

Postcard Decks Are Great for Selling Bait Pieces

A *postcard deck* is a group of advertising postcards mailed as a package to individuals whose names are on a mailing list. Although some decks are dedicated (all the cards are from one advertiser), most carry cards from many different advertisers. The advertiser pays a fee to have its card included in the deck.

The main advantage of postcard decks is the low cost. The cost-per-thousand pieces for a solo direct-mail package can range from $400 to $800 (or more), depending on the quantity mailed. (Some business-to-business marketers spend 75 cents to $2 or more per piece for fancier lead-generating packages.)

Running a postcard in a postcard deck with a circulation of 100,000 typically costs $2,000 to $3,000, so the cost is low—$20 to $30 per thousand prospects reached. That's about thirty times cheaper than a full-blown solo direct-mail package.

Another advantage of postcard decks is that the postcards are easy to produce. They don't require copywriting genius, cleverness, or creative design. Just about anyone, even those with limited resources, can put such a card together. (Some decks, hungry for advertisers, will even do the card for you, at low or no cost.)

The third advantage is that postcard decks are inherently a response medium, so if you're after pure response and don't care about things like awareness or image, they make sense for you.

What kind of response rate can you expect? Approximately one-quarter to one-half percent is common. With a postcard deck going to 100,000 names, therefore, this would translate into 250 to 500 inquiries.

If you paid $2,000 to run your card in the deck, that's a cost per lead of $4 to $8, which is tremendously lower than solo direct-mail. On a $700-per-thousand direct-mail package pulling a 2 percent response rate, your cost per lead would be $35.

If you are selling capital equipment or other expensive technical products with long purchase cycles, use the postcard to generate a soft lead. The headline would state the main benefit offered by the product (e.g., "Reduce Energy Costs Up to 40 Percent in Your Paper Mill"). The copy would briefly explain the product and offer a free brochure. The visual would be a photo, sketch, or diagram of the product.

If you sell a broad line of low-to-medium-priced products, and your catalog is your primary sales vehicle, use the card for catalog distribution. The headline should stress the offer and value of your catalog (e.g., "FREE Electronic Component Buyer's Guide and Reference Catalog!"). The visual should be a picture of the catalog.

If you have a low-priced product (under $300), it may be possible to sell it directly from a postcard. But test cautiously. One manufacturer of electronic equipment in the $79 to $400 range uses postcards frequently, but he also has tested offering products directly versus a free catalog offer. He finds the free catalog offer gets much more response and is more profitable over the long run.

Using Direct Mail for Trade Shows

Free informational bait pieces and other give-away items can be enormously effective in getting people to visit your trade show exhibits, especially when direct mail or e-mail marketing is used to deliver the offer to your prospects.

Direct mail, in the hands of a knowledgeable pro, can be a powerful promotion that builds both traffic, targets key prospects, generates sales leads, fills conference rooms, creates an awareness of an event and your participation in it, or gets the word out about your products and services.

Unfortunately, most trade show direct mail I see violates the fundamentals of successful direct marketing. For this reason, few of these mailings generate anywhere near the desired response. (How many of your mailings produce the results you want or expect?)

Here are 10 proven techniques for creating direct mail that *works*. Try them in your next letter or invitation and watch your response rate soar.

1. *The importance of the list.* Even the most brilliant package will flop if it is mailed to the wrong list. Selecting the right mailing list is the most important step in ensuring direct mail success. According to Freeman Gosden, Jr., author of *Direct Marketing Success*, list selection is twice as important as copy, graphics, and printing combined.[8]

   For a trade show invitation, the best list is key prospects and current customers within a 100-mile radius of the exhibit hall. Invite only those people who are genuine prospects for the products you are featuring in your display. One good source of names might be a list of people who have responded to ads about the product within the last six months.

2. *Executive seminars.* An even more select list of key prospects can be targeted to receive special invitations to hospitality suites, executive briefings, presentations of papers, seminars, and other special events held in conjunction with your exhibit. If the event is relatively minor, a notice about it can be included in the invitation to the exhibit. But, if the event is major (such as the opportunity to see a new product introduction), you can play it up in a separate mailing.

3. *Carry cards.* A carry card, mailed with the invitation, is a printed card the prospect can present at your booth to receive a small gift, or perhaps to enter a sweepstakes or drawing. I call it a "carry card" because the prospect must carry it with him to receive whatever is offered in the mailing.

   By printing your booth number on the card, you remind the prospect to visit you; the offer of the gift provides the incentive to do so. The gift need not be expensive or elaborate; perhaps you offer free information, such as a special report, or an inexpensive item such as a pen or tie clip.

4. *Get personal.* The more personal a mailing piece, the greater the response. One effective technique is to personalize each mailing with the prospect's name. A form letter, for example, can be made to look personal if produced on a word processor using a program that inserts the prospect's name and address.

   There are other ways of individualizing the mailings. Carry cards or invitations can be numbered in sequence; therefore, each person receives a unique number, which may be used to qualify him or her to receive a prize or other gift.

   Another technique is for salespeople to write brief handwritten notes to each prospect. The note, written in the margin of a preprinted form letter or on the flap of a formal invitation, adds a human touch to the communication.

5. *Urgency.* Direct mail is a medium designed to generate an immediate response. Therefore, your mailing must give the reader reason to read and act now. A "teaser"—a short message written on the outer envelope—is often used to urge the reader to open the mailing right away. For example, it can tell the reader that the envelope contains dated materials. It can stress the importance of attending the show or emphasize benefits. Or, it can tell the recipient to take action—for example, the teaser copy could read, "Urgent: open by November 15." Such a letter should be mailed so that it arrives a few days before the 15th.

   If you want the reader to RSVP your invitation, you should create a sense of urgency for this too. The close of an invitation to a seminar might say, "But hurry. Attendance is limited. Reserve your seat at this important briefing *today.*"

6. *Give them a choice.* Years ago, direct marketers discovered that they received greater response when the reader was given a choice. And this holds true in trade show promotion.

   For example, many of the people you invite will be unable to attend, even though they may have genuine interest in the products being displayed. Why not have your mailings do double duty by offering information or further action to those people who can't come to the show?

   You could offer to send them a brochure or a newsletter or to call on them in person and tell them what they missed. One exhibitor even offered to send a videotape of his exhibit! This technique can dramatically boost response.

   Always include a BRC or business reply envelope in mailings designed to elicit a response. Without these devices, response drops to near zero.

7. *Create an event.* Although it is difficult for our egos to accept, the truth is, your next trade show is not a major event in the lives of your customers. Your challenge, then, is to change their reaction from one of boredom to one of excitement.

   How? There are many possibilities. One exhibitor featured the Dallas Cowboy Cheerleaders in his booth. Another had an exciting multimedia presentation on a revolutionary new type of technology. An instrumentation manufacturer employed a magician to perform at his display. A major defense manufacturer hired a quick-draw fighter to teach people how to use a six-shooter (with blanks, of course!).

Once you've invented an event (one that generates real excitement but also ties in with your product or theme), make this the feature subject of your mailer. Just as publishers win subscribers by featuring a free gift or a price discount, a successful trade show mailing features the "gimmick" rather than the exhibit itself.

For example, a mailing designed to draw people to the gun-fighter exhibit might read, "MEET THE WEST'S FASTEST GUN-FIGHTER AT HIGH NOON AT THE AMCOM AIR SHOW—AND WIN A GENUINE, OLD WEST TEN-GALLON HAT." Here we are selling the sizzle rather than the steak.

8. *Exclusivity.* A powerful appeal of direct-mail—and of trade shows—is exclusivity. One study released by the Trade Show Bureau reported that *half* the people who attend trade shows go specifically to see new products and services that have not been shown before.

If you're introducing a new technology, a new product, or an improved version of an old product, play this up in your mailing. Emphasize both the importance of the product as well as the fact that the reader is having an opportunity see it *first*—an opportunity not extended to other people in the business. This sense of being exclusive, of being first, is flattering, and it can do wonders for your response rate.

9. *Completing the set.* A classic trade show mailing is one in which the prospect is mailed an invitation along with a single cufflink. The cufflink is a free gift, the letter explains, and the reader will be given the other cufflink (to complete the set) when he visit the manufacturer's booth at the show.

This is a powerful technique. If you can think of an appropriate variation that is relevant to your sales pitch, use it. An automobile manufacturer, for example, could mail key chains to important customers and enroll them in a drawing for a brand new car. But to win the car, they must bring the key chain to the drawing. The mailing stresses how you can add a key to your chain (and the car that goes with it) by visiting the show.

In another variation on this theme, Omron Electronics mailed a box containing a fortune cookie. The fortune inside the cookie predicted "A fortune in your future!" at the ISA show in Philadelphia. Copy on a carry card enclosed with the cookie reinforces the message: "Bring this ticket to Omron's Booth #R631 to collect a fortune."

Note that the nature of the "fortune" is never specified. In direct mail, you can often boost response by leaving a part of your story untold. This creates a sense of mystery, and many people response simply to satisfy their curiosity.

10. *Use a series of mailings.* A series of mailings can generate more response than just a single mailing. So it may pay to mail more than once to the same list of people.

Many exhibitors have used the following three-part mailing format with success. The first mailing is a simple postcard that "previews" the show. It is used to tweak the reader's curiosity and interest, but demands no response.

The second mailing is the full invitation package. It can consist of a letter, an invitation, a carry card, a reply card, a booklet or brochure, or any combination of these elements. The theory is that more people will read the full invitation if they are "warmed-up" with the postcard first.

The third mailing can be either a follow-up reminder or, if the reader has responded to the invitation, it can be a letter confirming the time, date, and location of the event.

Telemarketing—the use of telephone calls to follow-up direct mail—can dramatically raise response levels. But, it is expensive: A phone call generally costs about ten times more than a mailing piece.

You might want to save the telephone for targeting a small, exclusive list—say, your top 20 or 30 clients or customers. They would receive calls after the second or third mailing; the caller would repeat the offer of the mailings and urge prospects to attend your display.

If you have a series of invitational mailings, you can make the last effort an e-mail. An effective gambit is to send a last-minute e-mail reminder just a few days before the start of the event. (If you try that with paper direct mail, the mailing may arrive after the event is over.)

Bonus tip: Here's one thing to keep in mind. Even if you design your own invitation, it's a good idea to include an official show pass or registration form in the envelope, as well. Having a show pass gives your prospect the comfort and security of knowing he has the necessary paperwork to get him into the exhibit hall.

You should imprint your company name and booth number on the show pass, so the prospect will be reminded to visit you even if he throws away the rest of your mailing.

Radio Commercials Can Get Your Phone Ringing Off the Hook

Thousands of small businesses have successfully promoted themselves through radio advertisements; these include auto dealers, accountants, banks, boutiques, bars, clubs, lounges, restaurants, theaters, health clubs, and hairdressers.

If you wish to join them, ask the advertising sales departments of your local radio stations for help in planning your radio advertising. They can set up a schedule and budget, help you plan advertising strategy, recommend an ad agency to produce the commercial, and even help with writing of the commercial. Best of all, this free service comes with the price of air time.

Depending on the nature of your business, the radio salespeople may recommend drive time spots, late night commercials, sponsorship of program segments, or a combination of several alternatives. Naturally, as with newspaper and magazine advertising, you want to reach the greatest number of qualified prospects at the lowest possible cost per thousand.

Two major advantages of radio advertising are its short lead time and its minimal production costs. While television spots have to be performed in a studio, recorded on film or videotape, and sent to the station to be aired, a radio commercial can be written, handed to the announcer in script form, and read live on the air all in the same day.

Some companies do hire advertising agencies to produce more elaborate radio spots, using professional narrators, actors, singers, musicians, and sound effects. But for most small businesses, a well-written live commercial (one read by the announcer from a script) can get the word out . . . and eliminate production costs altogether. Often, the radio station's advertising sales department can help you write the script.

Here are eight tips specifically designed to help you write better radio commercials:

1. *Make it sound the way people talk.* Radio, after all, involves talking and listening, not reading and writing. By controlling the volume, tone, and inflection of her voice, the radio announcer can emphasize certain points and communicate in ways a printed page cannot. A natural, conversational style in radio helps keep listeners interested; awkward or stiff monologue sounds false and turns them off.

2. *Repeat the product name and the store name.* Ever since Pavlov rang a dinner bell for his hungry dog, people have known that repetition aids memory. To get listeners to remember your product or your

store, repeat the name. I recently heard a 30-second radio spot repeat the advertiser's name eight times! If you don't pound the telephone number into the listener's head so she can remember it until she gets to a phone, you won't get a high volume of inquiries.

3. *Use short words and short sentences.* There are two reasons for this. First, although grammarians hate to admit it, people do talk this way. They use short sentences, sentence fragments, and sentences beginning with the conjunctions "and," "or," and "but." Second, short words and sentences are easier to understand and remember. Listeners cannot grasp long, convoluted arguments and complex terms.

4. *Supply the visual.* The major disadvantage of radio versus newspapers, magazines, and television is that radio has no pictures. It is a medium of words and sound. The listener's imagination supplies the visual based on what the ear takes in. So, if it's important that the listener know what your product looks like, you must describe it in the copy. For example, in a radio spot advertising a line of home-baked pies that are packaged in red aluminum foil, end the commercial with a line like: "So, ask for the pie in the bright red wrapper at your favorite supermarket or grocery store today."

5. *Use sound effects.* A lifeguard's whistle, children laughing, the tinkling of the bell on an ice cream truck are some sounds that can add warmth, drama, and believability to radio advertising. Promoting stock car races at the local speedway? Your commercial should include the roar of engines revving up for the big race. Selling mufflers? Let listeners compare the sound of an auto before and after the new muffler is installed.

    One important note: Adding sound effects to your spot means you will have to prerecord your commercial; that, in turn, adds considerably to the cost of your radio advertising.

6. *Identify with the listener's situation.* In print advertising, you can use hundreds of words plus photos and diagrams to explain the benefits of your product in great detail. In radio and television, you have only 10, 30, or at most 60 seconds of time to hook the listener's interest and explain your selling proposition. Radio and television are better for eliciting an emotional, rather than a logical, response from consumers.

7. *Ask for a response.* Don't forget to mention your phone number or address. Most stations will also allow listeners to write to you, the advertiser, in care of the station. You can mention this, too, just in case

listeners forget to jot down your number. Repeat the phone number at least two or three times.

8. *Offer a bait piece.* Give the listener who responds something tangible to ask for. A New York commodities broker offers listeners a folder that includes an audiocassette, financial reports, charts, and graphs of the commodity being promoted. A firm promoting copyright, patent, and other services for amateur inventors offers callers a "Free Inventor's Idea Kit."

"Don't be afraid to experiment," says Burt Manning, vice chairman of J. Walter Thompson, one of the world's largest advertising agencies. "Radio's lower production costs are an invitation to do that. And if you make a mistake, you'll know about it fast, and you can fix it."[9]

Try a variety of different approaches in your radio scripts: drama, dialogue, humor, warmth, hard sell. Run the spots that do work; rewrite the ones that don't.

TV Advertising for Lead Generation

Television advertising can be expensive, and small businesses cannot directly compete with national advertisers and their Madison Avenue ad agencies, in either coverage or quality. To run a single 60-second spot on certain national, prime-time programs can cost more than $50,000, a sum that exceeds the entire year's advertising budget for many small companies. And production costs for the commercial can run anywhere from $40,000 to $100,000 (and up) if you hire an agency to produce the spot.

The Hair Club for Men has been running successful lead-generating TV commercials for decades for a fraction of this cost. Founder Sy Sperling says TV advertising does not have to be expensive to be an effective lead generator.

"Like most successful direct-response commercials, ours air late at night, early in the morning, or on the weekends, when air space is cheap," says Sperling. "Even today, we routinely buy air time on cable stations for $100 a spot, and our average production bill for a Hair Club commercial is $10,000. You can produce a good quality commercial for as little as $5,000."[10]

David Ogilvy has lamented that television is "an infernally difficult medium to use."[11] That's especially true when you can't afford the services of an advertising agency or professional director to guide you in the use of storyboards, answer prints, voice-over tracks, mixing, dubbing, transferring, and other technicalities. Certainly, we advise you to get professional guidance if you can afford it. But, realizing that you may have to do it yourself, we offer the following tips:

1. *Demonstrate the product.* Television is a visual medium. Take advantage of it by showing how the product works. If the product doesn't lend itself to demonstration, at least feature it prominently in the picture. Show off the product, its function, and its packaging, so your viewers will remember it. Sy Sperling uses before and after pictures to demonstrate his product, a hair replacement system.

2. *Make it lively.* Use action, dialogue, testimonials, and drama to make your commercial interesting to watch. Television programs provide viewers with pure entertainment, and they expect as much from the commercials.

3. *Make it memorable.* The average consumer sees thousands of commercials each month. Make yours memorable so that it sticks out from the crowd. Do not fret if viewers say they do not like your commercial; research shows there is no correlation between people's liking commercials and their being sold by them.

4. *Repeat the product name and the selling proposition.* Broadcast advertisements come and go quickly—60 seconds or less. Help consumers remember your message by repeating it at least twice. State your offer clearly at least once; repeat the phone number twice while showing it on the screen.

5. *Use an 800 number.* Encourage telephone response with a toll-free number and an attractive offer. The Hair Club for Men, for example, offers informational booklets on hair loss and what to do about it. Craftmatic Adjustable Bed offers a free guide on how to get a good night's sleep.

Radio, like magazines, delivers narrowly targeted audiences. Television is more like newspapers in that it reaches a broad consumer-oriented audience.

Print can accommodate detail; television cannot. For one thing, there's not enough time in a commercial spot for a lengthy explanation of a product's features and benefits; for another, television can't handle complex visuals such as tables of prices, long lists of retail outlets, and complicated graphs.

As a result, television is good for advertising simple products and services that the average consumer can buy: hamburgers, soap, records, clothing, rugs, automobiles, soft drinks.

Highly technical products and services that require a great deal of explanation generally do not lend themselves to promotion through TV commercials. Exceptions? Of course.

Generating Inexpensive Inquiries with Free PR

This is my secret weapon in public relations (PR) and the single most effective type of PR tactic I know of. It works as follows: You write a free booklet, report, or other bait piece. You then send out a press release that (1) announces the publication of your new booklet or report, (2) describes some of the useful information it contains, and (3) offers it free to readers of the publication or to the audience of the radio or TV show.

All three elements are critical. Editors are primarily interested in what's new, so if you are offering a new booklet on a topic, your headline should always begin "New Free Booklet" followed by a description of the topic, contents, or issue the information addresses.

Next, your press release should repeat (either word for word or edited) some of the key points highlighted in the booklet or report. This is done so the editor can run your release as a mini-feature article on the topic.

Put excerpts from your booklet into your release. Do not assume that the editor will read your booklet and pull out pertinent material for an article. The press release should be a self-contained mini-article ready to use "as is," without the editor's having to refer to any enclosures or other materials.

Finally, your free booklet press release must call for action. In the last paragraph, you say, "For a free copy of [title of booklet], call or write [your company name, address, phone]." Many editors will include that contact information and a call to action when running your release, and you will get many requests.

Some editors will not print such contact information, but you have no control over that. However, if you do not put in contact information and a call to action, no editors will tell their readers how or where they can request your booklet, and without such information, no one will contact you. So, always close with the call to action.

If your booklet is available on your Web site as a downloadable PDF, include the URL of the Web site or the specific page from which it may be downloaded. Reason: some editors who refuse to publish your mailing address or phone number will include your Web site URL.

Should you include a copy of your free booklet with the press releases you mail? Including a sample of the booklet may be desirable, but it is not necessary. I have had great success mailing press releases that did not include a sample copy of the booklet or report being offered.

The main benefit of leaving out the sample booklet is cost savings: Including a sample booklet can add another ten cents to 70 cents (or more) per release being mailed, depending on the cost to print the booklet and the weight of the booklet (which increases postage). For example, a tip sheet or slim pamphlet will add less cost than a bulky special report, book, or manual.

If the extra ten cents to 70 cents per piece is significant to you, omit the sample booklet and pocket the savings. Be sure to put a line after the close of your release that says, "Editor: Review copy of [Title of Booklet] available upon request; call Joe Jones at XXX-XXX-XXXX." Some editors may insist on seeing a copy before they'll promote it in their publication, so you should offer to send a copy free to any editor who requests it.

If your free booklet is slim and inexpensive, or if cost is not a factor, include a sample copy with each release you mail. It certainly can't hurt, and some editors may pay extra attention when they open the envelope and see your report or pamphlet.

Of course, your free booklet need not be an actual booklet with cover and staples; you can offer a free report, fact sheet, audiocassette, or other free bait piece in your release.

50 Lead-Generating Tips

What should you know when planning a lead-generating edu-marketing program? Here are a few pointers to guide you in the right direction:

1. How many steps are there in the buying process for this product? Where in this process does my mailing fit?
2. What can I tell my prospect that will get him to take the next step in the buying process?
3. Can I reduce selling costs by creating a mailing designed to produce a direct sale (a mail order) instead of an inquiry?
4. How many leads do I want to generate? Do we want a large quantity of "soft" leads? Or are we better off getting a smaller number of more highly qualified leads?
5. What happens if the mailing produces too many leads? Too few?
6. Is there a geographic region that my sales force does not cover? How can I respond to inquiries from this region?
7. What is the primary market for my product or service? (Which industry needs it most?)

8. Are there any secondary markets for the product large enough to justify a custom-tailored version of the mailing?
9. Who is my primary prospect within the target industry? What is his or her job title? Function?
10. Who are the other people (by job title) involved in the purchase decision for this product? What are their roles? (Who recommends the product? Who specifies it? Who has authority to approve the purchase?)
11. Must we reach all of these prospects? Or can we generate the desired sales result by targeting only one or two key decision-makers at each prospect organization?
12. If we don't know who we should be mailing to, how can we find out? From our sales representatives? Market research? Direct mail?
13. If we don't know what we should be telling our potential customers about our product, how can we find out?
14. Should we tailor versions of our sales letter either to vertical markets or various job titles—or both?
15. Should we tailor our brochure to specific markets or job titles?
16. What offer are we using in our current mailing? Is there a way to make the offer stronger or better?
17. Is the prospect in need of information about our product or the problem it solves? Can we package this information in a booklet or report and offer it as a response piece in our mailing?
18. Does our sales process involve a face-to-face meeting with the prospect? Can we legitimately call this sales meeting a "free consultation" and feature it as the offer in our mailing?
19. Do we allow the user to sample our product on a free trial basis? Should we be stressing this free trial offer in our mailing?
20. Do we offer our mail customers a free gift, price discount, free shipping and handling, or other money-saving incentive for responding to our mailing? If not, why not?
21. What reason or incentive can we give the reader to respond NOW and not later?
22. Can we use telemarketing to qualify sales leads generated by our direct mail program?
23. Can we use telemarketing to turn non-responders into responders?
24. Can we use telemarketing to identify and presell prospects before we send them our mailing package?
25. What format is best for our mailing? Self-mailer? Sales letter? Postcard?

26. Is there any benefit to personalizing the mailing?

27. What graphic treatment is appropriate for our audience? Should it be businesslike or bright and loud? Should it be "disguised" as personal correspondence or clearly marked (by use of teaser and graphics) as direct mail?

28. What copy approach should I use? Serious or breezy? Educational and informative versus hard sell?

29. Does my reader want or need a lot of information?

30. Can I reach these people with e-mail?

31. Is post card-deck advertising appropriate for my offer?

32. Should I use a single mailing or a series of mailings?

33. How many mailings should I send to my list before giving up on people who do not respond?

34. In a series of mailings, am I using a variety of different sizes and formats to gain attention for my message?

35. Are requests for more information fulfilled within 48 hours?

36. Are hot sales leads separated for immediate follow up by sales representatives or telephone salespeople?

37. What is the conversion ratio (the percentage of mail-generated inquiries that result in a sale)?

38. Are our salespeople competent? If not, what can we do to ensure better handling of sales leads?

39. Do salespeople follow up on all leads provided? If not, why not?

40. Do salespeople welcome direct mail leads or do they grumble about them? Why?

41. Are there qualifying questions we can add to our reply form to help salespeople separate genuine prospects from "brochure collectors"?

42. Can we afford to send a brochure to everyone who requests it?

43. Do we have a sufficient quantity of sales brochures on hand to fulfill all requests for more information—assuming we get a 10 percent response to our mailing?

44. Do we get a better quality lead by requiring the prospect to put a stamp on the reply card rather than offering a postage-paid BRC?

45. Do we get better sales results from prospects who respond by telephone versus those who mail in reply cards?

46. Does our fulfillment package or sales brochure provide the prospect with the information he asked for? And does it do a good job of selling our product or service?

47. Do we include a cover letter with the brochures and data sheets we send in response to mail-generated inquiries?

48. Do we include a questionnaire, spec sheet, or some other type of reply form with our inquiry fulfillment package?
49. Do we automatically send follow-up mailings to prospects who don't respond to the inquiry fulfillment package?
50. Should we be more vigorous in our program of follow-up mailings and phone calls?

9

Edu-Marketing Online

*"*I want to market my business on the Web, but how do I get traffic to my site?" one client asked recently. "And if I want to sell my product or service using e-mail marketing, who do I send the e-mails to?"

Here is one online marketing methodology that has proved effective for many different types of businesses—and it is based on edu-marketing and the offer of a valuable bait piece.

The primary concept is that online marketing works best when you e-mail to people who already know you. Therefore, successful online marketers build their "house file" or "e-list" (lists of prospects and their e-mail addresses) using the process outlined below, and then sell to those people via e-mail marketing.

To begin, build a Web site that positions you as an expert or guru in your field. This is the "base of operations" for your online marketing campaign. This Web site should include a home page, an "About the Company" page, your bio, and a page with brief descriptions of your products and services (each product or service description can link to a longer document on the individual item). You should also have an "Articles Page" where you post articles you have written on your area of specialty, and where visitors can read and download these articles for free.

Next, write a short special report or white paper on your area of expertise, and make this available to people who visit your site. They can download it for free as a PDF, but in exchange, they have to register and give you their e-mail address (and any other information you want to capture).

Also consider offering a monthly online newsletter, or "e-zine." People who visit your site can subscribe free if they register and give you their e-mail address. You may want to give the visitor the option of checking a box that reads: "I give you and other companies you select permission to send me e-mail about products, services, news, and offers that may be of interest to me."

The more "content" (useful information) on your site, the better. More people will be attracted to your site, and they will spend more time on it. They will also tell others about your site. You can even add a feature that allows your visitors to e-mail your articles to their friends—a good idea since it spreads the word about you and your site.

The model is to drive traffic to your site where you get them to sign up for either your free report or free e-zine. Once they register, you have their e-mail address and can now market to them via e-mail as often as you like at no extra cost.

The bulk of your online leads, sales, and profits will come from repeat e-mail marketing to this "house" e-list of prospects. Therefore your goal is to build a large e-list of qualified prospects as quickly and inexpensively as you can.

There are a number of online marketing options, which can drive traffic to your site:

1. *Google.* The world's largest search engine, Google facilitates 250 million Web searches per day for its users. As an advertiser, you can buy preference in Google's search engine, based on key word, on a cost-per-click basis.

   It could cost you as little as a dime a click or more than a dollar a click, depending on the popularity of the key word you want to buy. If the cost of the key word is 30 cents per click, and 100 people click on your site that day as a result of a Google search on the key word you bought, Google charges you $30. Google lets you put a limit on how much you spend per day, so the cost can fit any budget.

2. *Overture.* Another search engine that lets you buy preferential rating on key words. Overture reaches over 80 percent of active Internet users by displaying your business in search results on leading sites like Yahoo!, MSN, and Alta Vista.

   How do you determine what you can afford to pay? Say your product costs $100 and out of every 100 clicks on your site, you get one sale, for a total of $100. You can afford to pay $1 per hit if breaking even on the initial sale is your goal.

3. *Affiliate marketing.* Find Web sites that cater to the same market you do. Arrange for them to feature your products on their site and in

their e-mails. Online ads, e-mail blurbs, and Web pages talking about your product link to your site where the user can purchase the product under discussion. The affiliate receives a percentage of the sale ranging from 15 percent to 50 percent. To recruit affiliates or make money being an affiliate for other marketers, visit *http://www. affiliatesdirectory.com.*

Amazon.com runs one of the largest affiliate programs, enabling you to feature books on your site that are related to your topic and of interest to your audience; when the user clicks on the book page, he is automatically linked to *www.amazon.com* where he can buy the book online. It's a service for your visitors, and you earn a small commission on each sale.

4. *Co-registration.* In co-registration marketing, the user who visits a Web site is served a pop-up window containing a number of special offers; most frequently these are subscriptions to free e-zines. By arranging to have your e-zine or another offer featured in these co-registration pop-ups, you can capture many new names for your online database at a relatively low cost compared with traditional e-mail marketing.

There are a number of companies that can find such co-registration deals for you. One of these is VentureDirect Online, *www.venturedirect.com.* Another is E-Tactics, *www.e-tactics.com.* Be aware that many people dislike pop-ups and will set their browsers to block them.

5. *Banner ads.* Banner ads have seen a resurgence thanks to the increasing sophistication and popularity of the software application Macromedia® Flash®; in an attempt to recapture the attention of the overloaded Internet user, animation and effects in banners have become more sophisticated and dynamic. Banner ads can work but should be tested conservatively and cautiously, and don't get your hopes of a breakthrough up too high. Banner ads usually supplement other traffic generation methods, and are only occasionally a primary source of unique visits. Exceptions? Of course.

6. *E-mail marketing.* Sending solo promotional e-mails to a rented list of opt-in names is an expensive way to acquire new names. Say you rent a list of 1,000 e-mail names for $200, get a 2 percent click-through, and 10 percent of those sign-up for your e-zine. Your acquisition cost to acquire those two new subscribers is a whopping $100 per name. Business-to-consumer marketers have a better chance of success with careful testing of e-mail marketing, since consumer lists are more reasonably priced than business-to-business names.

7. *Online ads.* While sending a solo e-mail to a company's e-list can run $100 to $400 per thousand, a less expensive option is to run a small online ad in their e-zine. Cost can be as little as $20 to $40 per thousand. The e-zine publisher specifies the format and length of your ad, which are typically 100 words of text with one URL link. The higher up (earlier) your ad appears in the e-zine, the higher the response.

8. *Viral marketing.* At its simplest, viral marketing entails adding a line to your outgoing e-mail marketing messages that says, "Please feel free to forward this e-mail to your friends so they can enjoy this special offer." To work, the e-mail you want the recipient to forward must contain a special offer, either a free offer (typically free content) or a discount on merchandise. According to Bryan Heathman of 24/7 Media, 81 percent of viral e-mail recipients will pass the e-mail on to at least one other person.[1]

Another way to increase traffic is to optimize your site so your rankings are high in search engines. The key is to make your Web site findable by search engines that send out "spiders" and "crawlers" to scour the Web.

Some of the information those spiders and crawlers seek can be found in "meta tags"—words or phrases embedded within the html code used to create Web sites. Before you create your own tags, it's a good idea to take a look at those of others, especially competitors and colleagues.

You can easily open a window and view the meta tags of any Web site you visit. From your browser's tool bar, simply choose the "View" menu. Then click on "Source," and a window will open with html text that you can study. The most important meta tags are found near the top of the page in between codes like this: <head> and </head>. If you are creating your own Web site, depending on which software you use, all you have to do to add meta tags is type the words you've chosen in the appropriate places.

The key meta tags for marketing purposes are Title, Description, and Key words. These tags control what surfers see when your site is listed in the search engines, which means they will help people decide whether to visit your site.

"Title" is what your visitors see at the top of their browser windows when they are visiting your site, as well as what they will see in their bookmark lists. So make sure each page has a title that makes sense to visitors, not just to you. Be descriptive; failure to put strategic key words in the page title is often why Web pages are poorly ranked.

When your Web site comes up in search-engine findings, the meta tag identified as the "description" is often the opening statement people will use to decide whether to access the link. The description should concisely answer the question "What do you do?" For example: "XYZ Design provides client-focused, creative, and effective graphic design, art direction, and project management for marketing communications."

"Key words" are the terms your prospects and visitors will type into the search field when they are looking for talent. So consider the words and phrases they might use to describe your services. Put these key words in your meta tags. You also should include your key words in the first 25 words of your home page.

Here are some additional tips for selecting key words:

- Use plurals for your key words, but avoid excessive repetition.
- Misspell key words if misspellings are common. For example, DI-RECTV, a digital satellite television service, is frequently referred to as Direct TV. If your name is misspelled regularly, include that spelling in your key words as well.
- Don't always use obvious key words. Include phrases that may get fewer searches but higher results.
- Don't let your combined key words exceed 1,000 characters. The fewer key words, the greater impact they will have.

Maintaining a high ranking in search engines is a time-consuming process. And even with due diligence, these efforts may not get you into the top 30 listings, particularly if you're competing in a niche with well-established and better-financed competitors.

The best strategy is to register with the major search engines and free directories, and supply your information every time you find a site that offers a free listing. Have a seven-word description ready to copy and paste as well as ten key words. Devote a certain amount of time each month to maintaining your listings in databases and directories.

I had always thought a good strategy for making your Web site easy to find was choosing a domain name that is clearly descriptive of what you do; e.g., *http://www.divorceonline.com* if you are a divorce lawyer.

But Heather Lloyd-Martin, a copywriter specializing in search engine optimization, disagrees. "This doesn't really work," she says. "Plus, it encourages people to come up with those terrible domains like *www.make-money-online-with-internet-marketing.com*, which are spammy and are usually downgraded in the engines." She also downplays the importance of tags. According to Martin, "The search engines key on the content—so that's what's important. The title is also important for positioning and conversion off the search engine results page."[2]

If you want search engines to find you, avoid Flash or frame pages. "Search engines can find Flash or frame pages, but it's harder for them," says Lloyd-Martin. "Fast has indexed Flash® for a long time now, but it can be horrid for usability, and it won't gain the best rankings. Html is truly the best bet."

The key to success is to try a lot of different tactics in small and inexpensive tests, throw out the ones that don't work, and do more of the ones that are effective.

Another question that comes up is frequency: How often can you send promotional e-mail offers to your house e-list?

Every time you send an e-mail to your house file, a small percentage of the list will "unsubscribe," meaning they ask to be taken off your list. The number of people who unsubscribe is called the "opt-out rate."

Start increasing the frequency of promotional e-mail to your house file. As soon as the opt-out rate spikes upward, stop. You have now reached your maximum frequency.

Many marketers have discovered that the frequency of e-mail promotion to the house file can be much higher than previously thought. Some are successfully e-mailing different offers to their house e-list as often as two times a day or even more.

This is good news for marketers, since the more frequently you can e-mail offers to your list, the more money you can make.

Best of all, the profit on these sales to your house file is extremely high, since the e-mail promotion costs almost nothing. There are no postage or printing costs, and because you already own the names, you avoid the $100 to $400 per thousand charge incurred when renting outside e-lists.

Generating Internet Leads with Online Conversion

How do you make use of free bait pieces to increase online marketing results?

There are several models for doing so, the easiest of which to implement is called the "online conversion model." Online conversion means that you use the bait piece strategy to attract people to your Web site or some other location on the Web. At the location, they can find, read, and download your bait piece. When they do so, you capture their e-mail address, which they are required to give you in order to access your free bait piece.

The "conversion" part of the process refers to what you have to do to convert these people from freebie collectors to paying customers. In a nut-shell, here's an oversimplified version of how online conversion works:

1. You create some free content.
2. You offer people the free content online.
3. When they accept, you then upsell them to your paid subscription product—again, online.

Let's break down each step.

Step 1: Create some free content.

This is the easiest step. Just repackage some of your content as an information premium. The content does not have to be long. Repurposing existing articles works fine for this purpose. So do special reports specifically written for the online conversion campaign. Or the same reports you offer as premiums in postal direct marketing.

The premium is typically offered as a "free special report." It is usually available as a downloadable PDF file. Some marketers prefer to post the report as a multi-page html document on the Web.

Step 2: Offering the free content.

The most common way to offer the free content is by sending an e-mail to your house file. You can also test outside lists.

The e-mail offers the content as a "free special report." To get the free report, the recipient clicks on an embedded URL in the message text.

If the content is a downloadable PDF file, the recipient is brought to a short transaction page. He enters his e-mail address, and is then allowed to download and print the PDF file.

Within the PDF, be sure to include several links to an order page for the product you are promoting. Also add text encouraging the reader to share the document with friends and colleagues.

This is an example of "viral marketing." By encouraging readers to forward the PDF to others, you increase the number of potential customers reading your bait piece. And by including a link to the product landing page, you can actually generate orders even from people who did not originally visit your site to request the bait piece from you but rather, got it from a friend.

If the content is a series of sequential html pages, the recipient is again brought to a short transaction page. He enters his e-mail address, clicks Submit, and is brought to the first page of the micro site where the report is available to read as a posted html document.

Within the html report, put a number of links to a landing page or transaction page for your paid subscription product. Many readers may click on these links and order your paid product while they are in the middle of reading your free bonus report online.

Either way, the reader must give us his e-mail address to read the free report, which is the key to the online conversion method.

There are other methods you can use to generate leads for your online conversion campaign, as shown in Exhibit. 9.1. Some publishers have had great success with postcards. Others have used banners or online ads in e-zines.

Step 3: Converting the leads to paid subscribers.

Now two things have happened. First, we have captured the prospect's e-mail address, so we can market to him as often as we like at virtually no cost.

And second, we know that the prospect is interested in the topic of our content, because he at least requested a free article or report on it.

Since the content was free, we do not know at this point whether he will pay for more content on this topic. But he is a qualified lead in the sense that he is (a) interested in the topic and (b) responds to online marketing.

The next step is to send him a series of e-mails, known as the online conversion series, with the objective of converting him from a requester of free content to a subscriber or buyer of our paid content.

Planning the Online Conversion Series

While the online conversion process is still relatively new, experience so far shows that our online conversion series works best with between three to seven efforts.

Some marketers like every e-mail in the series to attempt to make a sale. That is, they all have a URL the reader can click to reach a page from which the product may be ordered.

Exhibit 9.1: Online Conversion Model

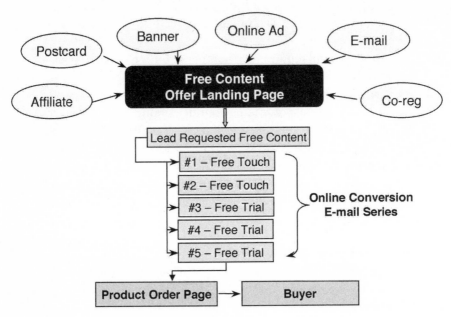

In the online conversion model, you drive visitors to a Web page where they can download a free bait piece, then follow up with a "conversion series"—a sequence of e-mail messages upselling them to a paid product.

Source: Robert Bly

Others like the first two e-mails to be simply goodwill, promoting the value of the information and encouraging the reader to actually read the free content, and in some cases, even giving him more free content. These are called "free touch" e-mails, because they touch the reader without asking him to purchase.

Subsequent e-mails in the series ask for the order; these are called "conversion e-mails." In a six-effort series, the first one or two e-mails might be free touch; the remainder, conversion e-mails.

When the reader clicks on the URL link in your e-mail, he may go either to a landing page or a transaction page. A landing page has a fair amount of descriptive copy about the product you are selling and your offer. It does a strong job of selling the reader on the value of the product. A transaction page has minimal description of the product. It is basically an online order form.

Some marketers always send the e-mail recipient who clicks on the link in the e-mail to the landing page, on the theory that the more sales copy there is, the more sales that will be made.

Other marketers believe that if the conversion e-mail is long and has a lot of sales copy, there is no need to repeat this in a landing page; and so they just send the prospect to a short transaction page.

The best offer for an online conversion effort is a free 30-day trial of the product. If you can set up your site so that the recipient's credit card is not billed until after the 30-day trial period, that's the best choice. Then you are truly offering a free trial or free 30-day subscription.

By comparison, if you charge their credit card as soon as they submit their order, it is not really a free 30-day trial; it is a risk-free 30-day trial. They are paying, but if they cancel within 30 days, they get a refund.

You can experiment with timing, number of efforts, and mix of efforts (free touch and online conversion) in your series. A typical series might go like this:

Day 1—e-mail #1, free touch. Thank the prospect for requesting your free content and reinforce its value.

Day 2—e-mail #2, free touch. Encourage the prospect to read the free content and highlight its value. Point out some especially good ideas, tips, or strategies it contains.

Day 4—e-mail #3, online conversion. Tell the prospect he can get more of the same content by accepting a free 30-day trial to your publication. Sell him on the publication and its value.

Day 7—e-mail #4. Remind the prospect that he can still become an expert on the topic by getting your publication and accepting your free trial offer.

Day 14—e-mail #5. Tell the prospect the free 30-day trial is expiring, resell him on the content you are offering, and urge him to act today. Tell him after that, it's too late.

Write your online conversion series e-mails the same as you would write other online and offline promotions to sell your products. Use the same copy, content, and organization. Get attention in the lead . . . generate interest . . . create desire for your product . . . and ask for the order.

One key difference: In your lead, always acknowledge that they are hearing from you as a follow-up to the free report or article *they asked you* to send them. This has two benefits.

First, they may feel slightly more obligated to read your message; after all, you did give them a gift. And second, if they liked the free content, it automatically puts them in a receptive mood for more of the same—even if they have to pay for it.

Every marketer who wants to generate leads or sales on the Internet should try an online conversion series. Just renting an e-list of opt-in names and asking them to subscribe won't work; people who are online tend not to buy from strangers. But send those same names an offer of a free article or report, and they will take you up on it. After all, what's to lose?

If you have targeted the right audience, and the free content you give is of high quality and value, then enough of the readers will want more of the same that they will be willing to accept a free 30-day trial of your product.

And if your product is of high quality and value, a large percentage of the buyers will not request a refund, and you will have successfully converted free content requesters to paid buyers—your goal in online conversion.

Publish Your Own E-Zine

If you want to market your product or service over the Internet, I strongly urge you to distribute your own e-zine free to your customers and prospects. There are several reasons for doing so.

First, the e-zine allows you to keep in touch with your best customers—indeed, with all your customers—at virtually no cost. Because it's electronic, there's no printing or postage expense.

Second, by offering potential customers a free subscription to your e-zine, you can capture their e-mail address and add them to your online database. You can then market to these prospects, also at no cost.

Whether you are generating leads or direct sales, there are two ways to sell your products and services to your e-zine subscribers. One is to place small online ads in the regular issues of your e-zine. These ads are usually a hundred words or so in length, and include a link to a page on your site where the subscriber can read about and order the product. Or, you can send stand-alone e-mail messages to your subscribers, again promoting a specific product and with a link to your site.

My monthly e-zine, The Direct Response Letter (*www.bly.com*), is not the most successful or widely read e-zine on the planet. Far from it. But marketing results and comments from subscribers tell me my simple formula for creating the e-zine—which, including copy and layout, takes me just an hour or two per issue to complete from start to finish—works.

I want to share the formula with you, so you can produce an effective e-zine of your own, sitting at your computer, without hiring a writer or designer, in just a single morning or afternoon.

When you are dealing with a free e-zine (as opposed to an online newsletter which the reader pays for), people spend just a little time reading it before they delete it with a click of the mouse.

I am convinced that most subscribers do not print out the e-zine, take it home, and curl up with it on the couch later to read. Therefore, I use a quick-reading format designed to allow the subscriber to read my e-zine online right when he opens it.

In this formula, my e-zine always has between five and seven short articles. They are usually just a few paragraphs each. Every article can be read in less than a minute, so it never takes more than seven minutes to read the whole issue, though I doubt most people do. I advise against having just a headline and a one-line description of the article, with a link to the full text of the article. All this clicking forces your subscribers to do a lot of work to read your articles, and that's not what they want.

I do not use html; my e-zine is text only. This way it is easy and inexpensive to produce. I don't "make a production" out of it; it's just straight type. Many readers have told me they like it this way, and that they don't like html e-zines, which look (a) more promotional and less informational and (b) seem to have more to read.

When preparing your text e-zine for distribution, type your copy, in a single column, in Times Roman or another easy-to-read typeface.

The column width should be 60 characters, so you can set your margins at 20 and 80. However, to make sure the lines come out evenly, you must put a hard carriage return by hitting "return" at the end of each line.

There are a variety of services and software programs for distributing your e-zine as well as your e-mail marketing messages to your online database. I use and recommend Bulking Pro (*www.bulkingpro.com*).

My frequency is monthly, though occasionally I do a second issue if there is major news that month.

I am a freelance copywriter. Let me show you specifically how having an e-zine helps bring in business for me.

I recently gave a speech on software direct marketing. It was recorded, so I had audiocassette copies made. In my e-zine, I offered the cassette free to any subscribers involved in software marketing—potential clients for my copywriting services.

Within 24 hours after I distributed the e-zine, we received over 200 inquiries from marketing managers at software companies requesting the tape, many of whom needed copy written for direct mail and e-mail to promote their software.

By comparison, most copywriters tell me that when they send postal direct mail to a list of prospects, they average a 2 percent response. At that rate, they would have to send out 10,000 pieces of mail to generate the 200 leads I got in an hour for free.

That's what an e-zine can do for you. Once you build your subscriber list, you have an incredibly powerful marketing tool and the most valuable asset your business can own: a database of buyers with e-mail addresses and permission to mail to them at any time.

Monitor the ROI from your e-zine carefully, especially with respect to the investment of your time you must make producing it. Is your free e-newsletter delivering a return on investment? If you're spending hours or days a month creating and delivering an e-newsletter whose primary goal is to generate leads or sales, and you're not showing a measurable bump in either, then stop the presses.

How much self-promotion versus useful how-to tips should be in your e-zine? According to Deb Weil, "Best practice guidelines recommended a 70/30 or even 80/20 ratio of content to promotion for e-newsletters."[3]

But if you're giving away too much free content and never "making the ask" for a sale, your readers may not be motivated to buy. Why should they? They've got a good thing going, and they'll enjoy it as long as you'll dish it out.

You might need to tinker with your ratio or experiment with gracefully intertwining a promotion with your content. If they're related, readers will want to learn more.

As for frequency and consistency of publication, it's all in the eye of your reader. For some people, receiving your e-newsletter once a month will seem frequent. For others, that much of the gap between issues means your newsletter will lack a recognizable punch. Better to stick to a consistent schedule, whether it's once a week, twice a month or less often. Bottom line: You'll never make everyone happy.

Copywriter John Forde offers the following tips for writing an engaging e-zine:

- Always remember that your reader is much smarter than you think. Even while educating or informing, never talk down. And never think the readers won't notice when you haven't done your homework.
- Your readers prefer stories to lists of facts. You'll find it a lot easier to hold onto human interest by putting plenty of human interest angles

into the articles you'll write (e.g., marketer Joe Vitale recently ran an article, "How Mark Twain Would Write Online." He could have just listed points. But instead, he gave his lesson a face we could all identify with.)

- Your reader expects profundity. The deeper you can take your reader, the more you can expand his mind, the greater your editor-reader relationship will be, the more he'll recommend your e-zine to friends, and the longer he'll stay active on your mailing list.

- Trust encourages action. Relationships like the ones we've been talking about are built on trust. The more the reader trusts you, the more genuinely he regards your message, and the more likely he is to take the action you recommend.

- Your reader expects imperfection. There's a reason we laugh hardest at comedians who aren't afraid to make fun of themselves. Showing an occasional weakness actually confirms your strength of character. And gives your writing a personal, human appeal.

- Your reader expects emotion. Getting personal means getting emotional. But be careful in two ways. First, realize that even zealots can only go so far. Be passionate about your position, but not crazed. Second, good writers express the full range of emotions over time (fear, greed, anger, desire, vanity, etc.) You can't fake this. But don't suppress it in your e-zine copy either.

- Give both need-to-know and want-to-know information. No question, the most valuable e-zines educate readers. But remember, your e-zine subscribers will want to be entertained as much as they'll want to be informed. Think of it like the difference between the college professor who bores listeners at a cocktail party ... and the master storyteller who builds a circle of guests around him, all leaning in to hear more.

- Reinforce the old, introduce the new. When you're writing an e-zine, it's true you're almost always "preaching to the choir." Which means a lot of your e-zine copy will appeal to the suspicions, opinions, and principles you and your readers already share. But just as much, you have to make sure you introduce, amplify, and illuminate a new direction for your readers to take. By repeating core ideas, you reinforce your reader's good feelings about your e-zine. By saying something new, however, you also provide understanding.[4]

Building Your E-Zine Subscriber List
Using "Safe Lists"

Online marketing expert Deb Weil recently asked me, "How do you know whether an e-zine is successful?"

"An e-zine is successful if it achieves its stated marketing objective," I replied. "Conversely, if you have no written marketing goal for your e-zine, you have no way to determine whether it is worthwhile."

The original goal of *my* e-zine was simply to update clients, prospects, book buyers, seminar attendees, and colleagues about things I was doing that they wanted to know about, such as publication of a new book or availability of a recent speech on audiocassette.

As a result, I kept it deliberately small: between sign-ups on the home page and e-mail addresses added from my database, circulation was about 2,000. And that was fine with me.

But my plans changed, and I suddenly wanted to get a lot more subscribers in a hurry. One reason was that a larger e-list would mean more sales of my books when announced in the e-zine. In fact, my publishers were concerned that with such a small circulation, sales of my books to my e-zine readers would be insignificant.

Also, a larger list would allow me to do cross-promotions with other e-zines, enabling me to reach a wider market for my books and tapes, as well as drive more people to my speaking engagements and Web site.

I called Peter DeCaro, my freelance web master, and gave him the task of adding new e-zine subscribers. To my amazement, within six weeks he had built my e-zine distribution list from 2,000 to more than 60,000 subscribers.

"How did you do it so quickly and inexpensively?" I asked Peter (the entire fee was around $1,000). "Safe lists," he replied.

As Peter explained it to me, the Internet users on what is known as a *safe list* have agreed to provide their e-mail address in exchange for the ability to regularly promote to the list's membership. It is known as a safe list, I suppose, because it is "safe" to send promotional material to these people—they have opted in and agreed to receive it.

Peter has joined numerous safe lists for the purposes of promoting his clients' offers, including me and my free e-zine. You and I can join, too. There's no exclusivity. Some safe lists are free to promote to; others require a fee. But the fee is a tiny fraction of what you'd pay to mail to traditional rented opt-in e-lists, which can run $200 to $400 per thousand.

What works in promotions targeted to safe lists? "Free offers tend to pull well in safe lists," says DeCaro. "So by offering a free report or some other freebie in your promotion, you establish credibility with the safe list sub-scribers and encourage them to investigate the source of the ad—you—further."

Some safe lists permit only text ads; others allow either text or html. Peter says html ads pull better on safe lists.

I asked Peter where one finds safe lists. He recommends several online directories that contain safe list listings, including *www.mailpro-network.com* and *www.101-website-traffic.com*.

Here's how our promotion worked: Instead of sending safe list subscribers directly to *www.bly.com* to simply sign up for the free e-zine right away, we first directed them to a special landing page offering a free bonus report as an extra incentive for subscribing to the e-zine. The copy on this landing page began:

> "For a limited time, you can get a **FREE** copy of my report offering recession-proof business strategies by clicking *here*. Apply these techniques to your own marketing and selling efforts during a recession or a down time, and you will survive—even prosper—while others struggle to get by. . . ."

A link at the bottom allowed the reader to click onto my home page to sign up for the e-zine. An autoresponder automatically fulfilled the subscriber's re-quest for the free report.

Peter suggests using a cgi-based autoresponder as opposed to a pay service. A cgi script is prewritten code that performs the autoresponder function of au-tomatically responding to e-mail requests. A good Web site that reviews differ-ent cgi autoresponder scripts is *www.autoresponder-review.com*. Many cgi scripts can be found on *www.scriptsearch.com*.

At this point you may be thinking that safe lists sound like an Internet scam and that the quality of the names can't be any good. This I don't know yet—it's too early for me to tell. I do know that the unsubscribe rate for safe list-acquired names is many times higher than people who subscribe to my e-zine either because they (a) know me or (b) signed up for it on *www.bly.com*.

What I *do* know is that if you're interested in quantity and not necessarily quality, safe lists can be an effective way to build your e-zine subscriber base in a hurry at very low cost.

10

Measuring and Improving Your Results

According to an October, 2004 study by Patrick Marketing Group, 81 percent of marketers surveyed said accountability had increased in their marketing organizations over the last 24 months—and 59 percent of those surveyed said marketing programs must show a return on investment.[1]

This chapter discusses how to monitor, measure, and analyze results from edu-marketing campaigns. Factors to be measured include: inquiries (raw numbers of leads); cost per lead; cost per order; total sales; conversion rate; brand image and awareness; company reputation; and sales force buy-in:

- *Inquiries*—If you send 1,000 sales letters to your target audience, and 20 people mail back the business reply card requesting your free white paper, your response rate is 2 percent.
- *Cost per lead*—Let's say the printing, postage, production, and mailing list cost to send out those 1,000 letters was $700. Divide $700 by 20, and you get a cost per lead of $35.
- *Cost per order*—Now let's say 2 of those 20 people place an order with your company for the product you are promoting. Divide $700 by 2, and your cost per order is $350.
- *Conversion rate*—The conversion or closing rate is the percentage of inquiries that convert into sales. If you generate 20 leads and get 2 orders, your conversion rate is 10 percent.
- *Total sales*—You generated two orders from the promotion. If they both ordered the same product and it costs $1,000, your total gross sales from the promotion are $2,000.
- *Brand image and awareness, company reputation*—Extremely difficult to

measure. Publishing edu-marketing materials undoubtedly builds awareness of your product and your company, but most marketers judge edu-marketing campaigns by easier-to-measure metrics such as inquiries and sales.

- *Sales force buy-in*—Does the sales force distribute your edu-marketing materials and report that customers find the content useful? Are they able to close at least 10 percent of the sales leads generated by your edu-marketing campaign?

But the most important factor to measure is return on investment (ROI). Quite simply, we want to know that every dollar spent on marketing has returned to us two, three, even four dollars or more in sales.

The only kind of marketing that consistently demonstrates a significant, positive ROI is direct marketing. And as you have seen throughout this book, edu-marketing is simply direct marketing built around the offer of free, valuable information.

Recently, there has been a trend in the advertising world towards direct response. Building brand is of concern to many marketers. But the economic realities of the past few years have caused marketing executives to change the way they are going about it. They have to be better than they used to be, and they have to justify their activities more thoroughly.

"Marketers want to know the actual ROI of each dollar," writes Diane Brady in *BusinessWeek*. "They want to know it often, not just annually. And increasingly they want a view of likely returns on future campaigns."[2]

To do this, they must employ strategies and tactics that produce measurable results. Direct response marketers have always known which programs are showing a direct impact on sales and which are not. Now traditional marketers are using the same techniques to strengthen their programs.

The difference between general advertising and direct response is simple to understand. Direct response ads are designed to generate a response from the target customer. To achieve this, the ad must contain three things:

1. A call to action.
2. An incentive to respond (in edu-marketing, this is our free bait piece).
3. A response mechanism.

The call to action tells your prospect what you want them to do, the incentive that rewards them for the desired behavior, and the response mechanism they can use to reply.

It is a simple formula, but it must be executed properly to work. Simply asking someone to call for "more information" and offering a toll-free number is not enough.

The most successful marketers place primary importance on capturing and qualifying leads at every point of contact. These strategies help them to view marketing spending as an investment, not an expense. That's the reason why market leaders advertise aggressively in difficult times. They understand the importance of strengthening their position and capturing market share when their competition is suffering.

Business-to-business marketers often see their challenges as distinctly different from marketers in other industries. The common claim is that their business is driven by personal relationships and long-standing deals between major sellers and buyers.

Barring major innovation, this would suggest a pretty bleak picture for anyone trying to improve market share. Yet every year, in nearly every industry, market share changes hands.

Good marketing begins with knowing your customers and responding to their wants and need more attentively than your competitors do. You need to understand what activities are really driving your sales. The marketing department must have ways of benchmarking the success of their efforts.

An important part of this is securing feedback, from your advertising and marketing programs. It is different than it used to be. We all remember a time when the reader service cards in trade publications would serve as a barometer for how our spending was paying off. Today, your customers can visit a Web site in less time than it takes them to fill in the reader service card.

You must develop a plan to implement tools and processes that allow you to learn from the actions and words of your customers and prospects. Some information will come directly from the sales force. Other information can be aided by technology. Technology can tell you which ads generate which calls and Web inquiries. Lead-capture technology, such as unique URLs and landing pages customized for specific offers, can build a database of names of callers and Web site visitors.

Online surveys are easy to deploy and can give you access to opinions and feedback that you are currently missing. Outbound telephone lead qualification can improve the quality of the leads that your sales team receives.

The tools at your disposal are better than they have ever been. Some new capabilities have evolved, but the ideas have been employed by good marketers for decades.

At its most basic level, advertising has always been about driving sales.

Although percentage response is the simplest way to measure the performance of a direct mail package, it's not the truest test. What you really want to know is: Was the promotion profitable? Did it make money? Lose money? Break even? So you can analyze not only number of replies received, but also gross sales and net profit generated.

Example: You use a lead-generating sales letter with reply card to generate inquires for a $2,000 business service. Your letter generates a 2 percent response. That's twenty replies per thousand pieces mailed. The cost of mailing the letter is $600 per thousand. To calculate the cost per inquiry, we divide $600 by twenty inquires and get $30 per sales lead.

Let's say 10 percent of twenty prospects buy the service. That's two sales at $2,000 per contact for a gross of $4,000. Your profit per thousand is the $4,000 in gross sales less the $600 per thousand mail cost, or $3,400. To put it another way, you're getting an almost 7:1 return on your investment ($4,000 sales divided by $600 mailing cost). For each $1 spent on direct mail, you make almost $7 in sales.

Another example: Let's say we are selling a $149 software product via mail order. The cost to manufacture and ship the product is $15 per unit. Therefore, the profit is $149 minus $15, or $134 per unit sold. Now, we have to print and mail a direct mail package to get orders. Our cost for mailing is $700 per thousand. To calculate the number of orders needed to break even:

Break even = Mailing cost per thousand divided by profit per order

For our example:

$700 mailing expense divided by $134 profit per order =
Break even on 5.2 orders per thousand pieces mailed

In terms of percentage response this comes to:

5.2 orders divided by 1,000 mailings × 100 = 0.52 percent

Therefore, we break even on the mailing with only 0.52 percent response rate. At a 1 percent response rate, we get $2 in income for every $1 spent on direct mail. At a 2 percent response rate, we quadruple our investment every time we mail 1,000 pieces.

How They Did It

Let's take a look at some real companies that have used the edu-marketing strategy and the results they have achieved:

Case Study: Studebaker-Worthington Leasing's Free Sales Training for Resellers

Studebaker was originally a car company making an automobile of the same name. The production of the Studebaker was short-lived, but the company merged with Worthington and began manufacturing industrial pumps.

Fred Weiss was the senior executive in charge of finance. When Studebaker-Worthington chose to divest itself of its leasing division, Weiss bought it and founded Studebaker-Worthington Leasing as an independent company specializing in financing for office equipment and, later on, for computer systems for businesses.

He had two immediate problems. First, his competitors, the giant leasing companies, had better sources of capital and, because of their volume, could offer lower rates than Studebaker. He could never be the cheapest source of financing or compete with them on price—or he would quickly lose his shirt.

Second, the large leasing companies could afford to have a sales force blanket the country, calling on prospects. As a small start-up, Studebaker-Worthington couldn't.

Weiss decided he could conduct leasing transactions remotely by mail, fax, and phone, eliminating the need for a sales force. He would let people know about his leasing services through direct mail. And he would offset his competitor's advantages—local account reps making personal visits and lower rates—with superior service and faster credit approvals.

But mailing to the millions of businesses that might need a new computer system some day would be cost-prohibitive. There were just too many of them. He had no idea when they would actually need a new computer. And the chances of his mailings reaching users at the precise time they were thinking of buying a new system were miniscule.

Weiss then implemented the channel marketing strategy that made him rich: He decided to target computer resellers rather than end-users. Almost all computer sales at the time (this was before Dell and Compaq), especially for systems integrating hardware and software, were made by resellers. And they were easy to reach by mail: CMP, a major trade magazine publisher, had a list of over 100,000 computer resellers.

Weiss still had no way of knowing when a reseller had a sale pending—although, since resellers were in the computer business, their volume of transactions would be greater, and so would the likelihood of them having a pending sale versus an end user.

Renting mailing lists gets expensive. Weiss knew that once he got a reseller on CMP's list to call him, he could capture the name for his database and "own" it as part of his house file. Mailing subsequent promotions to the house file is not only cheaper, but almost always generates a higher response than mailings to cold lists.

But how could Weiss generate a response not just from resellers who had a pending sale and needed a quote on a lease, but also from resellers who might use his financing services some day but not today?

Weiss decided to take the white paper marketing approach. He knew from his talks with computer resellers that, while they were good at programming and systems integration, many lacked organizational, sales, marketing, financial, and other basic business skills.

Fred decided to establish Studebaker-Worthington as a trusted advisor to computer resellers by providing them with useful sales training and other tools to help them run their businesses more profitably. He figured they would be grateful and would favor his company over other leasing firms when they needed to help a buyer get financing.

Also, as an experienced leasing executive, Weiss knew that leasing was a powerful strategy for closing sales for big-ticket items, such as computer systems. After all, what sounds more affordable to you—$10,000 or $362 a month? With leasing, you can quote the price as a low monthly payment instead of a big up-front purchase price, avoiding "sticker shock."

But most resellers never used leasing proactively to close sales. They only offered leasing when the customer asked for it. If Weiss could teach resellers to use leasing to close more and bigger sales, more often, he would create an increased demand for his company's leasing programs.

Weiss outsourced with a writer to create a short white paper, published in booklet form, "10 Sales Tips for Resellers." It presented, in a clear and simple fashion, real and valuable sales training to help resellers close more sales. Of the ten sales tips, two or three subtly promote leasing, by showing the reseller how to use leasing to overcome sales objections.

For instance, if the customer is afraid the system he is buying will be obsolete in a few years, the reseller can overcome that fear by offering a short-term lease. The reseller is instructed in the booklet to say to the customer, "At the end of the lease, you can trade in your old system for a more modern one. So your system never becomes obsolete."

Weiss sent out letters to CMP's reseller list telling the resellers about his services and offering the free booklet. Within about a year, several thousand resellers had requested the white paper, and Studebaker's transaction volume soared.

Based on the success of "10 Sales Tips for Resellers," Studebaker put out a steady stream of sales training materials and business tools, available free to resellers. These included booklets of sales tips, a sales video, another sales training program (this one on audiocassette; I wrote and recorded it for them), even free sales software—a contact manager for organizing leads and following up with prospects.

Today Studebaker is one of the most successful and profitable companies in the computer leasing industry, serving thousands of resellers nationwide. Fred Weiss recently retired to Florida a multi-millionaire, and his partner, Ken Paston, now runs the business. And he continues the consultative marketing program started by Weiss years ago, selling resellers by being their partner in business success.

Case Study: *Fortune* Magazine and Multiple Premiums

One approach you may want to test is offering multiple bait pieces in a single promotion. In his book *Secrets of Successful Direct Mail* (NTC, 1989), Dick Benson says, "Two premiums are frequently better than one."

A successful direct mail package selling a subscription to *Fortune*[3] offered three premiums. *Fortune Fax*, the primary premium, is a combination address book and daily planner and includes a credit-card size calculator. A second premium, *Fortune Financial Planner*, consists of a series of worksheets the subscriber can use to calculate cash flow, taxes, and net worth. *Investor's Guide*, the third premium, is a special issue of the magazine.

"We use multiple premiums to create an additional incentive to buy and also for display purposes," explains *Fortune* circulation director Ken Godshall. "If you have multiple premiums, the direct mail subscription agents give you more promotion space in their packages. So a second premium helps us get a greater 'share of mind.'"[4]

New subscribers who order through subscription agents or in response to

Fortune's TV commercials receive *Fortune Fax* and *Investor's Guide* but not *Financial Planner*.

Premiums for *Fortune* and other Time, Inc. magazines are purchased by a separate premium department at the company. Most items come from Hong Kong. By centralizing premium purchasing, Time enjoys substantial volume discounts. Godshall says the cost is approximately $4–$5 for *Fortune Fax* and less than $1 for *Financial Planner*.

"The *Fax* is an important part of our offer." Godshall says, "Our experience is that there are a lot of potential subscribers who need just a little extra something to make them subscribe. These relatively inexpensive premiums related to business are effective. They increase trial subscriptions, and we find we can sell more efficiently with a premium than without one."

Adds Godshall, "The *Fortune Fax* and *Financial Planner*, like most of the premiums we have used in the past [including desk items and financial software], relate to the interests of our target reader. We want *Fortune*-compatible readers—not people ordering just to get a free gift."

Like many publications, *Fortune* has increased its use of premiums over the past several years, and advertisers have occasionally expressed concern about the quality of subscribers generated through premium offers. Research, however, shows no evidence of a decline in the typical *Fortune* reader.

"We've kept close track of our subscriber quality over the years to make sure premiums haven't affected it, and basically, we don't think they have," says Godshall. "Median age has not changed that much; personal and household income have increased smartly in line with our competition; the percentage of managers reading *Fortune* has increased slightly; and the level of education is virtually the same as it was several years ago when we used premiums less extensively. Subscriber quality has not declined as a result of using premiums."

Market research designed to measure reader involvement also indicates no adverse effects from premium usage. According to Godshall, the number of hours readers spend with each issue has remained the same, while the number of times each issue is picked up and the percentage of subscribers who claim to have read three of the last four issues has increased slightly.

Most important, readers responding to *Fortune* surveys say that premiums are way down on the list of reasons they subscribe. Number one on the list is keeping up with business news, number two is to get information they can use on the job, and number three is that *Fortune* is enjoyable to read. Getting a premium was number 12 out of a possible 16 reasons featured in the research survey. "Apparently, the premium doesn't dominate the reasons they decide to buy," says Godshall.

No matter how successful the *Fortune Fax* may be, Godshall plans to continue testing premiums. The reason: after a major campaign or two, he says, the premium gradually becomes less effective as more of the target audience buys the magazine and gets the item. He estimates that the average *Fortune* premium will start to fatigue after one or two years of use. The magazine is currently testing an information premium that consists of three booklets containing reprints of past articles.

Although premiums have been a part of circulation promotion for more than a decade, Godshall notes that their use has grown dramatically during the past five years. He adds, however, that premiums have probably peaked and that magazines will use them on a more moderate basis in the future. Alternatives to premiums, he notes, include deep-discount offers, risk-free trial issues, short-term subscription offers, and sweepstakes.

"We all need some incentive to get the consumer to act," Godshall observes, "and every publication has one or more of these techniques in its arsenal of direct response marketing weapons."

Case Study: *Money's* Starter Kit

"Our current premium, which is a proven winner, consists of reprints of editorial material that is virtually timeless and of key interest to our readers," says Diane Potter, circulation director of *Money* magazine. "We offer a set of 'how-to' booklets that give subscribers a head start on getting a hold on their finances, and this is a natural extension of our magazine."[5]

The premium, called *The Financial Advisor*, is made up of three special reports: *How to Invest and Win*, *How to Retire Worry-Free*, and *How to Save on Taxes*. Each booklet contains 16 pages of reprinted articles from past issues, and the booklets are updated every six months to keep the information and topics timely.

Potter has conducted extensive premium testing and finds that for *Money*, the editorial premium works best. Merchandise premiums—including a calculator—were less successful than the reprints, and books performed even more poorly. In one split test on insert cards, Potter tested the *Financial Advisor* against an offer with no premium.

"The premium significantly boosted response and paid for itself," she observes. The current control mailing combines the *Financial Advisor* premium offer with a sweepstakes.

Based on test results, *Money* will continue to offer reprinted editorial as its premium. "Premiums do work," says Potter. "They can add value to a subscription offer and boost response. Premiums don't change who wants your magazine, but they do serve to convince fence-sitters—prospects who are undecided—to give you a try." While other circulation directors complain of depressed response rate, Potter says *Money* has never been stronger in terms of response or subscriber base.

Money's renewal efforts are a mix of premium and non-premium offers. The renewal premiums tend to be financial worksheets the reader can use to calculate net worth or manage tax payments.

"We find we can renew a premium-induced subscriber without a premium," says Potter, "but, as in any business, if you find something that brings in even more business and pays for itself, why not use it? Our readers are pleased with what the magazine offers, so if they can get more of it in a premium, they will."

Because the *Financial Advisor* is an editorial premium, *Money's* advertising department is not concerned about the effect of a premium offer on subscriber quality. "The advertising department views the premium as simply another statement from the consumer that our editorial is valuable," says Potter, adding that the *Financial Advisor* can, in a sense, be viewed as a "starter kit" for new subscribers. "Offering article reprints is a way of saying to the new subscriber, 'You've missed a lot of great editorial in the past; now you can catch up with it,'" she notes.

Another advantage of the editorial approach is low cost. "Editorial premiums are certainly on the low end of the price scale," says Potter. "We look for a premium to pay for itself—to break even or better—and the *Financial Advisor* does."

Interestingly, Potter does not necessarily recommend editorial premiums for every publication. "Each magazine must know its consumers and what's right for them," she observes. "The key is understanding your reader and the benefits your magazine provides to him or her—and speaking to those benefits when you sell."

Case Study: Steve McIntyre, The MFA Group[6]

It's not that he's financially independent (though he is doing very nicely, thank you) but that he doesn't consider what he does for a living as "work." He really loves what he does, and it shows in his products, services, and Web sites, and indeed, he owes a great deal of his success to the Internet.

The MFA Group is growing at such a rate that by the time you get to read this, the numbers will be well out of date, but here's the story at the time of this writing.

Steve grew up in the public accounting profession in the UK, joining a small firm straight from school in January 1980 as the office junior. After qualifying in 1983, he joined a national firm, and got a taste of marketing accounting services, which he really fell in love with.

From there, he became a partner in a firm for a number of years and then spent two years as a sole practitioner before selling out to a local competitor who made him an offer "too good to pass by."

At that point he turned to the marketing of accounting services, first as the director of marketing for a well known UK accounting firm, and in 1997 he went freelance.

He moved to Canada in 1998 and set up *www.marketingforAccounts. com* as a sideline income while working in the executive recruiting business. In 2002 he set up *www.awesomeclientservice.com* and in 2003 he left his $140,000-a-year job as vice president of a search firm to do his own thing full time.

But it was edu-marketing that helped Steve build his business. He wrote a few e-books about marketing for accounting firms and posted them on his site in 2000, and they started selling.

At first he used Armand Morin's e-book creator software but later upgraded and now produces everything as PDF files. He also used e-cover generator to create great looking cover images for his e-books.

His marketing site offered a free marketing newsletter and the first issue went out in November 2001, to just eight people.

Next, Steve started an e-marketing campaign, by going to institute Web sites and mailing CPAs from any listing he could find there. He also added them to his database.

Today he has over 5,000 opt-in subscribers to his free newsletter, which recently started its third year, and has a total of 16 products for sale through his credit card processor, clickbank, with numerous affiliates signed up either directly via clickbank (Steve doesn't get to know these affiliates) and some as franchisees (who Steve gets to know very well).

At the time of this writing an Australian office is being set up with a long time client and newsletter subscriber. Steve says his secret to marketing on the Net is focus. He only deals with public accounting firms, and there are easy to find lists of these companies if you know where to look and what to look for.

He also got his products carried by *www.accountingweb.com*—a portal for CPAs with around 50,000 members that gives him a great deal of credibility in his market.

Another neat idea is to visit industry chat boards and answer any marketing questions posted. Steve has acquired a large number of subscribers that way, many of whom turn into customers.

He also advertises now in *CA Magazine*, but his big breakthrough for other services came when he approached a national financial and accounting newspaper to write a human resources column for them.

Eighteen months later and he has 26 published articles to his name—and growing every month—all of which are posted on his Web site.

A self-taught Dreamweaver® and Fireworks® (software applications for building Web sites and Web graphics) expert, Steve built his own Web sites and has revised each one many times in the last couple of years to improve the look and feel of the sites and make them easier for visitors to use.

Last year he generated over $500,000 in revenues working from his home-based office, with little or no overhead and all the flexibility that working from home affords.

Case Study: Commercial Property Services

Commercial Property Services (CPS) is a real estate firm in Florida specializing in both commercial property as well as obtaining property tax rebates for clients.

President Sheila Anderson comments, "Our monthly e-mail to clients and contacts encourages responses. We often get questions back, by e-mail, can provide answers quickly, and it's a convenient way to stay in touch.

We use our monthly e-mails to announce what's been added to our Web site, with headings linked to different sections, where copy is posted. And, periodically, when a new article is added to our site, we enter that address on search engines permitting more than one listing. Takes only minutes to do it but spreads word about our company all over the world.

Even if we don't need more business, keeping our company's identity 'at the forefront' gives us sustainable demand, and that leads to referrals and reputation. We also mail overprints of articles, printed on card stock, to places and people who might be interested in what we had to say—also building reputation related to our business.

For an hour one day each month, we maintain a generic program, and then use direct marketing to reach our target audience. One fuels the other.[7]

CPS mails three postcards timed to an annual legal deadline related to their professional services. The postcards vary, using direct and informative descriptions of what the process is about. A free booklet is offered, interpreting the governing law.

An example of the first postcard can be seen in Exhibit 10.1.

Exhibit 10.1: CPS Post Card—Initial Mailing

PROPERTY TAX BILLING NOTICE for owners and tenants of land, buildings, and business, furniture, fixtures, and equipment in FLORIDA.

On January 1st, Government Assessors set taxable valuations for this calendar year, based on "mass appraisal techniques" using general assumptions about many properties at the same time. Public information indicates taxable values often are incorrect, raising questions about most tax rolls. To insure your individual taxes are set at constitutionally mandated "just value" and are accurate, owners and tenants must verify these mass taxable calculations and document January lst conditions of real estate and tangible investment property. For a FREE Booklet (with absolutely no obligation) on important property tax legislation, updates on the tax reduction process, and the necessary form, return this card to:

Property Tax Reduction Department
COMMERCIAL PROPERTY SERVICES, INC., Realtors
6595 Doral Boulevard, Suite 304-1 - Virginia Gardens, FL 33166
MAIL THIS CARD IMMEDIATELY FOR FREE BOOKLET AND INFORMATION, OR contact CPS now. Call 305-871-0017.
Visit Web site at *www.floridapropertytaxappeals.com*

Reproduced with the permission of CPS.

Case Study: Hewlett-Packard Oscilloscopes

Hewlett-Packard's (H-P) edu-marketing campaign for its line of oscilloscopes generated an 18.2 percent lead-to-contact ratio and a 5.6 percent lead-to-dial ratio.

Although 75.1 percent of the responses were from a trade advertisement offering a free white paper, a direct mail piece generated a larger "lead-to-inquiry" ratio (8 percent for the direct mail versus 3 percent for the magazine ad).

The direct mail piece, a tri-fold self mailer, had this headline: "Some engineers would give anything for practical, easy-to-use measurement advice. We'll give it to you for free."

There were five boxes on the tear-off reply card for the reader to check to request the following items:

1. Free "Scope Hints" booklet.
2. Competitive specs from leading manufacturers.
3. "10 Steps to Selecting the Right Oscilloscope" buyer's guide.
4. A phone call about an evaluation.
5. A phone call from an H-P applications engineer.

Of the leads generated, analysis showed that the customers who only checked the first box on the reply card turned into 15 percent of the leads.

"When the project originally started, we decided not to call on these customers because they were categorized as 'cold' inquiries," said an H-P marketing manager. "However, a study was put into place to have Hancock Information Group follow-up on these inquiries. As it turns out, it looks like these customers should not be neglected in upcoming projects as 15 percent of them were in the purchasing mode."[8]

In addition to calling these customers, priority was placed on calling back those customers who marked both box two and three on their BRC. The "Competitive Comparisons" and "10 Steps to Selecting the Right Oscilloscope" booklets were good indicators that customers were actively looking to purchase a scope. Further analysis also suggested that priority should be placed on those inquiries that are geographically located in the Northeast with subsequent follow-up in the West, Midwest, and Southeast.

For the number of inquiries received, approximately 25 percent of the contacts did not give their phone numbers and limited resources hindered attempts to locate phone numbers for these customers. Another 20 percent of the inquiries had either bad information (bad phone numbers, no names, customer no longer with company, etc.) or were international customers (H-P was following up with U.S. customers only).

Lastly, approximately 10 percent of the inquiries were duplicates (i.e., customers who responded to more than one ad). Although H-P had a high percentage of inquiries that could not be followed up on, this project was still considered a high volume project. Due to the high volume of inquiries received, it was not feasible to make more than one attempt to reach each customer.

Leads were forwarded to the appropriate inside sales engineer. If deemed necessary by the inside sales engineer, the lead was passed along to the outside field engineer (FE).

When the lead was forwarded to the outside FE, there was often a breakdown in the closed loop marketing process where status on the lead was not fed back. There was also a problem with forwarding leads that did not have an immediate time frame.

Because the inside sales team was booked to capacity, the leads that did not have an immediate time frame were often forwarded to be outside FE, increasing the probability that H-P's marketing department would not know the final status of the lead.

Case Study: Canon® Workstation

The target audience for this campaign was 4,300 users of the NeXTSTEP™ operating system. Chris Marlowe, the copywriter who promoted the mailing pieces, comments, "These would be excellent targets for the purchase of the new Canon® object station since the workstation was built to optimize the NeXT™ system."[9]

"We had an interesting situation. People who had bought into NeXT's computing system—both their hardware and software—felt left high and dry when NeXT™stopped making its workstations. So Canon® decided to create a workstation that looked and felt just like the old NeXT™ models—a workstation also designed specifically to enhance the latest version of NeXT™ software."

In fact, this was the key selling point. Introduction of the Canon® workstation would not only help NeXT™ retain its customer base for its software—

they had been jumping ship to other systems—but of course, it was an extremely fertile market for Canon®, who could sell them the hardware they were desperately needing.

The objective was to generate 1,000 leads for the Canon® object.station. The budget was a modest $16,000. "With a budget like this, all we could reasonably produce was a self-mailer—not exactly the vehicle of choice for high response," says Chris. "Nevertheless the challenge was ours, so we rolled up our sleeves and went to work.

Cornered into using a self-mailer format, where we couldn't hope for more than a measly 1 percent response, we decided to put all of our eggs in one basket—the offer basket. If we could come up with one hell of an offer . . . well, that might save the day.

Having recently tested CD offers in packages for other high-tech clients, we knew that right now, CDs were hot, and the right CD could really pull response. So we looked and looked for just the right CD.

Finally we hit pay dirt, with a CD made specifically for the NeXTSTEP™operating system! *The Fatted Calf CD* contained over 350 utilities, applications, and games. Its value was $30, and it was both exciting and utilitarian. With this CD, we had a chance to pull high numbers.

The self-mailer is supremely simple, yet it stood out against the backdrop of other mail with its oversize format and the heavy use of black. Inside, we capitalized on one of the most differentiating attributes of NeXT's hardware: their computers used to be black.

Showing that the Canon® object.station was black would soothe the anxieties of NeXTSTEP™ users, who would feel a mother's relief 'at finding her lost child.' But of course, our big advantage was the offer, and it didn't disappoint us! We got a 12 percent response off this little thing. Sales were $900,000, generating an incredible 5,455 percent ROI.

To sum up the metrics for this edu-marketing campaign:

Budget: $16,000
Format: Postcard
Quantity mailed: 4,300
Response rate: 12%
Number of leads generated: 516
Cost per response: $21.88
Conversion rate: 20%

Case Study:
Tektronix Free Bright Ideas Book

Oregon technology company Tektronix, Inc., had been getting less than 1 percent response from its self-mailers promoting its color printers, so they came to Rosen/ Brown Direct in Portland, Oregon, to create a more successful mailing program.

"When Tektronix first came to us it had been pulling anemic .50 to .75 percent response rates with self-mailer formats," says one of the agency's writers. "In early testing, we discovered that the biggest obstacle confronting Tektronix was the sophisticated corporate mailroom. Stuff just wasn't getting to the prospect. Thus our most important goal for Tektronix is discovering a foolproof strategy for tip-toeing through the mailroom, yet landing with a thud in our prospect's in-box."[10]

After doing some research, the agency decided to go oversized (9" × 12") and 4-color to impart a feeling of importance. The agency conducted a message test between two concepts as well. The main selling point was that having a color printer would allow you to make superior presentations.

Package # 1 took a fear-based approach, and showed a well-dressed professional behind bars. The headline was WANTED—FOR KILLING A GREAT IDEA WITH A BORING PRESENTATION. A full-color transparency was enclosed in this package.

Package #2 took a positive approach. The visual showed a professional "climbing the ladder of success." The headline was LADDER ENCLOSED. A unique involvement device was enclosed, a die-cut "corporate ladder" the prospect could climb with die-cut paper dolls. Each week that they used color in their presentations, they could climb one rung; making it to the top would mean more efficient work, which could earn them a promotion.

The copy for Package #2 painted pictures of career advancement via the use of Tektronix color presentation materials. Like the WANTED package, a sample color transparency was enclosed. (See Exhibit 10.2 for a sample information request sheet from Package #2.)

Package #1 outperformed Package #2, pulling a 10.56 percent response rate. Package #2 was also successful, generating a 6.73 percent response. In both packages, the offer was a free "Guide to Selecting a Color Printer." It continued to pull well over numerous mailings, including self mailers.

The objective of offering the bait piece was to get professionals who make internal and external presentations to request additional information on the company's line of color printers. Tektronix's sales force would then follow up the hottest leads, the "A" leads; the "B" and "C" leads went into a database for future use.

Case Study: The Million-Dollar Pool Builder

Hal Slater is the producer of the Millionaire Pool Builder program, details of which are at *http://www.upxel.com*. He is a builder of Web sites specifically for home improvement contractors. "One of the unique features of the sites we build is the inclusion of a form to capture lead information with the offer of a free Yardscape Design Guide (see Exhibit 10.3) in PDF format," says Hal.[11]

"On *http://millionaire.upxel.com/clientlist.php* you will find links to a number of our clients using this system.

"The first sites we did, like Atlantis Pools, get 20 to 25 design guide requests per month during the high season (spring and early summer) and five to six requests per month in the off-season.

"Approximately 80 to 85 percent of the entries are complete even though we have no required fields. Most builders are too busy to call the requesters, but the autoresponder seems to drive a few prospects to call the builders."

Case Study: Ghostwriting Articles for Trade Journals

According to a study by Siegel & Gale, trade articles enjoy the highest credibility ratings. In fact, articles top the list over all other information sources, including staff written stories in the *Wall Street Journal*, *BusinessWeek*, and *Newsweek*.

Articles penned by engineers, describing how they solve a customer's problem, generate trustworthiness. They're powerful endorsements, and the result is influence that can bring more business to an engineer's company.

Because readership in a single trade publication ranges from 50,000 to half a million, the potential to favorably sway thought is enormous. Engineer

Exhibit 10.2: Information Request Form

FREE COLOR PRINTER COLOR BOOK
Information   Request Form

Climb the ladder faster and stay ahead of the pack in the quick-to-change world of business graphics with *Bright Ideas: A Guide to Color Printers for Business Graphics.*

Bright Ideas is an informative guide that shows you how to harness the considerable power of color to create the most effective reports, transparencies, and other presentation materials. You'll also learn about:

- Use of Overhead Transparencies vs 35mm Slides
- Presentation Style for Audience Type
- Today's Color Output Technologies

Yours FREE! Value $9.95.
An exclusive offering
of Tektronix, Inc.

Detach Here

☐ **YES!** I want to learn more about the Tektronix line of Top-Rated Color Printers so I can get up the Corporate Ladder faster. Please rush me additional information along with my FREE Phaser 200e sample color transparency and my FREE copy of: *Bright Ideas: A Guide to Color Printers for Business Graphics.* (Offer expires December 31, 1993.)

MINI-COLOR PRINTER SURVEY
Please circle the letter of the answer that best applies.
To receive your FREE guide and transparency, all questions must be answered. Thank you.

1. What is your current desktop computing environment:
   a. PC   b. Mac   c. Workstation

2. Are you planning on purchasing a color printer in:
   a. 0-3 mos.   b. 3-6 mos.   c. Longer than 6 mos./not sure
   d. No purchase plans, but please send me a copy of *Bright Ideas; A Guide to Color Printers for Business Graphics.*

3. Have funds been budgeted for the purchase of a color printer?
   a. Funds currently available   b. Funds not yet allocated
   c. Gathering information for budgeting   d. Not sure

   If funds are not yet available, when does the next budget period begin?_____

4. What is your involvement in this purchase decision:
   a. Recommend or specify purchase
   b. Influence decision   c. Approve purchase
   d. Have no involvement

5. Please write your daytime phone number:
   (_____) _____ Ext. _____

6. Name/Address:

MAIL, FAX or PHONE YOUR REQUEST TODAY
MAIL: Fill out this form, fold and mail in the enclosed envelope.   **FAX:** Fill out this form and fax to (503) 682-2980.
PHONE: Just call 1-800-835-6100.

Tektronix

Reproduced with permission, courtesy Xerox Corp.

A Homeowner's Guide

Yardscape Design

Gazebos and Patio Covers

Pools and Spas

Outdoor Cook Centers

Soil and Plants

Elevations and Grading
Drainage and Irrigation

Patios and Walks
Fencing and Lighting

Pool builders give away this "Pools and Spas" design guide to attract potential customers who may want a new pool built.

Reproduced with permission. Copyright 2003 ACT San Diego, CA 92164-4671

Jennifer Borkovich notes how a published article about her work at Coding Products recently secured new contracts. She says, "Another company had end users completely locked up. Before the story ran, those users didn't know we even existed. We gained ten new clients—a very significant number in this small market."[12]

For engineers, the payback from publishing a case study article can be significant: job security, recognition, promotions, and even raises. For example, co-principles Pat Whitcomb and Mark Anderson of Stat-Ease, Inc. say, "Years ago, we wrote up ideas on process monitoring and control. They developed into an article published by *Chemical Engineering Progress*.

"It got picked up by the home office of Henkel in Düsseldorf and reprinted with other articles published by Henkel scientists worldwide. That gave us valuable visibility within this multinational corporation, which led to promotions and higher salaries."[13] And after Mary Kay Inc.'s Renee Wickham had a trade publication article appear that featured her work, the recognition helped her career. She explains, "I was promoted to Director of Quality Assurance, and the article played a big part."[14]

Appendix A: Resources

Content Sources

Federal Citizen Information Center
Pueblo, Colorado
http://www.pueblo.gsa.gov/
Reports and booklets on consumer topics, most of which are published by the U.S. Government Printing Office (GPO) and are not copyright protected, which means you are free to reprint and distribute them, as long as you credit the GPO as the source.

Insurance Media Consultants
1600 Bedford Highway, #100-114
Bedford, Nova Scotia, Canada B4A 1E8
http://www.insurancenewsletters.com
Prewritten newsletters and articles for insurance marketers.

Vendors

You may want to hire vendors—copywriters, proofreaders, graphic designers, Web designers, e-zine distribution specialists—to handle various aspects of your marketing programs. We continually update our list of recommended vendors. Simply go to the Web site *www.bly.com* and click on Vendors.

Web Sites

www.bitpipe.com
Online archive of IT-related white papers.

www.bettermanagement.com/default.aspx
White papers on business and IT strategy and management.

http://itpapers.techrepublic.com/
Another Web site with IT white papers.

www.cooperresearchassociates.com
Cooper Research Associates (CRA) specializes in writing white papers for IT and other technology clients.

www.itpapers.com
Largest collection of technical white papers on the Internet.

www.ezine-universe.com
Directory of e-zines searchable by topic.

www.printingforless.com
Printer specializing in promotional newsletters.

www.sprintgraphics.com/website/index.cfm
Printer specializing in booklets.

Appendix B: Model Documents

Sample Press Release

FROM: Unique Truck Equipment, P.O. Box 8798, Grand Rapids, MI 49518
CONTACT: Dick Stillwell, phone 1-800-777-4855

For immediate release

New FREE expanded 40-page Truck Safety and Maintenance Products Buyer's Guide Available from Unique Truck Equipment

Unique Truck Equipment, a supplier of specialty truck products to fleet managers nationwide for over half a decade, has just released the new edition of its quarterly publication, the *Unique Truck Safety and Maintenance Products Buyer's Guide.*

A $5 value, the new buyer's guide is available free of charge to professionals in trucking and transportation—drivers, mechanics, managers, owners, and purchasing agents.

The expanded 40-page guide features specialty products designed to help fleets increase productivity, reduce maintenance costs, minimize down-time, and maximize worker and driver safety.

Products featured range from the Tiger Stud Installer, which enables mechanics to install 10 studs in under 30 minutes without taking the hub off . . . to the Back Buddy, a patented device that prevents back injuries when servicing heavy duty drums. Other items include yoke pullers, slack adjuster pullers, bolt-on steps, dollies, tire inflators, transmission jacks, torque sticks, oil-drain systems, organizing systems, safety training videos, and more.

One added bonus: According to Dick Stillwell, president of Unique Truck Equipment, competitive pricing is guaranteed. "If you ever find one of our products advertised at a lower price, we'll match it for up to 30 days after your purchase. That way, you always get a competitive price on every product you buy from us," says Stillwell. All purchases come with a 30-day money-back guarantee of satisfaction.

For a free copy of the *Unique Truck Safety and Maintenance Products Buyer's Guide,* contact Unique Truck Equipment, P.O. Box 8798, Grand Rapids, MI 49518, phone 800-777-4855, fax 616-245-4918.

Sample Lead-Generating Sales Letter

Dear IT Professional:

It's ironic.

You were hired because you're an expert in IT . . . a subject about which many of your company's senior executives are almost completely ignorant.

Yet you can't implement any significant IT solution without running it by them, explaining it to them, convincing them that it's the right thing to do, and getting their approval to go ahead with it.

Well, if you've ever had a great IT initiative killed by a blockhead non-techie who just didn't "get" what you were talking about, I have some good news for you:

Now you can get even the most stubborn and argumentative senior executives to support your IT initiatives . . . and give you the resources you need to implement them . . .

. . . with *Influencing Others: How to Effectively Sell Your Ideas*—a new FREE CD-ROM learning system from the ABC Group.

In this informative CD workshop, you will discover:

- 10 ways to transform any business customer from an *adversary* into an *ally*.
- The only 2 things you'll ever need to "sell" your ideas to senior management.
- The 4 dimensions of behavior . . . and how to control each—no matter what the situation.

Since 1981, the ABC Group has helped more than 150,000 IT professionals dramatically improve their interpersonal skills . . . and their relationships with their business clients. Now, we want to help you do the same.

For your FREE copy of *Influencing Others* on CD . . . and a free information kit on ABC Group's interpersonal skills workshops for IT professionals . . . just complete and mail the enclosed reply card today.

Or, call me now at (XXX) XXX-XXXX or visit [URL]. There's no cost or obligation of any kind.

Sincerely,

John Smith, Vice President

P.S. Our clients include AstraZeneca, Avon, Blue Cross, Coca-Cola, Dell, Disney, Fidelity, John Hancock, Kraft, 800-Flowers, and hundreds of other organizations, large and small.

Sample Query Letter

John Koten, Editor
Inc.
375 Lexington Avenue
New York, NY 10017

Dear Mr. Koten:

My small company, Center for Technical Communication (CTC), has a marketing director, sales manager, office manager, controller, bookkeeper, shipping manager, and administrative assistant. Yet we don't have a single employee on the payroll.

How is this possible? Outsourcing. All of these functions are performed by independent contractors. Once a strategy embraced mainly by a downsized corporate America, outsourcing is now being used by small businesses of all types—from accounting firms to petting zoos.

I'd like to write an article for Inc., "7 Smart Secrets of Savvy Small Business Outsourcing," on how small businesses can use outsourcing to increase their ability to serve customers without adding staff or overhead. Topics include:

* types of services that can be outsourced (and what should not be)
* how to determine whether to outsource a particular function or task
* where to find—and how to select—reputable third-party service firms for outsourcing
* negotiating contracts, fees, and payment arrangements
* how outsourcing can improve business results while reducing capital investment and operating costs
* equipment and technology that can make outsourcing more efficient
* examples of small businesses that have successfully outsourced functions previously handled in-house
* moving toward the concept of a "virtual business"—90% outsourcing, with all business partners connected via the Internet
* a sidebar of major national outsourcing firms with contact information and services offered.

By way of introduction, I am the author of more than 100 magazine articles and 50 books including *101 Ways to Make Every Second Count* (Career Press). My articles have appeared in *Cosmopolitan*, *Amtrak Express*, and *New Jersey Monthly*.

I can have this article on your desk in 3 to 4 weeks. Shall I proceed as outlined?

Sincerely,

Bob Bly

Notes

Introduction

1. Weil, Deb, "White Papers: B2B Email Marketing's Best Friend," *ClickZ Today*, 8/8/01. © WordBiz.com, Inc.
2. Stelzner, Michael, "How to Write a White Paper" at *http://www.stelzner.com /copy-HowTo-whitepapers.php.*

Chapter 1

1. Pritikin, Robert C., *The Amazing Advertising Business* (New York: Simon & Schuster, 1957), pp. 48–49.
2. Sewell, Howard H., President, Connect Direct, "Lead Recycling: A More Cost-Effective Approach to Marketing for High-Tech Companies," (Connect Direct Inc.: Redwood City, CA, Connect Direct Inc, *http://www.Connectdirect.com*), p. 2.
3. Quote is from e-mail sent to the Author by John Clausen, 12/2/03.
4. Riegel, Nicole, Letter to the Publisher, *Internet Marketing Report*, 11/26/03, p. 7.
5. Copley, Nick, "How to Write High-Impact White Papers," *Software Success*, 3/31/03, pp. 1, 3. © Copyright Softletter 2004. All rights reserved. Reprinted by permission of the publishers. *www.softletter.com.*
6. Ibid.
7. Quote from personal e-mail correspondence to the author from Donny Lowy, 1/13/04.
8. Polish, Joe, "4 Secrets from a Marketing Wizard to Bring in More Business," *Bottom Line Personal*, 5/15/04, p. 7.
9. Dobkin, Jeffrey, "Lessons in Successful Advertising," *PMA Newsletter*, 9/04, p. 31.
10. Coe, John, *The Fundamentals of Business-to-Business Sales and Marketing* (New York: McGraw-Hill: 2000), p. 104.
11. Cited at Starch online: *http://www.ciadvertising.org/studies/student/99_fall /phd/hyogyoo/public_html/starch/references.html*; and D. Starch, An Analysis of Five million Inquiries (Cambridge, MA: The Compiler, Starch 1930).
12. Sewell, Howard H., President, Connect Direct, "Lead Recycling: A More Cost-Effective Approach to Marketing for High-Tech Companies," p. 2.
13. Quote from personal correspondence between with author and a Hewlett-Packard Marketing Manager.
14. Palmer, Parker, *The Active Life* (San Francisco: Jossey-Bass, 1990).

15. Uhlan, Edward, *The Rogue of Publishers Row* (New York: Exposition Press, 1956).
16. Quote from personal correspondence between author and Jamie Whyte, 9/4/04.
17. Hubert Bermont at American Consultants League, *www.americanconsultants league.com*.
18. Parker, Roger, *www.onepagenewsletters.com, RogerCParker@aol.com*, "Education-Based Marketing," *Guerrilla Marketing & Design*, July 2003, *www. gmarketing-design.com, www.onepagenewsletter.com*, or e-mail RogerCParker@ aol.com. Reprinted with permission.
19. Joe Vitale, Interview with Bob Serling for *The Ultimate Guide to Selling Your Services Online*, Copyright © 2004 Joe Vitale and Bob Serling. See also Serling, Bob, *The Ultimate Guide to Selling Professional Services Online*, Consulting Success, Copyright © 2004 Bob Serling.
20. Miller, Elissa, Senior Consultant, "The Steak Behind the Sizzle: Effective Marketing Using White Papers," *The Business-to-Business Marketer*, March 2003, pp. 4–5. Reprinted with permission © 2003 by Elissa Miller and Hoffman Marketing Communications, Inc., *www.hoffmanmarcom.com*.
21. Ibid.
22. Levison, Ivan, "5 Ways to Make Your Fulfillment Piece Irresistible," *The Levison Letter*, 5/1/03. Ivan Levison is a freelance direct response copywriter. For a free subscription to this monthly e-newsletter for marketers, visit *www. levison.com*.
23. Aurel Gergey, quote from personal interview, 3/20/04. *www.gergey.com /konzentrate.php*.
24. Miller, "The Steak Behind the Sizzle," *The Business-to-Business Marketer*, p. 5.

Chapter 2

1. Flesch, Rudolph, *The Art of Readable Writing* (New York: Harper & Row, 1949), p. 179.
2. From Wally Bock Web site: *http://www.wallybock.com/*.
3. Nicolle, R., *Practicality: How To Acquire It* (New York: Funk & Wagnalls Company, 1915).
4. Quote from John Forde is from personal conversation 2/10/04.
5. Quote from conversation between author and Sy Sperling 11/8/99.
6. Kern, Russell, "Leverage the B-to-B Buy Cycle," *Target Marketing*, 2/05, p. 22.

Chapter 3

1. Quote from conversation between author and Michael Masterson, 10/7/04.
2. Spock, Benjamin, *Dr. Spock's Baby and Child Care* (New York: Simon & Schuster, 1992).

3. Quote from Gary Blake, Director, The Communication Workshop, personal conversation, 6/4/99.
4. Schwartz, Eugene, *Breakthrough Advertising* (Stamford, Connecticut: Boardroom, 2004), p. 3.
5. Phelps, Russ, "How to Keep Your Creative Juices Flowing," *DM News*, 9/20/04, p. 14. Russ Phelps is a copywriter/marketer and author of "7 Steps to Killer Ad Copy," from which this is excerpted. Contact him at *www.russphelps.com* or call 858-0831-1668.

Chapter 4

1. Burnham, Richard, "Engineers as Credible Marketers," *The Business to Business Marketer*, 1/04, pp. 1–3. Richard Burnham has written, co-authored, and ghostwritten hundreds of trade publication articles for companies and individuals. He may be reached at *RABURNHAM@PublicationCoordination.com*.
2. Finnell, Gwyn, Senior Writer/Marketing Consultant, "Creating White Papers that Drive Sales," Hoffman Marketing Communications, Inc., *www.hoffmanmarcom.com*. Reprinted with permission of Hoffman Marketing Communications.
3. Burnham, "Engineers as Credible Marketers," pp. 1–3.

Chapter 5

1. O'Sullivan, Mike, "7 Tips to Craft a Downloadable White Paper," *WordBiz*, 11/19/03. Reprinted with permission. © Copyright Mike O'Sullivan and WordBiz, Inc.
2. Copley, Nick, "How to Write High-Impact White Papers," *Software Success*, 3/31/03, pp. 1–3. © Copyright Softletter 2004. All rights reserved. Reprinted by permission of the publishers. *www.softletter.com*.
3. Bacchetti, Jerry, Quote from the author's interview with Jerry Bacchetti, 7/5/85.
4. Menzel, D. H., H. M. Jones, and L. G. Boyd. 1961. *Writing a technical paper*. New York: McGraw-Hill Book Company.
5. Butler, J.A.V., *Gene Control in the Living Cell*, New York: Basic Books, 1968, p. 1.

Chapter 6

1. Bencivenga, Gary, "Bencivenga Bullets," a free e-zine of response tips, 1/8/04.
2. Parker, Roger, *www.onepagenewsletters.com*, *RogerCParker@aol.com*, "Education-Based Marketing," *Guerrilla Marketing & Design*, July 2003, *www.gmarketingdesign.com*, *www.onepagenewsletter.com*, or e-mail RogerCParker@aol.com. Reprinted with permission of the author.

Chapter 7

1. Benun, Ilise, "Tips on Tip-Writing," *Quick Online Marketing Tips*, email dated 4/30/03 and "How to Write a Great Tip," *Quick Online Marketing Tips* email dated 5/20/03.
2. Quote from personal correspondence between author and Fern Reiss, 8/7/98.
3. Robert Bly, "Making Your Prospects Sit Up and Take Notice," *DIRECT*, Feb. 2000, p. 249.
4. Quotes from author's personal interview with Craig Evans, 8/14/87.
5. Ibid.
6. Phillips, Michael, "Classes Can Be a Marketing Tool," *Bottom Line Personal*, 10/1/04, p. 15.
7. Quotes from author's interview with Gary Blake, 10/15/98.
8. Quote from author's interview with David Yale, 7/14/01.
9. Quote from personal correspondence between author and Steve Yoder, 1/6/04.
10. Gittomer, Jeffrey, "Spring It On: An Interview with Jeffrey Gittomer," *Sharing Ideas*, Spring 2004, p. 5.
11. Amy Bly and Robert Bly, "In Search of Ink," *Business Marketing*, June 1986.
12. Ibid.
13. Ibid.
14. Ibid.
15. Ibid.
16. Ibid.
17. Quote from personal correspondence with Christopher Cain, 3/7/04.
18. Quotes from author's interview with Ken Ball, 2/6/04.
19. Weil, Deb, "Business Blogging Starter Kit"; *www.wordbiz.com*.
20. Quote from author's interview with Paul Chaney, 10/30/04.
21. Quotes from author's interview with author Marc Orchant, 11/2/04.
22. Quotes from author's interview with B.L. Ochman, 11/8/04.
23. Quotes from author's interview with Max Blumberg, 11/22/04.
24. Quotes from author's interview with Jennifer Rice, 11/29/04.
25. Slaunwhite, Steve, *WordBiz* e-newsletter, 3/24/04, p. 1.
26. Hibbard, Casey, President, Compelling Cases, *casey@compelling-cases.com, www.compelling-cases.com, www.compelling-cases.com*, "8 Ways to Recycle Success Stories," *Software Success*, 7/15/03, p. 2.
27. Suggestions from author's personal correspondence with Steve Slaunwhite.
28. Lewis, Herschell Gordon, *Direct Mail Copy That Sells*, Englewood Cliffs, NY: Prentice-Hall, 1986.

Chapter 8

1. Levison, Ivan, "5 Ways to Make Your Fulfillment Piece Irresistible," *The Levison Letter*, 5/1/03. Ivan Levison is a freelance direct response copywriter. For a

free subscription to this monthly e-newsletter for marketers, visit *www. levison.com*.

2. Caples, John, *Tested Advertising Methods* (Upper Saddle Ridge, NJ: Prentice Hall, 1997), p. 11.
3. Quote from author's interview with author Perry Frank, 10/3/04.
4. Quote from author's interview with Sean Lyden, 3/7/04.
5. Quote from author's interview with Roscoe Barnes, 2/22/04.
6. From a personal interview with Cheryl Markstahler, 11/5/04.
7. Quote from author's interview with Kimberly Park, 4/2/04.
8. Gosden, Freeman, *Direct Marketing Success* (New York: John Wiley, 1989).
9. Robert Bly and Gary Blake, *Dream Jobs* (New York: John Wiley & Sons, 1983).
10. Quotes from author's interview with Sy Sperling, 3/9/02.
11. From David Ogilvy comments at *http://www.rcw.raiuniversity.edu/mass communication/MACM/advertising-mangement/lecture-notes/lecture-12.pdf*.

Chapter 9

1. Heathman, Bryan cited statistic from the book *Internet Direct Mail* by Steve Roberts and Robert Bly (Lincolnwood, IL: NTC Business Books, 2001).
2. Quote contained in personal correspondence between author and Heather Lloyd-Martin, 9/8/03.
3. Quote from author conversation with Deb Weil, 10/5/04.
4. Forde, John, The Copywriter's Roundtable #17, "Nine Cardinal Rules of E-zine Rhetoric," 9/14/04.

Chapter 10

1. Maddox, Kate, "Marketing Accountability Demand Increases," *BtoB*, 11/8/04, p. 4.
2. Brady, Diane, "Making Marketing Measure Up," *BusinessWeek*, 12/13/04, p. 112.
3. Benson, Richard V., *Secrets of Successful Direct Mail* (Lincolnwood, IL: NTC Business Books, 1989), p. 2.
4. Godshall, Ken, Quotes throughout *Case Study: Fortune Magazine and Multiple Premiums*, from interview with author; in Robert Bly, "Subscription Premiums," *Circulation Management* (April 1988) pp. 38–44.
5. Potter, Diane, Quotes throughout *Case Study: Money's Starter Kit*, from interview with author; in Bly, "Subscription Premiums."
6. McIntyre, Steve, Quotes throughout *Case Study: Steve McIntyre, The MFA Group*, from interview with author via email, 1/14/04.
7. Anderson, Sheila, Quotes throughout *Case Study: Commercial Property Services*, from interview with author, via e-mail, 12/2/03.

8. Statistics and quotes throughout *Case Study: Hewlett-Packard Oscilloscopes,* from private correspondence with copywriter Sharyn Nisssen, 12/5/03.
9. Marlow, Chris, Quotes throughout *Case Study: Canon® Workstation,* from interview with author via mail, 12/10/03.
10. Quotes throughout *Case Study: Tektronix Free Bright Ideas Book* from author interview with a Rosen/Brown Direct writer; from Chris Marlow, via email, 12/10/03.
11. Slater, Hal, Quotes throughout *Case Study: The Million-Dollar Pool Builder,* from interview with author, via email 12/2/03.
12. Quotes from personal correspondence between author and Jennifer Borkovich, 12/16/03.
13. Quote from author conversation with Pat Whitcomb and Mark Anderson, 12/7/03.
14. Quote from author conversation with Renee Wickham, 12/22/03.

About the Author

Bob Bly is an independent copywriter and consultant specializing in business-to-business, high-tech, industrial, and direct marketing.

Bob has 25 years of experience writing ads, brochures, direct mail packages, sales letters, publicity materials, e-mail campaigns, white papers, booklets, special reports, newsletters, e-zines, and Web sites for such clients as Associated Air Freight, Philadelphia National Bank, Value Rent-A-Car, Timeplex, Grumman, AT&T, IBM, Lucent Technologies, Medical Economics, and EBI Medical Systems.

He has won a number of industry awards including a Gold Echo from the Direct Marketing Association, an IMMY from the Information Industry Association, two Southstar Awards, an American Corporate Identity Award of Excellence, and the Standard of Excellence award from the Web Marketing Association.

Mr. Bly is the author of more than 50 books including: *The Complete Idiot's Guide to Direct Marketing* (Alpha Books), *The Copywriter's Handbook* (Henry Holt), *Public Relations Kit for Dummies* (Hungry Minds; with Eric Yaverbaum), *Internet Direct Mail: The Complete Guide to Successful e-Mail Marketing Campaigns* (NTC Business Books), and *Become a Recognized Authority in Your Field in 60 Days or Less* (Alpha Books).

His articles have appeared in such publications as *Cosmopolitan, Chemical Engineering, Computer Decisions, Business Marketing, New Jersey Monthly, The Parent Paper, Writer's Digest, City Paper, Successful Meetings, Sharing Ideas, DM News, Amtrak Express,* and *Direct Marketing.*

Bob Bly has taught copywriting at New York University and has presented sales and marketing seminars to numerous corporations, associations, and groups including: the American Marketing Association, Direct Marketing Creative Guild, Women's Direct Response Group, American Chemical Society, Publicity Club of New York, and the International Tile Exposition. He has been a guest on dozens of radio and TV shows including CNBC and CBS's *Hard Copy,* and has been featured in periodicals ranging from *Nation's Business* to the *Los Angeles Times.*

Bob is a member of the Business Marketing Association, Newsletter and Electronic Publishers Association, and the American Institute of Chemical

Engineers. His e-zine, Direct Response Letter, goes to more than 60,000 subscribers monthly.

For more information, contact:

Bob Bly
Copywriter
22 E. Quackenbush Avenue
Dumont, NJ 07628
Phone: 201-385-1220
Fax: 201-385-1138
e-mail: *rwbly@bly.com*
Web: *www.bly.com*

Index

About TEXERE

Texere, a progressive and authoritative voice in business publishing, brings to the global business community the expertise and insights of leading thinkers. Our books educate, enlighten, and entertain, and provide an intersection where our authors and our readers share cutting edge ideas, practices, and innovative solutions. Texere seeks to cultivate, enhance, and disseminate information that illuminates the global business landscape.

www.thomson.com/learning/texere

About the typeface

This book was set in 10 pt Giovanni Book. Giovanni Book is the work of designer Robert Slimbach, whose goal was to create a face of classic old style proportions that was nevertheless thoroughly contemporary. Giovanni was given a modern feel with slightly shortened ascenders and descenders, a slightly larger x-height, and optically lighter capitals.

Library of Congress Cataloging-in-Publication Data

Bly, Robert W.
   The white paper marketing handbook : how to generate more leads and sales with white papers, special reports, booklets, and CDs / Robert W. Bly.
      p. cm.
   Includes bibliographical references and index.
   ISBN 0-324-30082-4 (alk. paper)
   1. Communication in marketing. 2. Market segmentation. 3. Advertising.
4. Selling. I. Title.
   HF5415.123.B585 2005
   658.8′2—dc22

                                                    2005021939